SEX WORK
SEX WORKERS

in Australia

Movie still from Doerthe Jansen's *Let Me Rescue You Before Someone Else Does* (Quality Productions, Australia). This short film has been screened in 20 film festivals and was granted a certificate of merit at the Cork International Film Festival in Ireland. Above photograph by Geoffrey Downs.

Cinematic images of prostitutes are rarely factual representatives of sex workers. Female prostitutes are usually shown as gutter-bred women, for example, *Whore*, or as a perpetual victims (*Hustling*), as gangster's molls (*Mona Lisa*) or as whores with a heart of gold (*Irma la douce*), as oversexed (*Walk on the Wild Side*) or as undersexed (*Klute*). They are often depicted as melancholic (*Winter of Our Dreams*), good-time gals (*Crimes of Passion*), or as heartless (*Lola*). Most are seen as hating their work (*Broken Mirrors*) and are killed off in the end(*Waterloo Bridge*) or rescued by some nice man 'taking them away from it all' (*Pretty Woman*). Male prostitutes are treated little better and are usually seen as shadowy background figures in squalid surroundings (*The Detective*). Their male customers are often identified as lonely, sleazy and into kinky sex (*Midnight Cowboy*), while the clients of gigolos are usually beautiful women (*American Gigolo*). Jansen's *Let Me Rescue You* is a critique of the popular image of prostitutes. The illustration above is a fantasy scene clearly showing the dichotomy of the virgin/whore stereotypes of the male imagination. From the 'fallen women' and 'brazen hussy' stereotypes of the earlier cinema more recent films are beginning to depict the realities of sex work (*Prostitute; Working Girls*) (see Perkins 1989).

SEX WORK & SEX WORKERS

in Australia

Edited by

ROBERTA PERKINS
GARRETT PRESTAGE
RACHEL SHARP
FRANCES LOVEJOY

UNSW
PRESS

Published by
UNIVERSITY OF NEW SOUTH WALES PRESS LTD
Sydney 2052 Australia
Telephone (02) 398 8900
Fax (02) 398 3408

National Library of Australia
Cataloguing-in-Publication entry:

Sex work and sex workers in Australia.

  Bibliography.
  Includes index.
  ISBN 0 86840 174 9

  1. Prostitution – Australia. 2. Prostitutes – Australia – Employment.
  3. Prostitutes – Australia. I. Perkins, Roberta.

306.740994

Printed by Southwood Press Pty Limited

Available in North America through:
ISBS Inc
Portland Oregon 97213-3644
Tel: (503) 287 3093
Fax: (503) 280 8832

CONTENTS

FOREWORD

COMPASSION RATHER THAN COMPROMISE IN LAW REFORM

Prostitution is an ancient and enduring institution which has survived centuries of attack and denunciation. In many countries in the past prostitution has not been illegal, nor is it in some societies today. For example, in Germany, Holland and Denmark female prostitutes are accepted by law as long as they ply their trade in designated areas and fulfil other requirements, such as licensing and payment of taxes.

In Australia, prostitution laws differ widely between jurisdictions. The shape and form of prostitution in each State and Territory are substantially determined by the laws that operate and the enforcement practices that result from those laws. Although laws criminalising prostitution may have little lasting effect on the numbers of people who choose to buy or sell sexual services, these same laws and enforcement practices determine whether sex workers seek their clients on the streets, in escort agencies or in brothels.

Not that politicians or policy-makers care particularly about the conditions that sex workers are working under. Despite the clear evidence from the Fitzgerald Inquiry in Queensland indicating the almost inevitable association between police corruption and the criminalisation of prostitution, sex work continues to be heavily criminalised. The effects of this reach well beyond police vulgarism. As *Sex Work and Sex Workers in Australia* points out, many prostitutes continue to be exploited as a result of laws that lead to physically dangerous working conditions.

Nowhere is this better illustrated than the Queensland Labor Government's *Prostitution Laws Amendment Act* 1992. The government's stated purpose was to reduce the influence of such criminal activities as drug-dealing, money-laundering, violence and extortion. Some commentators have intimated that the government's tough stance may have had more to do with Premier Wayne Goss's 'moral' opposition to prostitution on the grounds that it degrades women. Whether the underlying motive was to stamp out 'pimps and parasites' or to stop men using prostitutes, the legislation is very dangerous for sex workers.

The Act is aimed at the criminal control of all forms and all participants, in what is called 'organised' prostitution. The new law makes it a crime for any person to be found without reasonable excuse in a place used for prostitution by two or more prostitutes; for example in brothels, escort agencies, massage parlours or other commercial sex venues. Anyone who knowingly allows premises to be used for prostitution or knowingly participates in the provision of prostitution can be imprisoned. It is also a criminal offence for a printer, publisher or newspaper proprietor to knowingly advertise prostitution.

What this legislation has done, by criminalising 'organised' prostitution, is to drive prostitution underground. This has attracted criminal interests and sabotaged preventative public health programs. In addition, the new legislation has forced sex workers who wish to operate legally to work on their own at home. This enforced privatisation of prostitution has disturbing implications for the privacy, security, welfare and personal safety of sex workers. Indeed, a great number of Brisbane sex workers have been bashed, raped and severely harassed following the implementation of this new legislation.

Not that legal brothels necessarily offer protection for sex workers. Marcia Neave, in discussing the failure of prostitution law reform in Victoria and elsewhere (Chapter 3) indicates that where there is an oversupply of people working as prostitutes and 'permit' laws govern the location of brothels grossly humiliating forms of sexual service (including pressures for unsafe sex) prevail. Indeed, the approach of Australian law-makers in this area seems to be that, although prostitution is inevitable, the industry should be tightly controlled and those who sell sexual services should be segregated from the rest of the population. It is the strict regulation of the sex work business — undoubtedly more strictly regulated than any other business sector — that often leads to many of the unsavoury aspects of selling sex for money.

The alternative to regulation and control is to have minimal or no regulation or to make prostitution absolutely illegal. These alternatives are also far from satisfactory, as the situation in several Southeast Asian countries demonstrates. Clearly, there has to be some regulation and control, but I would suggest that it has to be regulation and control based on compassion for the sex worker. What is remarkable in the Australian context is that when governments establish regulatory frameworks for sex work they rarely consider the needs of sex workers. The police position is given prominence, and so is that of moral entrepreneurs and business groups. But, both in the submissions to parliamentary committees establishing new legislation and in the final regulatory frameworks themselves, the safety, health and industrial conditions of sex workers are all but ignored.

Nowhere is this concern more required than in dealing with Thai sex workers. As Linda Brockett and Alison Murray point out in Chapter 10, the development of an Asian sex industry in Sydney reflects the increasing mobility of female labour within the region and the establishment of sophisticated recruitment and 'immigration' systems. Yet many of these Thai workers remain marginalised by their often illegal status and are forced to submit to unsafe sex practices. These Thai women, like many of their Australian male and female co-workers, are forced to submit to industrial and health-and-safety working conditions that would not be allowed in other sectors of the labour market.

Yet, as this book clearly demonstrates, it would be narrow minded to assume that there are only negatives attached to life in the sex industry. For example, among Thai sex workers in Australia a great number have made enough money to return to Thailand and settle down in quite comfortable circumstances. For them, presumably, the traumas of migrating and working in a new country have been worthwhile.

Indeed, sex work is clearly attractive to many of its workers. Roxy Blain in Chapter 6 is quite clear on this point: 'Mostly I feel that sex work has given me more confidence, financial security, independence and a better understanding of both men and women'. She adds: 'I am happy and secure in myself and in the relationships I have outside of work'.

Of course, this is the message that the media do not want to hear. Jeddah Jakobsen and Roberta Perkins are quite correctly cynical about newspapers and electronic media that emphasise the 'down side' of prostitution but ignore the benefits. As they point out in Chapter 2, there are sex workers who enjoy what they do and find considerable benefits from working in a business that pays well and has flexible hours. A great deal of the gloss obtained from these conditions, though, is taken away by public and press stereotyping of sex workers and by a distorted understanding of the history and role of such workers in Australia.

Hopefully, *Sex Work and Sex Workers in Australia* will help to redress some of the distortions. The book is edited by people with a long and intimate knowledge of prostitution in the Antipodes. An academic reader on prostitution in Australia is long overdue, especially when there have been so many recent legislative changes to prostitution laws, inquiries into the sex work industry and major research projects planned on HIV/AIDS and other health issues. Fortunately, this book is no barren and dry collection of academic musings. Some of the chapters sparkle with stories from the streets and the brothels — illustrative examples of an industry full of life, vitality and humour. Certainly there is sadness too, but much of it is created by hostile and moralistic parliaments, assisted by their bureaucratic underpinnings, which appear hellbent on considering every point of view except those of the sex workers themselves.

While *Sex Work and Sex Workers in Australia* is a sound academic reader on prostitution, it contains much more than just the laws or the history or the research evidence. The book is replete with humanity and most of all with insight. Though sex workers do not need pity or paternalism, they do require — especially from law-makers — compassion and understanding. Let us hope that these pages reach the hands, and the hearts, of at least some of those who craft the regulatory framework that governs sex work and the lives of sex workers.

Paul R. Wilson,
Bond University,
1994

INTRODUCTION

Garrett Prestage
&
Roberta Perkins

A great deal of research into sex work has taken place in this country over the past decade, but little of it is easily accessible to the general reader or to students interested in studying the sex industry. This book brings together in one cover the most recent research done by experts in their respective fields. It is the first time a multidisciplinary reader on sex work has been produced in Australia and, to the best of our knowledge, anywhere in the world.

Prostitution has been defined in various ways but, in the broadest sense, it is the exchange of sexual activities for material gain. Yet this raises other questions of definition, the most fundamental of which is: 'What constitutes sexual activity?'.

Another basic issue in understanding prostitution is 'exploitation'. This concept lies at the heart of the current use of the term 'sex work', in preference to 'prostitution', by those involved in doing that work. The concept also underscores the problem of locating male homosexual prostitution within a broader analysis of the sex industry.

TERMINOLOGY AND PERCEPTION

Terminology and perception are on-going issues in prostitution that need to be addressed before any proper discussion of the subject can begin. We will commence the reading with some comments as a way of introducing the reader to the complex world of sex work and its participants.

'PROSTITUTION' OR 'SEX WORK'?

The use of the term 'sex work' has two significant consequences. It avoids the use of a more pejorative term, as 'prostitution' has come to be. It also emphasises its position as a form of labour: the implication is that, although sex work is concerned with sexual behaviour, it is in fact merely another form of work and those performing it are primarily motivated by the conditions of their work rather than by some particular sexual interest.

By locating 'sex workers' within a 'sex industry' they are necessarily made equivalent to any other person performing a service and exchanging their labour for material gain. Such a perspective does not carry with it any necessary implied exploitation — the exchange can be relatively equal. The key to the issue of exploitation for 'sex workers' is the manner in which their work is organised: it is an issue of industrial relations. Those sex workers who are self-employed directly exchange their labour for whatever the market will bear and they retain the entire return from this exchange themselves. However, if they work within a setting where they are able to retain only a portion of the income derived from their labour (such as in a parlour or through an agency), then the particular circumstances might be viewed as exploitative. Even so, the use of the term 'sex work' reduces the issue to one merely of industrial relations, and there is little implication that the work itself is necessarily exploitative or that it carries with it any particular moral considerations.

On the other hand, 'prostitution' is a term which conveys powerful images to do with morality. Also, despite the relatively widespread use of the term 'sex work' within the sex industry and by those with a professional or academic interest in the industry, the fact remains that it is the much more pejorative term 'prostitution' which remains in common usage in the broader society and particularly in the mass media.

'Prostitution' is a term which has a very strong association with the concept of exploitation, but the exploitation suggested by the use of that term has much less to do with industrial relations than it does with 'moral relations'. It is widely believed that 'prostitutes' are necessarily exploited because they must use their sexuality in order to derive an income (cf. de Beauvoir 1979, p 578). This rarely requires explanation because it is generally inconceivable that the 'prostitute' would choose to do this. The term 'sex work' is morally neutral on this matter because, by locating it within the arena of industrial relations, it simply avoids the issue of choice.

In the case of 'sex work', the relative value in the exchange relates only to the labour involved and the return from that labour. It is possible to view this exchange as being relatively equal where the sex worker is self-employed. The association with notions of 'moral exploitation' becomes far more relevant when 'prostitution' is the term being used. Nonetheless, it is interesting to note that at no time is the *client* ever considered as possibly being exploited through the transaction. The client is always thought of as having the greater power in the exchange while the 'prostitute' is often viewed as a victim.

The term 'sex work' emphasises the 'work' rather than the 'sex': sex is viewed merely as a product of the work rather than as an activity in itself. 'Prostitution' as a term is not often related to the work, although it is questionable whether the sex involved is given any emphasis either. In fact, if anything is associated with the use of the term 'prostitution' it is probably just the notion of exploitation: 'to prostitute oneself' can relate to the selling of sex but more often suggests the selling of one's very being, giving up one's very identity for material gain.

Yet, regardless of whether one calls it 'prostitution' or 'sex work', the fact remains that the occupation is one which involves the performance of sexual activities as labour. The difficulty is that these concepts are all very much dependent on the perspective of the persons involved and how they view themselves in relation to their behaviour, and the ways in which that behaviour is viewed by others.

Under certain circumstances prostitution may not actually be work and this would very much depend on the way the individuals who practise prostitution view themselves and what they are doing. The important factors include whether the individuals see their sex work as a 'job', whether they practise prostitution regularly or in an organised manner, whether they derive a substantial proportion of their income from prostitution, and whether they engage in prostitution primarily because the working conditions suit them.

In order to classify prostitution as either sex or work (or indeed both), both terms must be clearly defined and the activity which is described as 'prostitution' must correspond to either or both of those terms. Superficially, this would seem to be not too difficult.

PROSTITUTION AS WORK

According to Marx, work consists solely of tasks performed from which a use-value can be derived and for which one is compensated in goods or services (Marx 1976, p 998) — work constitutes those tasks from which a person derives an income. Tasks which are performed primarily because they give pleasure to oneself are considered to be recreational and, even if some income is derived from them, such tasks are rarely viewed as 'work' (Burns 1973, pp 40–54). Also, other tasks which are performed irregularly and from which only a small portion of one's income is derived, might not be called 'work': they might be seen as 'favours', or they might be viewed merely as tasks which have little or no consequence beyond the fact that they are being performed.

The problem with the definition of work is that it is very much associated with issues of identity. Berger and Luckmann (1966) argue that concepts of self and identity are constructed in relation to social activities (which are themselves based in social relations). In modern industrialised societies work is the primary basis of social relations because it determines social values. For this reason, work is central to most people's self-identity: it is a core element of one's sense of who one is and where one fits in society. Work is what one does in one's 'job' and one's job is what determines, to a large extent, one's place in social relations. In writing about working-class culture Paul Willis (1979, p 187) argues that work is the key arbiter of social relations:

> It is also specifically working-class cultural forces from the place of production which help to mould the whole of class culture. Production is not simply the engine house of the social totality producing, somehow, its 'effects' elsewhere on the social plane. Production and its relations is social and cultural to its very roots,

to its very surface. It is the privileged site and generator of working-class culture both because of its massive presence and also because the struggle there *fixes*, organises in a particular combination, those discourses and external influences which play over the place of work — helping to develop them in a particular way, clinching certain features, even when appearing manifestly outside of production. Work is where the demands of capital must be met but from the resources not simply of potential *abstract* labour but from concrete, cultural forms of labour power. Whatever 'free' play there is in cultural forms articulates always around this most central point of reference. Non-work supplies many of the categories and meanings for work but it can only be understood in relation to work and is finally shaped by it.

Those who derive an income from performing an activity which they do primarily because it gives them pleasure (as many in the arts might see themselves as doing), often claim that they do not, in fact, have a 'job' and that, therefore, they do not 'work': they merely derive an income from that which they do because it is who they are. In fact Marx (1975) argued in the 'Economic and Philosophic Manuscripts' that wage labour, or work, is defined by its loss of artistic and creative character. This is highly problematic for a simple understanding of the concept of 'work' and it is an issue to which we will return.

Similarly, when people perform a task outside their 'job' in exchange for which they receive a material reward, it can be viewed in many ways. If they view it as a pleasurable task, then the receipt of goods or services may simply be held to be fortuitous and nothing more. If the task is not particularly pleasurable to them, and is not a task organised on a regular basis or from which they derive any more than a small compensation, then it may be relatively meaningless to them: a 'chore' which they happen to have performed and for which they happen to have received a small reward. Although it may be classified as labour it is difficult to view this as 'work' because of its highly circumstantial and temporary nature. Certainly the performance of such tasks is unlikely to be viewed as a 'job' or to affect individuals' sense of themselves in their occupational role.

Is prostitution always work? Given the complexity of the concept of work the answer can only be 'maybe'. This also is an issue to which we will return.

PROSTITUTION AS SEX

The concept of sex is possibly even more complex. Even simplistic definitions are difficult to determine. Gagnon and Simon (1973a) suggest that psychosexual development is not just a mere shaping process whereby the individual is the passive receptor of external influences who adjusts and conforms to a particular and accepted form of sexuality. They claim that the meanings, and even possibilities, of sexual acts for any individual are determined by the social context and that what is sexual is so defined, in this way becoming a script for the individual's sexual behaviour.

This account of sexual behaviour as 'scripted' behaviour means that it is '… symbolically invested behaviour through which the body is eroticised and through which mute, inarticulate notions and gestures are translated into a sociosexual drama' (Gagnon and Simon 1973b, p 5). Adults respond to children's behaviours with their own, more socially defined, sexuality and thereby invest those behaviours with sexual meanings. This is integral to the individual's sexual development. Moral values are assigned to sexual behaviours, through social processes, which the individual interprets variously. This indirectly shapes the individual's understanding and interpretation of sexual activities and events and, ultimately, the individual's sexual identity (Gagnon and Simon 1973a, pp 34–8).

One might say that sex involves activities which provide genitally based pleasure to the participants. However, individuals will often engage in activities that give them no physical pleasure simply because they give pleasure to their partners. In such cases the only pleasure derived is emotional — certainly it cannot be genitally based, at least not in any direct sense. It is clear from this that sex can encompass a broad range of activities in which individuals engage as part of their sexual lives. Perhaps the common factor is what may be termed 'erotic fantasy': any activity can be sexual if it arises from erotic fantasy — if it encourages a feeling of titillating pleasure and desire, even though there may be no physical basis to that pleasure. This being the case, sex is very much dependent on the way in which individuals interpret their desires and behaviour.

Prostitution is performed in a variety of ways and out of a variety of motivations. The question then arises: Does prostitution always involve sex? Certainly it depends on both the circumstances and the perspective of those involved; and it is likely that in most cases this perspective would be very different between the sex worker and the client. Does prostitution itself form a part of erotic fantasy? If it conforms to either the circumstances or the perspectives of those involved, then certainly the particular form of prostitution being performed by the sex worker in question includes sex. However, if that sex worker does not include prostitution within her or his range of erotic fantasies and if the activities performed are simply viewed as performing a service with little or no erotic pleasure derived from them, then it is quite possible that that sex worker may argue that there is no sex involved, at least for him or her on that particular occasion.

NAMING PROSTITUTION

Naming an activity has implications. The recent renaming of prostitution as sex work is clearly intended, among other things, to remove the activity from the arena of illicit and socially unacceptable behaviour and to separate the activity from issues of exploitation. This is commendable for the purposes of defending and promoting the industrial rights of sex workers and for giving the activity an imprimatur of acceptability. However, it is fraught with problems, not least of which are the issues of definition of both sex and work.

If an individual is taking money for sexual activity but does not view this activity as either work or sex, what does this mean for the notion of the category of 'sex work'? This is the fundamental problem with any definition or redefinition of a category. The individuals who perform the activity of sex work must actually identify their behaviour with the components of that activity, and this is not necessarily the case. Indeed, it is commonly the case that, as the term 'sex worker' gains wider circulation within the sex industry, individuals in the industry refer to themselves simply as 'workers' — as though they are consciously avoiding the use of the word 'sex' in relation to their behaviour. This may partly be due to a sense of shame or it may be due to a feeling that what they are doing is not truly sex, at least for them. Whatever the reason, there are clearly unresolved problems with the use of the term 'sex work'.

An associated problem is that which the use of the term itself sought to avoid. Because the term sidesteps the issue of exploitation implied by the word 'prostitution', it leaves the issue unresolved. 'Sex work' may allow the activity some degree of acceptability in certain circumstances — such as when the industrial rights of sex workers are being considered — but only while those specific issues are being dealt with in isolation. In the meantime the underlying problems of moral condemnation and social marginalisation remain, resurfacing from time to time, and building on a continuing social tension between widely held and longstanding social attitudes about sexuality and prostitution on the one hand and the desire for fairness for all regardless of their particular choices on the other. At least the use of the term 'prostitution' forced these issues to the fore and challenged conservative social attitudes and beliefs.

This is not to suggest that the use of the term 'prostitution' is necessarily any less complicated or fraught with difficulties. It is, of course, the term of popular usage and it is a term which has the clearest resonance, even now, for workers, for clients, and for the broader community. However, usage is not a sufficient argument in itself.

An issue of primary concern is that of inclusion and exclusion. Many advocates of prostitutes' rights believe that the term 'sex work' more effectively covers a broader range of individuals than is the case with the term 'prostitution'. Many people who work in strip clubs or as performers in explicit sex films, or even in massage parlours or similar situations, do not consider themselves as 'prostitutes' nor do they necessarily associate their behaviour with that activity. Prostitute advocates feel that 'sex work' is a broader term which can include all such individuals and others who might perform some sort of sexual activity for a material reward. This is certainly true of some people in certain sections of the sex industry, but not of all — and in fact, as we have argued above, without a recognition that what they are doing involves both sex and work, many may not even associate their behaviour with sex work. Certainly many who engage in casual prostitution on an irregular basis, particularly many of the boys, do not consider themselves as sex workers and are as unlikely to identify with that term as they are with the term 'prostitute'. On the other hand, we have already acknowledged that most of those who engage in prostitution as their primary source of income and who do so on a fairly permanent basis, particularly the women, prefer to call themselves 'workers' rather than 'sex workers'. And this is very likely related to a disinclination to view their own activity as involving sex.

The politics of terminology has its own problems and there is no clear resolution of 'prostitution' versus 'sex work', although it seems that 'prostitution' remains the word of common usage and carries with it the benefit of more challenging social attitudes toward the activity itself. 'Sex work' is a term which appears to have greater force when used in a more academic sense — as a means of describing the activity for semi-official purposes and as a morally more neutral means of addressing the rights of individuals involved in the activity.

THE POLITICS OF CATEGORISATION AND IDENTITY

There is an associated issue in the politics of terminology which has some relevance here. It relates to the use of the word 'queer'. There has been a movement to adopt this word to encompass all persons who do not correspond to the dominant heterosexual and masculinist hegemony. The debate over the use of this word in preference to existing words such as 'gay', 'lesbian', 'bisexual', and 'transsexual' has been most widely, and heatedly, canvassed within the gay and lesbian communities. The all-encompassing intent of the word would logically mean that it should include those engaging in prostitution, as quite clearly prostitutes do not conform to the predominant sexual values of society, in that they sell sexual activity rather than engage in it for romantic reasons, within the confines of a committed heterosexual loving relationship. However, it could also be argued that even the clients of prostitutes could similarly be included within the broad sweep of this word, as they too are using socially proscribed means of engaging in sexual behaviour by purchasing sexual activity outside a committed heterosexual loving relationship.

Regardless of who is included and who is not included in the term 'queer', the problem is that the whole notion of a 'Queer Agenda' or 'Queer Politics' has little relevance to those to whom it is intended to appeal. It is intended to underpin coalitionist politics and to provide the basis for a more broadly based challenge to the sexual norms of society. This intent is neither new nor especially appealing as a basis for a social movement.

The sexual liberation movements of the late 1960s and early 1970s also argued strongly for such broadly based social challenges, and looked to a future where sexual categorisation of individuals would be meaningless because everyone would be free to do as they desired without social disapproval — and a 'natural' polymorphous perversity would prevail (cf. Altman 1971). This broad agenda has remained the underlying ideology of all movements for the defence and extension of sexual rights since then, whether stated explicitly or not. The 'Queer Agenda' provides us with nothing new in this regard except that it creates a new social category of 'queer' with which all those who do not conform to socially prescribed sexual norms are expected to identify. The social movement for broadly based challenges to those sexual norms is intended to be based on this 'queer' identity. This is a fundamental shift.

Social movements are issue-based, but individuals come to associate themselves with movements either through an identification with a movement's political agenda or on the basis of an identification with a social category whose rights are being addressed by that movement. Personal identity relates to core aspects of oneself and is based primarily on one's social and personal relationships. Sexuality is central only when one develops those relationships on the basis of one's sexuality, as is commonly the case with gay men and lesbians (cf. Prestage and Hood 1993).

Categories of persons exist through social definition, whether positive or negative, on the basis of stereotyping (T. Perkins 1979). The terminology used to describe such categories can be imposed through social institutions or by other social forces, or else can be adopted by those who identify with the category themselves. This is the distinction between the more clinical term 'homosexual', which carries with it certain negative stereotypes, and the term of more common usage, 'gay', which has a clearly positive sense of self-assertion of identity by a social movement. Such terms which describe a social category and which correspond to and reflect personal identity arise out of usage by individuals who perceive a common interest with others within the relevant social category. Such commonality is subcultural in origin and is based in common language and meanings and symbolism (Hebdige 1979). Studies of non-gay-identifying and non-gay-attached men who have sex with men have shown consistently that even when behaviours are identical between individuals — in this case sexual interaction between men — this does not necessarily mean that those individuals share a common identity or even a common perception of their behaviour (Hood et al. 1994). The crucial issue is the meaning those individuals ascribe to their own behaviour and the behaviour of others, as well as to the interplay of social forces which interact with their own personal relationships.

This being the case, terms which describe a social category must resonate with the actual experience of the individuals concerned as well as describing a set of individuals with whom they feel they share a common experience. Terms which arise out of social movements themselves are usually the most effective as objects of personal identification in this regard. Yet even these terms do not necessarily relate to all persons whose behaviour corresponds to that of the social category — as has been seen in the case of homosexually active men.

A Prostitute Identity

The terms used to describe prostitutes consist of three types, none of which is entirely adequate. First, there are terms of abuse such as 'whore'. Clearly these terms are not an adequate basis for assertion of a positive identity based on prostitution or sex work. Second, there are terms which are similar to the first type in that they are common vernacular with generally derogatory meanings attached to them, such as 'hustler' or 'hooker'. But, they are not usually used as terms of abuse. Finally, there is the term 'sex worker'. As we have noted, it carries with it no particular moral stance and has been used largely by advocates on behalf of the sex industry to describe individuals within that industry. It is not, in fact, used as a positive assertion of identification with a negatively stereotyped social category, as is the case with the term 'gay'.

The term 'prostitute' sits uneasily among these three sets of terms. It is not a term of abuse, although it can be used as such because it seems to carry with it more negatively stereotyped associations than do the other terms of common vernacular. Yet it has also been used as a semi-official means of describing those who perform sex work. It is the most widely used term and it seems to convey much of what is generally understood about prostitution (mostly negative). The main problem is that a common term has not been developed or even co-opted by prostitutes to describe themselves, one with which they can comfortably identify both as a group and individually.

The difficulty in trying to include prostitutes within a broader category called 'queer' is precisely that the term simply has no resonance with them. The issues of concern to gay men, lesbians, bisexuals and transsexuals do not necessarily relate to those of prostitutes; nor do prostitutes, especially heterosexually identified female prostitutes, necessarily see themselves as having similar interests to these other groups. In fact, like most heterosexually identified men who have sex with other men, they generally view themselves as very ordinary and normal people and those particular behaviours which might set them apart from the norm (according to others) are not viewed as relevant to their sense of who they are and how they relate to other people in their lives. A term such as 'queer' is actually offensive to such people.

In truth, the term 'queer' is often offensive to a large number of gay men and lesbians and many transsexuals. It is traditionally a term of abuse; but most gay men, lesbians and transsexuals also view themselves as being fairly ordinary and normal people who happen to share certain interests with others who behave sexually or interact with people in similar ways to themselves. But, this perception of shared interests does not, and need not, extend to all persons whose sexuality and gender-related behaviour does not conform to socially prescribed norms. They may all come together on an issue of common concern. Or they may be generally supportive of each other's rights. But, they do not identify themselves as necessarily being in a similar situation or as being the same sort of person. To attempt to create an 'umbrella identity' for all these groups is simply not possible and, especially when any such attempt involves the use of a term generally regarded as being derogatory, it is actually offensive to the individuals concerned.

This approach is certainly not an answer to the dilemmas of terminology for prostitutes.

The particular situation of transsexuals is perhaps relevant here. The term 'transsexual' has been problematic. It is a term which was created by professionals in the social and medical sciences and it carries with it an implication both of the medical definition of those persons and an association with sexuality rather than gender. For this reason transsexual advocates have encouraged the use of the term 'transgender'. Yet, this is also a difficult word to use as the basis of an identification with a social category or with a social movement. It is a cumbersome word, especially when used as a noun. Also, the word is based on the term 'gender' which does not refer to persons but to a social division, making it especially difficult for individuals to feel comfortable in identifying with it. And, like 'transsexual', the word remains fairly clinical and academic. Common vernacular uses terms such as 'drag' to describe transsexuals. These terms are both demeaning and derogatory, and they are inappropriate because they merely refer to the superficial appearance of individuals rather than to the serious lack of synthesis between current gender identity and ascribed gender at birth. Yet there is a term — 'trannie' or, sometimes, 'trany' — which is gradually emerging as a word used by transsexuals themselves. The word is simple, it relates to the more serious clinical and academic terms without being cumbersome, and it implies a positive assertion of identity by 'trannies' themselves. One might expect that this term will gradually become the transsexual equivalent of 'gay'.

There has been no similar evolution in the use of words to describe prostitutes. Perhaps the reason this is the case is that they have not regarded themselves, in general, as sharing a common identity. Certainly the differences between male and female prostitutes are such that there is some difficulty in viewing them as being in a similar situation. In some ways transsexual prostitutes are also in a unique situation and it may be fair to say that their shared identity as transsexuals, regardless of whether they are involved in the sex industry or not, is so important to their sense of themselves that identification with other, non-transsexual, prostitutes is problematic. Indeed, even among the women, the differences between private or brothel workers and street workers are often perceived as so great that many see little commonality with the other group.

To sum up, it is probably fair to say that the term 'sex worker' has some relevance when talking about the broad range of persons working within the sex industry as a whole, and that this usage of the word is especially appropriate in an academic or similar discussion of the topic. The term 'prostitute' has greater currency as a term with which most people who engage in sexual activity in exchange for material reward can identify, but it is both limited in its ability to include various categories and is associated with negative stereotypes. However, these are the only terms we have at this stage and we cannot *impose* a more suitable term. Indeed, it might be that there is no ultimate commonality of identity for all those involved in the sex industry. While we as researchers and other interested professionals use various inclusive terms, we must remember that our descriptions might be of groups of people who in fact belong to discrete social categories.

THE BOOK IN OUTLINE

As a multidisciplinary reader this book is intended for a broad and diverse readership. Accordingly, it should appeal to scholars and students in many different fields of study — not to mention the general reader with an interest in prostitution (perhaps a fascination) who wishes to learn the truth behind the mythology. The book is divided into four parts, each referring to a particular aspect or set of related aspects of the sex industry.

Part I deals with historical and legal matters. Our historian is Raelene Frances, who is writing (or perhaps we should say rewriting) a comprehensive history of prostitution in Australia, of which her Chapter 1 in this book is merely a synopsis. Raelene's analysis of past sex work challenges the conventional histories by taking into account rural and frontier prostitution, as well as the more familiar urban sex industry. And she has included sex workers much too often overlooked in the writings on sex work: Aboriginal, Japanese and other non-Anglo women recruited for the commercial sex trade. Another break with historical tradition is oral history, and in Chapter 2 Jeddah Jakobsen and Roberta Perkins provide a rare glimpse of the past from the sex worker's point of view. What emerges is women with a strong sense of their own history, one which is in great contrast to the documented evidence of the print media, the court records and the words of authority figures.

Our legal academic is Marcia Neave, best known in this field for her role as the Inquirer appointed by the Victorian Government in 1984 to investigate prostitution in that state. Her Chapter 3 on the prostitution laws in Australia unravels the complex web of legislation across the country. Indeed, it well illustrates the present contradictory and preposterous situation state by state. Finally in this part, there is Chapter 4, written by a senior police officer once stationed in the heart of Sydney's unofficial red-light district of Kings Cross. Mike Lazarus was the instigator of a unique move in the annals of law enforcement when he brought together former antagonists — prostitutes, residents and police — for regular discussions on mutual problems.

Part II is titled *Inside Views* because it includes chapters written by those involved in the sex industry. Roxy Blain's Chapter 5 recounting her experiences as a sex worker illuminates the great variation in modes of operation in different types of sex work and the vast differences in treatment by police in three states. In Chapter 6 our male worker, Steven Goodley, indicates how different sex work is for a young man — though, on close examination there also appear to be many similarities with Roxy's account. Chapter 7 by Caroline Barlow provides the reader with a rare glimpse into the life of a member of the most maligned group of people in the sex industry, the parlour (brothel) owners. In keeping with the gradual elimination of sexist language, female parlour owners are no longer referred to as 'madams', at least not in Sydney.

Part III covers a vast field: the social and health aspects of the sex industry. Roberta Perkins' Chapter 8 on female prostitution looks at the social and working lives of sex workers by drawing on the statistical findings of her own quantitative research covering a span of nearly ten years. In Chapter 9 on male and transsexual prostitution Garrett Prestage takes a different approach, discussing the social vagaries of various forms of sex work and posing some tantalising questions on sexuality and gender behaviour for the reader. Chapter 10 on Thai sex workers, written by Linda Brockett and Alison Murray, is a revealing account of migrant prostitution in Sydney, spiced with personal comments by the women and providing a very different profile from the usual sensational material in the tabloids.

Chris Harcourt's Chapter 11 on public health is packed with information. Her omnibus approach to the subject alerts the reader to Australia's sexual health concerns in prostitution and compares these with global epidemiological findings. Another area of popular misconception is the use of drugs in prostitution. Rachel Sharp's Chapter 12 brings us the facts about intravenous drug use among female sex workers, but leaves room for discussion on the issue. In Chapter 13 on AIDS education Carol Stevens describes the problems found in communicating prevention practices to sex workers. In the final chapter (Chapter 14) in this part Barbara Sullivan presents a stimulating and persuasive dialectical argument in favour of a feminist perspective of female prostitution.

Part IV is titled *Working with Workers* for in it social workers, health workers, research fieldworkers and outreach workers tell us about their daily interaction with sex workers. Louise Webb and Janice Elms are social workers from other countries who have been involved with prostitutes both overseas and in Australia, and in Chapter 15 provide valuable information for social workers intending to work among sex workers. Ingrid van Beek is director of the Kirketon Road Centre (KRC), an essential health service to inner city street prostitutes and others. She tells us in Chapter 16 about the success of KRC and why it is important. Amanda Wade and Gabrielle Mateljan are research assistants who have done years of fieldwork among sex workers in New South Wales. In Chapter 17 they impart valuable lessons for fieldworkers hoping to do research on prostitution. Geoffrey Fysh, who manages Sex Workers Outreach Project (SWOP), an important government-funded service for prostitutes in New South Wales, outlines in Chapter 18 the advantages and disadvantages of this kind of service. A brief conclusion (Chapter 19) completes the book.

ACKNOWLEDGEMENTS

Putting together a volume of this magnitude requires the assistance of many more hands (and minds) than we four editors could marshal alone. There are a large number of people to whom we owe a great debt of gratitude. To begin with, we must thank all 19 contributors (whose personal details may be seen in the list of contributors at the end of the volume) whose efforts in producing the chapters have collectively resulted in the first multi-disciplinary academic reader on prostitution in this country.

Rachel would especially like to thank her husband Mervyn for his patience and understanding, and her staff at the University of New England for their valuable assistance. Roberta would like to express her gratitude to her workmates at Macquarie University, and both she and Frances wish to record their appreciation of Bruce Johnston at the University of New South Wales for his invaluable advice and assistance during the transfer of the material to computer. Garrett thanks his colleagues at the National Centre in HIV Epidemiology and Clinical Research for their support.

We thank Doug Howie and the University of New South Wales Press for their insight in foreseeing what a valuable contribution this volume could make to social, legal, health and other studies in prostitution research, as well as to community knowledge of the sex industry. We particularly thank our funding bodies, especially the Commonwealth AIDS Research Grants Committee, the National Health and Medical Research Council and the NSW AIDS Bureau for having the courage to see the value of researching prostitution and for the generous funding which has made much of the work reported in this volume possible.

We should not forget the part played by various state governments, whose inquiries into prostitution have brought a fresh community consciousness to the subject and paved the way for serious discussion. This book is but one outcome of the growing maturity in debates on sex work.

Finally, but certainly not least, we owe a huge debt of gratitude to the sex workers themselves, especially those who contributed to this volume through their interviews, their participation in surveys and their ready supply of information. It should also be recognised that sex workers and their organisations, through their continual assertion of their basic human rights to work and to sexual expression, have more than any other source opened the way for works such as this to approach the issues with a well-informed scientific rationale that reflects, we hope, the perceptiveness and candour of the sex worker's view of the world.

PART I

HISTORICAL
& LEGAL
PERSPECTIVES

1

THE HISTORY OF FEMALE PROSTITUTION IN AUSTRALIA
Raelene Frances

When local councillors and other prominent citizens planned appropriate ways to celebrate the 1993 Kalgoorlie Centenary, a group of Hay Street sex workers suggested a brothel museum as a fitting tribute to the longstanding contribution of the prostitution industry to the town's economic and social life. While the city aldermen were not quite ready for such an idea, its conception raises a number of issues about the history of prostitution in Australia. Most obviously, the sex workers were drawing attention to the hypocrisy of the official disapproval of their industry alongside the open toleration, even encouragement, of the Hay Street brothels as a facility for local men and as a tourist attraction for the town. Equally important is the idea of prostitution as a subject for historical investigation and representation. What kinds of objects and texts could be included in such a museum?

The changing physical environment of prostitution is an obvious starting point. One scene might depict the interior of an 1890s hessian tent (through which enterprising policemen could poke spyholes in their quest for conclusive evidence of commercial sex), equipped with a wooden box on top of which washbowls contain water costing almost as much as a 'short-time' with the tent's occupant. Next to the basin, a handful of metal tokens struck with the silhouette of a young woman on one side and a name and address on the other. The only other furniture is an iron bedstead, above which is pinned a medical certificate signed by the local doctor proclaiming the prostitute (a young French woman) free of venereal diseases. Draped across the end of the bed, a collection of lacy underwear, silk stockings, high-buttoned boots and brightly coloured clothing. Moving forward in time, the next scene might contain an interior of a weatherboard and iron house, 1920s. Cleanly but basically furnished, it has a basin with cold running water in the corner. Through the door a bathroom, with chip heater, is visible. On the dressing table lies an Italian newspaper left behind by the last client. The final scene shows a street view of the same room in the 1970s, framed by a car window. The top half of the door opens independently of the bottom (in the manner of a horse stabledoor) to reveal a scantily clad woman sitting inside, lit by coloured lights. In the background the watchful eye of an older woman, expensively dressed and bejewelled, surveys the prostitute and the onlooker.

Such a display, while potentially very evocative and illuminating about the changing working conditions and even to some extent the working relationships of goldfields sex workers, nevertheless could not elucidate the more complex issues associated with the changing nature of prostitution over time. It would require considerable amounts of text to explain the complex range of factors which shaped, and still shape, the sex industry: changing economic options for women; changing sexual practices and values within the prostitute and non-prostitute community; technological changes; developments in medical treatment; shifts in the general economic climate; wars; racial ideologies; and, probably most importantly, changing state interventions in the form of legislation and its administration by the police, courts, prisons and other government agencies. This chapter will explore this complex history and the way in which it has been dealt with by Australian historians. It will look exclusively at female prostitution, since male prostitution is virtually absent from the historical record and entirely absent from the historiography.

PROSTITUTION IN PRECOLONIAL AUSTRALIA

It is a conventional wisdom that prostitution is the oldest profession and that it has existed in all societies in all times. The case of Aboriginal society before the European invasion refutes the latter claim. As far as we know, prostitution, in the sense of the exchange of sexual services for goods or money, did not exist in traditional Aboriginal society. Most (but not all) Aboriginal societies did practise some form of polygamy, but this was not prostitution. Nor was the ritual exchange of women as a sign of friendship between different groups of people (Williams and Jolly 1992, pp 9–19). The earliest hints we have of commercialised sex are with the Macassar fishermen who visited the northern shores of Australia on a seasonal basis from at least the 1670s. There were certainly sexual liaisons between these fishermen and local women, and cases of Aboriginal women returning to Macassar with their lovers. There is also evidence of a barter system whereby Aboriginal people exchanged local goods for rice, calico, alcohol and fishing equipment. Oral histories record some cases of women being exchanged for dugout canoes but it is unclear how widespread this was, or indeed whether it was in the period before European contact or in the later period (the trade did not end until 1907) when Aboriginal societies and economies were under greater pressure (McKnight 1976).

PROSTITUTION IN THE CONVICT ERA

Historians are on firmer ground when talking about prostitution in the post-invasion period, although our knowledge is by no means complete here either. As feminist historians have shown, prostitution was an integral part of the social and economic system of the early convict colonies. The numerical predominance of males on the first convict ships (amongst both convicts and gaolers) was from the outset perceived as a social and political problem: those in authority believed that 'without a sufficient proportion of that sex [female] it is well known that it would be impossible to preserve the settlement from gross irregularities and disorders' (Martin 1978, pp 22–9). Women were needed as an antidote to sexual deviance (read sodomy), rape of 'respectable' (read upper class) women, and rebellion. It was thus a matter of considerable urgency to find female sexual partners for the European colonists. Aboriginal women were obvious candidates for this role, and indeed Arthur Phillip, the first Governor, hoped that in time Aboriginal men would 'permit their Women to Marry and Live' with the convicts (Rutter 1937). In the short term, however, this was not practicable and, as subsequent events were to show, liaisons between convict men and Aboriginal women were to cause much interracial tension (Reynolds 1982). Having toyed with and rejected (on humanitarian grounds) the idea of luring Polynesian women to Sydney, the authorities turned to the possibility of bringing in significant numbers of women convicts. The issue here was not miscegenation, as it was to become by the end of the nineteenth century. Class considerations were paramount. The favourable response later on to Japanese prostitutes was based not just on their quietude but also on the fact that they didn't appear to have half-caste babies very often.

The plan was only partly successful. Only one quarter of the convicts transported on the First Fleet were women. If we add gaolers and officials to the numbers of males, women were outnumbered by roughly six to one in the convict settlements until the increase in free female immigration in the 1830s (Carmichael 1992, p 103). To achieve even this level of comparability in the numbers of men and women, the authorities had to transport women on much less serious offences than those for which men were transported (Robson 1963, 1965; Oxley 1988). But, the supply of female offenders was still not sufficient to keep pace with that of male convicts. This meant that, if the intention to use these women as sexual partners for convicts was to be fulfilled, some or all of the convict women would have to have multiple male partners. Indeed, in Phillip's opinion, 'the lusts of the men were so urgent as to require the prostitution of the most abandoned women to contain them' (Rutter 1937). The fact that 12 percent of convict women were recorded as prostitutes before leaving Britain no doubt predisposed them to continue their former occupation in the colony (Robson 1963). Other conditions in the penal settlements encouraged widespread prostitution. In the early years of the settlement no provision was made for housing for female convicts and a woman's best chance of accommodation was through striking up a liaison with some man. Those who could not or would not attach themselves to one man found the temporary bartering of sex for accommodation just as effective. Women were also the frequent targets of male violence and many found it necessary to seek the protection of one man, in return for sexual favours, against the sexual demands of other men. Limited opportunities for female employment in the early years, where the major demand was for male muscle-power, also placed pressure on women to prostitute themselves as one of the few ways in which they could earn a livelihood. According to Anne Summers, the result was a situation of 'enforced whoredom', either to one man or to many. (Summers 1975, pp 267–85; see also Alford 1984, p 44; Aveling 1992).

There is considerable debate about the exact level of prostitution in convict society (Lake 1988). Historians such as Lloyd Robson (1965), Alan Shaw (1966) and more recently Robert Hughes (1987) have tended to accept the judgements of contemporary officials who condemned the female convicts generally as 'damned whores', possessed of neither 'Virtue nor Honesty'. But the evidence upon which this judgement is based is problematic. How can we know, for instance, whether the frequent allegations of universal whoredom reflected the class- and sex-based prejudices and preconceptions of literate officials more than actual practices in the colony? As Michael Sturma has pointed out, middle and upper class commentators tended to see working class women as prostitutes simply because their behaviour transgressed their own class-based notions of feminine modesty and morality. For instance, long-term de facto relationships were a common and accepted part of early nineteenth century working class culture, but from the perspective of the middle or upper class observer, these women were prostituting themselves, albeit to 'one man only' (Sturma 1978). Such men were also shocked by working class women's open and aggressive sexuality compared to that of 'virtuous' women of their own class (Daniels 1993). Early feminist historians such as Anne Summers and Miriam Dixson have ironically reinforced this picture of wholesale whoredom by incorporating the stereotype as a key element in explaining Australian women's current low status in

relation to Australian men. Women were compelled into prostitution by State policy and structural factors rather than their own personal 'vice' but they were, by these accounts, prostitutes nonetheless (Summers 1975; Dixson 1975). Portia Robinson (1985), writing in the mid-1980s, presents the opposite view of the women of
Botany Bay as good wives, good mothers and good citizens. If they
were prostitutes, she says, it was as a result of their criminal environment in Britain rather than conditions in Australia. On the contrary, Australia offered women the chance for redemption
(Robinson 1988, p 236).

In the final analysis, it is impossible to know exactly how many
women engaged in commercial sex during the convict period.
Despite this, prostitution obviously was a key institution in convict
society, providing one of the few economic options for women who
supplied a high level of demand for sexual services in a dispropor-
tionately male population (Alford 1984). There is a sense, too, in
which the actual numbers of women working as prostitutes is irrel-
evant to an understanding of the place prostitution played in colonial society. What is more important is the fact that those in authority believed it to be widespread yet, apart from ritual expressions of
disgust, showed a high degree of toleration for the practice. As
noted earlier, this toleration reflected the official belief that prostitutes provided a necessary outlet for the powerful lusts of working
class men. It was also accepted because the women who provided
this service were, from the point of view of the ruling class, the
'other' — working class women with values and behaviour mark-
edly different from those of women of their own class. The sharp
contrast between the speech, dress and behaviour of convict
women and the demeanour of middle and upper class women also
helped mask the extent to which sexual services were exchanged
for financial gain across social classes. Because of this, convict society, particularly in the earlier decades, was noticeably more tolerant
of women of 'easy virtue' amongst its upper echelons than was contemporary British society or later colonial society.

Deborah Oxley (1988, p 87) makes another important point in
identifying prostitution as a structural part of the capitalist patriarchy which characterised colonising society. Working class wom-
en's role in this society was primarily to reproduce the working

class: future, past and present. An intrinsic part of this role was the provision of sexual services to men, through marriage, force or payment. Sex was commercialised and turned into a commodity.

The convict era was thus crucial in setting the pattern for the history of prostitution in Australia. It saw the establishment of the sex industry as an important part of the life experience and work options of women within colonising society; it was also during this period that the extent of prostitution came to be used as a gauge of the worth of colonial women and of the success of colonial society more generally. Prostitution assumed a rhetorical and symbolic significance quite apart from its importance as an avenue for women's economic survival.

PROSTITUTION ON THE COLONIAL PASTORAL, MINING AND MARITIME FRONTIERS

Meanwhile, as prostitution of European women flourished in the penal settlements, wherever the white colonisers intruded on Aboriginal lands sexual contact between white men and black women occurred soon after. In some cases this was the result of Aboriginal people extending traditional hospitality to visitors. That is, Aboriginal women were lent to the intruders in the expectation that friendly relations would ensue. In some cases, too, Aboriginal women became more regular companions for white men, often as a deliberate strategy to incorporate the newcomers into the Aboriginal kinship system. It was also, no doubt, sometimes a matter of personal preference on the part of Aboriginal women, who welcomed the novelty the white men provided and perhaps also wished to cast in their lot with the ascendant power in the region.

All too often, however, sexual interaction was coercive and violent, with Aboriginal women being conquered and taken in the same way that Aboriginal lands were. In the aftermath of dispossession Aboriginal women were often left with little choice but to engage in prostitution, either for money or for goods, in order to survive as individuals and to contribute to the survival of their kin. They formed the pivot of what Deborah Bird Rose (1992, Ch. 19) calls 'an economy of sex'. As access to hunting grounds was increasingly prevented and sources of food became rapidly depleted, Aboriginal people were forced to participate in the white economy to survive. In the early colonial period, where convict labour was readily available, Aboriginal women's sexuality was often the only saleable item possessed by the survivors who eked out a precarious existence on the edges of white society. In the north, the labour of young men was also valued, but here the almost total absence of white women placed Aboriginal women in even greater demand. They were indispensable as domestic workers as well as performing a wide range of non-traditional women's work, such as stock work and mining, in certain areas. For all these workers, satisfying the sexual demands of their co-workers and bosses was usually considered part of the job. The more fortunate were able to obtain something in exchange for their sexual favours — such as extra rations which were shared with their kin in the camp. The less fortunate were treated as sexual slaves, confined for the use of white managers and stock workers. Ann McGrath (1984a, 1987) relates the Northern Territory practice of keeping a number of young 'stud gins' locked up in a chicken-wire enclosure as an enticement for white labourers, who were otherwise reluctant to work in the so-called 'womanless North'.

While this practice contributed to the economy of the pastoralists, the relatively benign practice of exchanging sex for extra rations contributed enormously to the survival of Aboriginal groups dispossessed by pastoralism and mining or living in areas where the bush tucker was radically depleted.

But it was not just Aboriginal women who were engaged to satisfy the lusts of men in the North. In the late nineteenth century Japanese and, to a lesser extent, Europeans and Australians operated brothels, especially in ports and mining centres. The more southerly the location the greater the proportion of Australian and European women and the fewer the Japanese found in sex work. The earlier goldrushes in Victoria and New South Wales, by contrast, were served almost entirely by prostitutes from Britain and Australia. Japanese brothels were a prominent feature of waterfront life in ports such as Broome, Darwin and Thursday Island, where the inmates catered for the wide range of nationalities engaged in the pearling, pearl-shell and fishing industries, as well as those employed on cargo and naval vessels. The role these women played in the economic life of the ports was as great as their contribution to its social facilities. Brothel-keepers were often in partnership with pearl fishermen, the proceeds of prostitution being used to finance the purchase and outfitting of Japanese pearling luggers (Hunt 1986; C. Moore 1992; Sissons 1976–77).

Aboriginal women were also involved in prostitution in the maritime industry, though their case is somewhat special. In Western Australia, for instance, until legislation in 1871 prohibited the practice, they were employed both as divers and prostitutes on the pearling luggers which operated out of ports such as Broome and Roebourne (Hunt 1986; Reynolds 1990). On shore, women from local areas and others abandoned by drovers, miners or troopers far from their own country, waited in the mangroves at the river mouths to sell their wares to the fishermen as they came ashore with their earnings. Again, state intervention attempted to outlaw this practice. It would be naive to think, however, that legislation put a stop to the trade in Aboriginal women's sexuality. This continued, albeit in a more clandestine fashion.

The frontier has had a special legacy in the way in which prostitution is treated by sections of Australian society into the present. There is still a certain 'out of sight out of mind' mentality regarding sexual relations between women of Aboriginal descent and non-Aboriginal men which extends to commercial sex, especially in rural areas. For most of the twentieth century Aboriginal women were controlled by the various state 'protection Acts' rather than the civil and criminal laws which were used to police non-Aboriginal prostitution. They were thus put in a separate category to other prostitutes. In some ways this had negative consequences for the women concerned, since the powers of the Chief Protectors of Aborigines were far more far-reaching than those of the police in relation to non Aboriginal prostitutes (Huggins and Blake 1992). In other ways their separateness was more positive. The fact that Aboriginal women usually traded sex in fringe-camps or on isolated stations rather than city streets meant that they escaped many of the moves by police and criminal organisations to control their activities and earnings. The balance of these factors must have varied considerably with the experience of individual women.

The frontier years also had ramifications for non-Aboriginal sex workers. The legacy is clearly evident in mining towns such as

Kalgoorlie, where prostitution is openly carried on under the virtual supervision of the police. As in colonial days, the police (and apparently the majority of the local community) consider the brothels a necessary part of life in a mining town where men still outnumber women. This acceptance and semi-official control has been a mixed blessing for the women concerned. The vigilance of the police ensures that criminal elements are kept away from the brothels and their inmates, making sex work in Kalgoorlie much safer than probably anywhere else in Australia. However, this security comes at the price of excessive intrusion into the personal relationships and movements of sex workers. As one former Kalgoorlie prostitute recalled of her years in a Hay Street brothel in the 1970s, after fleeing Sydney because of violence from the 'big fellas': 'Oh no, you weren't allowed to have boyfriends. Not in Kalgoorlie… The police won't let you… I tell you what, I couldn't cop that, not being *free*' (Frances 1993, p 14). In addition to having their personal relationships vetted, sex workers were forbidden to shop in the town after midday and were not allowed to use the local restaurants, hotels, swimming pool or cinemas or to go to the racecourse. This situation persists to the present day (Cohen 1994).

DEMAND AND SUPPLY IN URBAN PROSTITUTION

The sale of sexual services was not, however, simply a product of the sex imbalance in convict society or on the frontier. On the contrary, prostitution flourished in every late nineteenth century city in Australia even where the sex ratios were more evenly matched. Of course, there were the perennial demands for commercial sex from enclaves of men, such as in the merchant marine and the armed forces. But colonial cities supplied other customers. In this case the demand came from white men who sought sexual release with prostitutes because, in the context of prevailing moral codes, 'respectable' women were not available to meet these demands. Middle class men, enjoined to defer marriage until they had attained a sufficient level of financial security, were not willing to stay virgins until they married in their late twenties or thirties. Single women of their own class were not generally willing to engage in premarital sex because to do so would spoil their marriage prospects. After marriage, the desire to limit family size, increasingly evident in Australian middle class families from the 1870s, meant that many couples severely curtailed their marital sexual activity. Men, 'naturally', it was thought, sought carnal solace in the arms of prostitutes. Bourgeois Australians had inherited from England the same double standard of sexual morality which insisted on women's chastity before marriage and faithfulness afterwards in the interests of guaranteeing the paternity of the heirs. While men were expected to have strong sexual urges and extramarital sex was winked at on their part, respectable women were generally expected to feel little sexual desire of their own and were condemned should they seek gratification outside the marital bed. Working class men too were increasingly subject to this bourgeois code of morality, and because of relatively high wages in Australia may have been able to afford prostitutes' services more readily than were their British counterparts.

The supply of prostitutes in the late nineteenth and early twentieth centuries came principally from the working class. Despite the rhetoric of the working man's paradise, wages and conditions for Australian women were far from heavenly. While the growth of manufacturing in the major urban centres in the late nineteenth century did open up new opportunities for women as paid workers, the options were still very limited and none of them very alluring. In 1900 domestic service was still the most popular female occupation, offering women a life of confinement, hard work, low wages and the strong possibility of sexual harassment from male employers and their sons. Women who preferred the freedom of the factory had a narrow range of female jobs open to them, all of which paid around half the male rate for similar occupations. For young women living at home, this was just enough to make the effort worthwhile. For older women, or those without family or friends to supplement their wages, life was difficult to say the least. Women with dependents found it almost impossible to subsist and support their children or other relatives on factory wages, while the logistics of balancing childcare and paid work outside the home were daunting.

Prostitution was attractive to many such women because, like outwork for the clothing industry, it offered them the chance to work from home. The increasing work opportunities in shops and offices offered slightly higher status but usually not much more in the way of remuneration. Even if a woman took only one paying customer a day, at the going rate of two shillings and sixpence for a short-time (at the bottom end of the market) she would earn more in a week than as a skilled tailoress or a lady typist. In times of economic depression the gap between respectable and unrespectable earnings was even wider (Scates 1993, pp 40–1). Given these economic realities, it is hardly surprising that there was always a ready supply of women to meet the demands for commercial sex in Australia's colonial cities. No doubt there were also women drawn to the prostitute's lifestyle for its own sake, as offering a more enjoyable and freer way of earning a living than other kinds of feminine work. Historians have been slower to recognise this aspect of prostitution than they have the economic one.

'CLEANING UP THE STREETS'

The forces propelling women into sex work were therefore almost as strong in the post-convict era as they were during the earlier colonial period. But, late nineteenth century Australians were increasingly less willing to allow the open, uncontrolled activities of streetwalkers on their city streets and of bawdy houses in their neighbourhoods. The period from about 1870 through to the First World War saw concerted efforts by legislatures and police forces in all the colonies to 'clean-up' their streets, and prostitutes were a major target of this cleansing operation.

How can we explain these moves to reform urban street life in the late nineteenth and early twentieth centuries? There is no one explanation which covers the situation in all colonies, but certain common processes are identifiable. And these relate to transformations in the management of urban space common to cities in other English-speaking countries at about the same time. The growth of an urban middle class which accompanied the industrial expansion of the nineteenth century created a class of leisured wives and daughters who sought to use urban space in new ways, most notably by shopping and promenading in the central business districts. A variant of this was the fashionable Melbourne pastime of 'doing the Block', or promenading around the Collins, Swanston, Bourke and Elizabeth Streets block of shops. With more 'respectable' women using the streets, the presence of what they regarded as 'nuisances' had to be minimised and preferably eliminated. Hawkers, beggars and drunks were all targets of this campaign, but prostitutes were especially targeted. The reason for this is obvious: while it might be annoying for a bourgeois woman to be accosted by beggars and so on, it was extremely embarrassing for her to have to encounter 'fallen women' and, worse still, to be mistaken for one of their number and propositioned by men (Davies 1989; also Walkowitz 1992). The attack on street culture can also be seen as part of a broader middle class assault on working class behaviour generally, aimed at reforming those aspects of life which did not fit with the demands of an ordered, industrial society (Daniels 1984).

Colonial legislatures were thus responding to similar pressures on other recently industrialised societies when they introduced a series of legislative changes which sought to give the police greater powers to control street life. Prostitutes were especially affected by changes to the vagrancy clauses of the police offences Acts, such as occurred in Victoria in 1891 and New South Wales in 1908, which made soliciting by women an offence for the first time (Arnot 1987; Golder and Allen 1979–80). Other legislation at both municipal and state/colonial levels imposed new penalties on brothel-keepers.

It should be noted, however, that the aim of this legislation was not to suppress prostitution entirely. Indeed, legislators generally accepted the inevitability of prostitution as a social institution — a 'necessary evil', as it was often referred to. Assuming that men's sexual instincts would find some outlet, politicians argued that it was better that they were satisfied by prostitutes than translated into the seduction or rape of 'respectable' women. The best one could do was control its more offensive side-effects. As Western Australian Attorney-General Walter James explained during the passage of the *Police Amendment Act* in 1902: 'I realise … that it would be undesirable to entirely suppress it [ie prostitution], even if we had the power to do so… On the other hand I do not believe in its being carried on in an open, flagrant and almost insulting manner. I believe it should be kept in restraint' (Davidson 1980, p 41). James's remarks sum up the dominant attitude of Australian authorities to the issue of prostitution from the late nineteenth century until the present day.

Pressures specific to new societies also saw increasing efforts to control the operation of prostitution in colonial Australia. Kay Daniels (1984) charts the changing attitude of the authorities to prostitution in Tasmania after the middle of the century, when colonial legislators were concerned to minimise the visibility of prostitution as part of the transition from a convict to a free society. The passing of convict society saw a change in the attitude of middle class people to prostitution. While the sexual exploitation of convict women was widely acknowledged, it was accepted as a reflection of the immoral nature of the women themselves, who were not ordinary women but 'whores'. With the move to a 'free' society, prostitution came to be seen in the same light as many other aspects of working class culture: as a social problem to be dealt with by civic authorities. Alongside sporadic (and largely unsuccessful) efforts to 'rescue' prostitutes was an increasing array of legislation designed to control prostitution.

Similar concerns were evident in Kalgoorlie in the early 1900s. Here the intensely masculine, frontier-style town, with large numbers of alluvial prospectors, was being replaced by a more family-oriented society based upon wage-labour in deep mines. 'Respectable' residents became increasingly dissatisfied with the open displays of the town's many prostitutes, who solicited throughout the central parts of the town in broad daylight as well as at night. Such behaviour was considered inappropriate in the presence of increasing numbers of 'respectable' women and children so moves were taken by the police which eventually localised the brothels and severely curtailed the public movement of sex workers (Davidson 1980, 1984).

CONTAGIOUS DISEASES LEGISLATION

Other pressures also affected society's willingness to intervene in the lives of prostitutes. Health considerations, for instance, became increasingly important in the context of British imperial expansion in the latter half of the nineteenth century. While venereal disease was not a new phenomenon in that century, governments saw it as an increasingly serious problem, especially as it affected the fitness of the nation's military personnel. Prostitutes were targeted as the major carriers of VD and the most vulnerable to control. In Britain, the government enacted the controversial Contagious Diseases (CD) Acts of the 1860s which aimed to provide a pool of disease-free prostitutes for the use of troops in English garrison towns. The British military authorities also wanted similar legislation introduced in ports regularly visited by its troopships. Governments in New Zealand, India, Singapore, Canada and South Africa bowed to this pressure, as did the government in Tasmania in 1879 (Warren 1993; Backhouse 1985; Van Onselen 1980; Macdonald 1986; Arnot 1987, 1988; Daniels and Murnane 1979). Other colonies, notably Victoria and Queensland, introduced such CD Acts without any direct pressure from the military, their intention being more clearly designed for the protection of the civilian (male) population (Evans 1984; Arnot 1987). It is clear that many in the colonies saw the CD Acts not only, although primarily, as a health measure. They were also a way of controlling prostitutes' behaviour generally. As the editor of the Perth *Sunday Times* argued in 1909:

> A CD Act is wanted in Western Australia for several reasons. It is wanted in the interests of morality and public decency; it is wanted for the protection of the prostitutes themselves; it is wanted because syphilis is becoming dangerously prevalent and because the only effective means of checking it is to put the women of the town under some restraint (Davidson 1980, p 65).

Like the British legislation, the colonial laws provided for compulsory examination of prostitutes and their forcible detention in so-called lock hospitals if found to be suffering from a venereal disease. Unlike the British legislation, however, the colonial versions were not geographically specific but applied to women throughout the colony as well as in the ports. The laws were obviously discriminatory, applying only to women and not to the men who must have infected them. While some politicians conceded the injustice and illogicality of this, none was prepared to extend the Act to cover men. As the premier of Queensland, William Kidston, candidly admitted, 'In a Parliament, however, which was composed of 72 men, no seriously minded man would propose to introduce such an innovation' (Evans 1984, p 142). Not all colonial governments were so insensitive to the civil rights of women. South Australia, for instance, prided itself on doing things differently from the former convict colonies, its Advocate General declaring that CD-style legislation was not in accordance 'with the sentiments of the Colony', representing as it did an infringement on the rights of women and official condoning of immorality (Horan 1984, p 115). Western Australian legislators were likewise sensitive to lobbying from religious, feminist and civil rights groups and deleted sections from the 1911 *Health Act* which provided for compulsory notification and treatment of venereal disease, fearing that this was a version of the CD Act (Davidson 1984, pp 178–81). Those colonies which did introduce and enforce the CD Acts were arguably influenced by their heritage of female convictism. As Kay Daniels says of Tasmania, the upper classes

> ...seem not to have had a finely developed sense of the rights of working-class women. Decades during which the mere accusation that a woman was a whore had been sufficient to deny her protection and civil rights had no doubt blunted colonial sensibilities and left a society more anxious than most to draw a dividing line between the prostitute and the 'respectable' woman (Daniels 1984, p 79).

The issue of the control of venereal disease raises important questions about not just the legislation on a colony's statute books but also the ways in which it was administered. Different emphasis and interpretation could result in radically different implementation of essentially similar laws, with significantly different consequences for individual sex workers. In Queensland, for instance, the *Act for the Suppression of Contagious Diseases* of 1868 was not applied universally but only to particular centres of population, largely because of the cost, the limited facilities and the fear of a backlash of organised protest (Evans 1984, p 142). However, within the gazetted areas women who found their names on the police list were subject to regular medical examinations and if diagnosed as having syphilis or gonorrhoea were incarcerated in special lock hospitals for periods of from three to six months. Inmates in these hospitals were treated more like prisoners than patients, subject to strict rules and regulations in the hope that such discipline would bring them 'to a sense of their past degradation' (Evans 1984, p 143). Recalcitrant patients could be placed in solitary confinement, placed on a diet of bread and water or even removed to the lock-up and visitors were not permitted. Medical treatment was largely ineffective, given that there was no effective cure until the introduction of Salvarsan treatment in 1912 gave relief to some victims of the disease. (More effective treatment was not available until the use of penicillin from the 1940s.) For Queensland prostitutes, the legislation was enormously intrusive, forcing them to keep on the move to avoid police notice or to relocate outside the gazetted areas. Once caught in the web of official notice life could become a tedious series of imprisonments in the dreaded lock hospital.

By contrast to the Queensland situation the Victorian contagious diseases legislation, embodied in the *Act for the Conservation of Public Health* of 1878, was never brought into operation. According to Meg Arnot (1987, pp 10–20) this was primarily due to the activities of an organised and articulate lobby group galvanised by the Women's Christian Temperance Union. But, this did not mean that diseased prostitutes were free from official harassment. On the contrary, the Victorian police had ample flexibility under the vagrancy clauses of the *Police Offences Act* to cover this contingency. As plainclothes constable Albert Tucker explained to the 1906 Royal Commission on the Victorian Police Force: 'When we know that a woman is suffering from syphilis and is soliciting about the streets, we get hold of her and lock her up, charge her under the Vagrancy Act, and inform the magistrates in the morning, and they will send her to the gaol hospital' (Arnot 1987, p 15). A similar strategy was employed by the Western Australian police after the deletion of the compulsory VD clauses from the 1909 Health Bill (Davidson 1984, pp 178–81).

Concerns about the spread of venereal disease became especially acute in times of war when authorities became alarmed at the effect on the fighting potential of the armed forces. In such circumstances, officials were prepared to take drastic action in the interests of national security. In Perth, for instance, several cases of syphilis amongst recruits at Blackboy Hill during late 1914 were attributed to prostitutes in Roe Street brothels. The police immediately instructed the Government Medical Officer, Dr Blanchard, to examine all the brothel inmates and report his findings. Any women found to be diseased were prosecuted as vagrants. This initial inspection was followed by regular fortnightly checks, paid for at the cost of a guinea a visit by the prostitutes. The police and medical authorities had in effect introduced a system of regulation of the Roe Street inmates without any legislative sanction whatsoever.

The Second World War saw even more drastic official harassment of professional sex workers and so-called 'good-time girls' who provided sex for servicemen on a less commercial basis. Under the National Security (Venereal Diseases and Contraceptives) Regulations of September 1942, the chief medical officer in each state was empowered to compel any person whom he had 'reasonable grounds' to suspect of suffering from a venereal infection to undergo a medical examination. If found to be infected the person could be detained in a stipulated hospital or other 'suitable place'. Although men were also technically covered by these regulations, in practice it was women who were its main targets. The regulations were applied with special enthusiasm in Queensland, where large numbers of Allied troops were either based or passing through during the war. Queensland women designated as 'common prostitutes' were already subject to regular medical surveillance and compulsory confinement and treatment under the 1937 *Public Health Act*; the National Security Regulations extended this medical surveillance to the rest of the female population. Information given by infected troops was used as the basis to 'contact and dispose of' any woman allegedly suffering from venereal disease (Saunders and Taylor 1987, pp 157–61).

'BLUDGERS' AND 'WHITE SLAVERS'

Other aspects of the increasing State intervention in the prostitution industry had serious consequences for sex workers. Changes to the vagrancy laws across Australia in the early 1900s made living off the proceeds of prostitution an offence under the various Police Offences Acts. The targets of these laws were 'bludgers' or pimps, men constructed in the popular imagination as villains who debauched and enslaved innocent girls and young women, then lived off their immoral earnings. Concern about this practice was fuelled by sensationalist reports in the London press of an international 'white slave traffic' which lured innocent young girls to a life of shame in Continental and Oriental brothels. Similar reports

appeared in the press across the English-speaking world throughout the 1890s and 1900s, prompting legislation to deal with the
organisers of this 'trade in human flesh'.

In most cases these stories had racist overtones, with the villains being portrayed as 'foreigners' of one sort or another, corrupt-
ing the wholesome morals of women of British origin and descent.
Australia was no exception to this pattern. In Western Australia, for
instance, the villains were usually French or Italian, with the occasional 'Afghan buck' thrown in for additional colour. A few sensational cases involving Italians added fuel to these beliefs (Davidson
1980, pp 24–5). Ironically, the police were rarely successful in
apprehending and convicting 'white slavers', although there is certainly historical evidence of the existence of syndicates who traded
in prostitutes, with or without the full knowledge and consent of
the women concerned (Davidson 1980). Indeed, a deputation of
concerned feminists who lobbied the 1914 Premiers' Conference in
Melbourne regarding the international traffic in women and girls
were refused admission and told that the premiers did not believe
in the existence of such a trade (Davidson 1980, p 71). The men
who became the targets of this legislation were generally less vil-
lainous types — the husbands and relatives of prostitutes who willingly contributed their earnings to the upkeep of people they lived
with and loved. Very often, too, the 'bludger' of popular imagination was in reality a necessary assistant to the prostitute, providing
protection against violent clients and a less obvious way of soliciting custom. The legislation rebounded on these women, who could
no longer support family members or use their help without fearing the prosecution of their menfolk (Golder and Allen 1979–80;
Arnot 1988, p 54). One can see this attack on 'bludgers' as the most
extreme form of a move throughout Australian society from the late
nineteenth century to sharpen the definition of men as breadwin-
ners and women as dependents.

THE TWENTIETH CENTURY

All these State interventions in combination had profound effects
on the ways in which prostitution could be practised in twentieth
century Australia. The increasing illegality of so many aspects of
prostitution and related activities meant that police had more

control over what prostitutes did and where they worked. In Western Australia this power was used by the police, in collusion with magistrates, medical authorities and local governments, to establish red-light districts in major population centres such as Perth and Kalgoorlie. The breadth and flexibility provided for by the vagrancy laws meant that police could virtually dictate the behaviour of prostitutes and brothel-keepers on pain of imprisonment. While this policy meant severe infringements on the ability of sex workers to choose the location of their workplaces, it also had ramifications for the structure of the sex industry. Before the policy of localisation (ie up to about 1915) it was possible to be a freelance prostitute, operating as a streetwalker or independently in a house or flat. With the advent of the Hay Street brothels in Kalgoorlie and those of Roe Street in Perth, it became increasingly difficult for women to operate outside the tolerated brothels. In order to escape police harassment women had to become either brothel inmates or keepers. While this meant big profits for the few who became keepers, for the majority of sex workers the change spelt a 'proletariatisation' of their occupation as they gave up self-employment for the position of brothel employees, handing over half their earnings to the madam (Davidson 1980). Police ensured that organised criminals were kept away from the tolerated brothels by using the vagrancy provisions against 'bludgers' to deter any men other than customers from associating with the inmates.

A similar process of proletariatisation occurred in New South Wales over the same period, although it took a different form. Hilary Golder and Judith Allen (1979–80) describe how the increased police powers encouraged corruption in the police force, with individual officers accepting bribes to administer the law selectively. Organised criminal gangs, already in existence to control the gambling industry as well as the opium and illicit liquor traffic, seized this opportunity to extract protection money from freelance prostitutes, brothel-keepers and individual pimps, since they were the only ones with enough capital to pay either the police or the new heavy fines. Increasingly, sex-workers were forced to relinquish their former independence for the dubious protection of criminal networks. As Golder and Allen (1979–80, p 19) argue, this meant that

...the individual lost control over when, for how long, with whom and for what amount or kind of payment she worked. Her work could be deployed and incorporated into the service context of the drug, liquor or gambling traffic, whether she liked it or not. Increasingly she could be pushed into positions of risk, both as regards rival underworld gangs and the agents of the state. And where pimps survived, they tended to survive as employees of the criminal interests and acted in a managerial or supervisory capacity.

The changes to the New South Wales *Summary Offences Act* in 1908 thus provided the structural preconditions for the rise of the rival 'gang queens', Tilly Devine and Kate Leigh, who dominated Sydney prostitution from the 1920s to the 1940s.

The changes which occurred in the late nineteenth and early twentieth centuries set the framework for the operation of prostitution for most of the twentieth century. Only since the late 1970s have governments started experimenting with new ways of treating prostitution, generally moving towards less punitive models of legislation. These changes reflect changes in public attitudes towards sexual relations between consenting adults generally and a greater awareness of the deficiencies and injustices embodied in the previous approach. The evolution of new approaches is an ongoing process and the end of the twentieth century promises to be another crucial period in the history of Australian prostitution as state governments and local councils grapple with the various civil rights, health and planning issues associated with prostitution (Gerull and Halstead 1992). What is certain is that we will continue to see 'the State' behaving in complex and sometimes contradictory ways. Different levels of government (federal, state, local) have different priorities and responsibilities and these are not always compatible. Likewise, different state agencies (eg police, child welfare, health, prisons, military) have different agendas which sometimes coincide but at other times work in opposition to each other.

RESISTANCE

Although State activities have been enormously important in influencing the nature and experience of prostitution in Australian cities, they are by no means the only factor explaining changes in the industry over time. For instance, the State does not simply apply its policies to a passive prostitution industry. Sex workers have been able in the past, and will no doubt continue in the future to resist and negotiate attempts to control them. Since the 1980s this has been expressed most effectively through organised groups such as the Australian Prostitutes Collective and the Scarlet Alliance, but even before this there is evidence that prostitutes acted individually and collectively to protect their rights and to shape their working lives. Roberta Perkins (1991) notes the way in which Sydney street prostitutes acted collectively to retain certain working conditions, such as the refusal of 'kinky' services to clients. Oral evidence from my own research on Kalgoorlie reveals a similar collective control of the services offered in Hay Street brothels until the late 1970s (Frances 1993).

Individual acts of resistance are harder for the historian using written sources to uncover, but occasionally we get glimpses which suggest that prostitutes did not always accept the official view of their lives and behaviour. Prostitutes in Western Australia, for instance, complained to higher officials if they felt police officers were abusing their powers and these complaints appear to have been taken seriously and acted upon. Individual women also frequently abused arresting police in terms which reversed the supposed moral value of prostitute and policeman. Thus a Parramatta woman shouted at police who arrested her in a hotel in 1879: 'God bugger the police, they are a lot of bloody scoundrels' (Golder and Allen 1979–80, p 21).

OTHER FACTORS

Popular attitudes and practices regarding sexuality and morality must also be recognised as a factor in the changing nature of prostitution. Different class and demographic patterns also affect the type of clientele seeking the services of prostitutes and hence the type of services demanded. Kalgoorlie sex workers, for instance, comment on the less complicated demands made by the miners and 'bushies' who form the bulk of their customers. Into 'good old-fashioned sex', they make fewer demands on the women's time and ingenuity, in sharp contrast to the 'deviants' amongst the Perth businessmen who frequent prostitutes in that city (Cohen 1994, p 17). But even Kalgoorlie has seen an expansion in the variety of its services over the last 20 years. Ex-prostitute Rita, talking to me in 1978, described how things had changed in the nine years since she began working in Hay Street: 'I did it nine years ago and it was just ordinary, straight, prostitution. But now, there's that many per-versions, that many things … they've got a whole big menu (laugh-ing)' (Frances 1993).

This transition reflects the changing nature of the demand for prostitutes' services. Essentially, prostitutes provide services which men cannot get easily elsewhere. Where there are large numbers of single men and few available women this tends to be simple sex, the kind they would expect to enjoy with girlfriends or wives. In the past, clients were also drawn from single men who could not expect their girlfriends to contravene prevailing sexual mores by engaging in sex outside marriage and from married men whose wives did not want to have sex for fear of pregnancy or because of ill health. A relaxation of social taboos concerning extra-marital sex and better contraception has meant that more men can find sexual partners without having to resort to prostitutes. Those who do still seek a prostitute's services are thus often temporarily away from their womenfolk (like miners or servicemen) or seeking sexual activities that their wives/girlfriends are unwilling to engage in. As non-prostitutes become more sexually adventurous, prostitutes are sought for increasingly bizarre kinds of services, a situation which is resisted and resented by many sex workers.

Other factors independent of legislation have affected the demand for and supply of prostitutes. Social and economic crises such as wars and depressions have had particular importance in this respect. In both the 1890s and 1930s depressions more women were drawn into prostitution, as both single and married women sought other ways to make money when they or their husbands were unable to find enough work at their regular occupations. The population of Perth's Roe Street brothels rose from 50 to 70 during 1930, as both single and married women took desperate measures to survive the economic downturn (Davidson 1980, p 110). The increased numbers of women selling sexual services and the reduced spending power of men in the community meant that earnings for individual prostitutes and madams suffered consider-ably during this period.

The reverse happened during periods of economic boom, such as goldrushes and during wars, both of which brought large concentrations of men with money to spend. During wars especially the increased numbers of women, particularly young women, willing to engage in sex with soldiers was more than offset by the easy earnings available from men who were intent on having a good time before leaving for the battle zone. Many women took advantage of high wartime earnings to amass considerable amounts of capital which they used either to retire from prostitution or to expand their interests in the industry. Two notorious Roe Street madams of the interwar years, Mary Ann Collins and Josie de Bray, made their fortunes from brothels in Fremantle and Perth respectively during the First World War (Davidson 1980, p 100). The Vietnam War was also a boom time for Sydney sex-workers, as Rita recalls: 'I had more money than I've ever had in me bloomin' life. I had trips all over Australia. Went everywhere. I had a ball. Money was no worry' (Frances 1993).

Changing immigration policies were also important in influencing both the supply of prostitutes and customers. The female emigrant ships of the nineteenth century carried many single women who found their way on to the streets and brothels of Australia's young cities, inspiring the concern of reformers like Caroline Chisholm. Mass immigration of men from particular ethnic groups at different periods in our history has created special demands for the services of prostitutes, since racial prejudice amongst Anglo-Celtic Australians often prohibited their mixing with non-prostitute women. The Chinese and Pacific Island workers of the nineteenth century are the most obvious example, but later arrivals of Italian and Yugoslav workers in the twentieth century had a similar effect. Immigration restrictions could likewise restrict the supply of sex workers to meet these demands. While Japanese prostitutes played a large part in catering to non-white clients in the nineteenth century, especially in the north and on the Western Australian goldfields, the *Immigration Restriction Act* of 1901 meant that most returned home, along with their countrymen (Sissons 1976–7). Certain immigrant groups could also operate successfully as entrepreneurs in the prostitution industry. The Japanese in northern Australia mentioned previously are one instance; the Maltese in the back lanes of East Sydney in the 1960s is another (see Perkins 1992).

While factors such as these explain the changing dimensions of prostitution over time, other themes have retained a remarkable constancy or resilience. The gender bias of most of the laws about prostitution and their implementation is all too apparent from the preceding discussion. The class nature of prostitution and the enforcement of laws against it are also especially evident. The economic forces propelling women into prostitution have acted most strongly against working class women, but not exclusively. Prostitutes have been drawn from all sections of society and have operated in ways which have usually reflected their different social origins. Almost invariably, the targets of police harassment have been those least able to defend themselves: the streetwalkers and inmates of 'lower class' brothels who cater to a wide clientele. Middle class sex workers, operating as call girls, escorts or, in earlier times, in exclusive brothels, have had a much easier time of it, being able to work more discreetly and having more powerful friends to intervene on their behalf. Even when middle class women did come under official notice, as happened during the venereal disease surveillance of the Second World War, they were treated differently from their working class sisters. While the diseased street prostitute was sent to the lock hospital and treated as a prisoner, middle class sex workers contracting the disease were sent to private hospitals and treated as patients (Saunders and Taylor 1987).

Racial and age biases have also been evident in the way the law has been administered. Older women have generally been more vulnerable to arrest, both because they are generally forced to solicit more frequently to maintain their earnings and because the public and the police regard their presence as more offensive than that of younger women. On the other hand, very young women were considered in need of protection and reclamation and were also more likely to receive official attention (Golder and Allen 1979–80). Racial discrimination is a more vexed issue. In some situations prostitutes of non-Anglo-Celtic descent were less likely to be prosecuted. Japanese women, for instance, largely escaped prosecution in Queensland because they were seen to provide 'suitable outlets' for the sexual passions of 'coloured' male labourers. It was far preferable, in the eyes of the authorities, to have Asian women servicing this trade than European women (Evans 1984, p 139). Japanese women in Western Australia also enjoyed a remarkably prosecution-free existence, probably for similar reasons, even though their customers were often white. The logic here still seems to have been that it was better for Japanese women to perform this 'degrading' work than it was for Australian women. The high profile of Japanese, French and Italian women in Western Australia also encouraged politicians in the mistaken belief that 'our social conditions' meant that the supply of Australian women for prostitution had given out (Davidson 1980, p 137).

A final recurring theme refers both to the historiography and the history of prostitution in Australia. Because of its illegal, clandestine nature, prostitution presents particular challenges and opportunities to the historian. The frequent contacts between some classes of prostitutes and officialdom mean that historians often have more knowledge about the lives of prostitutes in the past than about their more 'respectable' sisters, about whom few written records survive. But such records present their own problems: they are a partial account only, in that not all sex workers are represented in the police record. And they present the picture from the official perspective rather than from the point of view of the woman herself. Occasionally historians are blessed with diaries or reminiscences of such women, but these are very rare indeed. The historian of prostitution needs to be especially imaginative in the use of the surviving written record, listening hard for the voices of women who do manage to get recorded. For the more recent past the task is made easier by the use of oral history, where prostitutes can speak their own stories in their own words. The work of Roberta Perkins (1989, 1992) on Sydney's 'working girls' from 1985 onward is an indication of how rewarding such research can be for the historian. Similar studies in other Australian cities would greatly enhance our knowledge of the history of prostitution in this country since the Second World War. Such studies would not just provide analysis of changing trends; they could literally restore the voice of prostitutes to history. Interviews of this kind could provide the raw material for 'playback' oral testimony as a feature of our hypothetical museum of prostitution.

2

ORAL HISTORY
OF SEX WORKERS IN SYDNEY
Jeddah Jakobsen and Roberta Perkins

This chapter looks at the personal histories of female prostitutes in a period of over sixty years, and compares them with the 'press' that sex workers received in mainstream Sydney newspapers at the same time. In doing so it illustrates some ways in which morality is socially constructed and invoked by society's more powerful groups, in order to support their ideas on legal and social control, as well as providing an insight into the world of prostitutes in the past. We have not dealt with male sex workers in this chapter, because the greater turnover of men than of women in prostitution and the higher concentration of youth in male sex work has resulted in less depth of oral history. Also, the moral reaction and social controls pertinent to male prostitution tend to focus on homosexuality rather than on prostitution, and this is reflected in press accounts of male sex workers.

SEX WORKERS AS 'BAD WOMEN'

Foucault (1980) discusses the constitution of sexuality as a 'moral domain', looking at the conditions under which we humans complicate the meaning of what we are, what we do, and the world in which we live. Practices such as stigmatising, criminalising or otherwise punishing, silencing and excluding the women who trade in sex form the basis for distinguishing prostitutes as 'bad' in the moral domain. The sources of prostitution history for conventional historians, such as official documents, police records, legislative instruments and the media, have reinforced this bias in covert ways. For example, police and court records continue to interpret prostitutes as criminals, and arrest data used by the media to indicate an active prostitution population fail to take into account the high proportion of arrests of recidivists. The political implications of the police, politicians and moralists manipulating the media in this way are obvious. When prostitutes have limited access to the media, as a result of their 'invisibility', the behaviour, lies or misrepresentations of these manipulating groups go undetected. Prostitutes are silenced by clamourous moral crucifixion whereby they are presented as irresponsible and brazen, with the morals of a dog, being low in intelligence and spreading like a pestilence. Their silence ensures that whispers of the injustice and corruption of the conservative groups remain unheeded. The oral history of prostitutes, despite being fraught with the difficulties of wariness and suspicion on the part of the women, offers a great opportunity to balance the picture and to let us reflect on how the power to define morality has been used and abused.

The fluidity of moral concepts can be seen in changing attitudes to sex workers as reflected both in language and in legislation. Prior to the *Prostitution Act* of 1979, which legalised street soliciting and sex work in a brothel or a private flat, the prostitutes were outsiders: 'fallen women' and 'criminals' who were finger-printed and had 'KP' ('Known Prostitute') stamped across their records. But in New South Wales in the 1990s these former criminals have increasingly been seen more positively, as workers in the sex industry with their own representative organisations.

While there is a burgeoning feminist debate about whether this acceptance of sex work as ordinary work by ordinary women is an entirely desirable development, when we look at conditions and attitudes towards sex workers in the 1960s and 1970s, and the increased vulnerability to violence and unwilling involvement in police corruption that these conditions and attitudes fostered, it is clear that societal inclusion has clear advantages for women working as prostitutes. When they are able to speak for themselves, sex workers emerge as women with lifestyles and attitudes not dissimilar from those of most other women. In a survey of 280 female prostitutes across New South Wales in 1991, Perkins et al. found that only 44 percent of the women were single, while 16 percent were married, 18 percent were in de facto relationships and 25 percent were divorced or separated. A third of the women had children. They had an average age of 21, 43 percent of them had white collar fathers and 79 percent of them still followed a formal religion (Perkins et al. 1991). In an earlier study (1985–86) 14 percent of the prostitutes held an HSC, 8 percent had matriculated, 14 percent had a diploma or trade certificate and 3 percent held a tertiary degree (Perkins 1991, p 180). The assertion that prostitutes are ordinary women, nonetheless, confronts the popular and press view and undermines practices and arguments for exclusion, separation and control.

COPS, CRIMS AND BROTHEL-KEEPERS

In the 1960s it was easier for the anti-prostitution lobby to accuse sex workers of associating with criminals and ne'er-do-wells, for the criminal stigma of sex workers at the time left them with little choice but to mix with crims and pimps. But as one sex worker, Karen, also points out: 'Lots of girls were having affairs with policemen. If you weren't a favourite, it wouldn't have been easy to work' (Perkins 1992, p 178; hereafter all comments by sex workers throughout this chapter come from this book). Transferring affections between crims and cops seemed easy, for as Karen recalls, 'After I broke up with the policeman I was on with a famous crim.' The favourite villain of the day was multi-brothel owner, Joe Borg. The press presented him as a gangster and standover tyrant, whose death by explosives in his car in 1968 was viewed as a blessing. Lisa, a prostitute who worked for him, saw him very differently: 'There were no gangs, Joe worked for himself and he was a lovely man, very fair with the girls.' The insights provided by oral testimony, particularly from the 'old girls' — as the younger street prostitutes of the 1980s would refer to the brothel

workers who had worked in East Sydney since the 1950s — reveal a group of women with far greater economic freedom than most other women. And in the earlier period of the 1950s and 1960s they also possessed much greater sexual freedom, even though outside their work and their marriages this may have been limited to policemen and gangsters. The price for this economic and sexual freedom, though, was high: arrests, which in the 1960s averaged 25 per woman per year; and brutality from pimps and more often from clients, sometimes resulting in death and always a legal and social stigma.

We can speculate on whether decriminalisation opened the way for more opportunities for women at the top of the industry. In 1993 post-feminist sex worker, Annabelle, comments: 'I wouldn't work in a brothel run by a man'. The advantage of female management is cited as an inducement in advertisements for workers in sex trade publications. Donna from the New South Wales North Coast suggests that 'a woman in charge [of a brothel] knows how to handle [any potentially violent] situations so everyone calms down'. Nowadays there are even lesbian-run brothels with a male clientele. Such speculation about the rise of female bosses also occurred in the late 1960s, at the beginning of the women's liberation movement. The *Sydney Morning Herald* of 3 October 1968 quoted the Chief Secretary of the Liberal Government, Mr Willis, as saying that 'there were two or three Mrs Bigs and Mrs Sins, who are bigger than Mr Big or Mr Sin in the field of organised prostitution'. These women were usually ex-prostitutes who, having worked during the war and the postwar years, gradually gained ascendancy in the late 1960s and early 1970s. According to Karen, they were tough businesswomen:

> Four women were running the houses, so I went to work for them. They just about ran prostitution [in Darlinghurst] for many years, collecting men in their cars and bringing them up to us in the houses in which we worked. They used to charge us for the cars, for a sitter and for the rent as well. A job was six pounds [$12] then, but we had to pay 20 pounds [$40] rent and five pounds [$10] for the sitter, and hardly ending up with anything. They really ripped us off, while the girls on the streets only had to worry about renting a

hotel room for the night. Because we were in the houses and had to make a certain amount we had to take whatever men were brought in, and they were horrible types too.

Lisa left Sydney to work in Perth for five months in 1969. When she returned she found one woman dominating Darlinghurst:

> Everybody was back on William Street, but this time driving cars. You had your own car and you would pick a client up and take him back to a house run by the only woman now allowed to run houses. If anybody else tried to get a house the police closed in, and if you had a boyfriend or husband he was arrested for living off the earnings. You had to work for her. If you didn't you had some terrible misfortunes in your life. I have no idea why she alone was allowed to operate houses. All I know is she was able to do it when others couldn't.

Women have been prominent in management at other times — such characters as Tilly Devine, who ran houses of prostitution in the 1930s. She was one of the few newsworthy items in our search of newspaper records of the immediate prewar and post-war periods, and we know through her stories that prostitution thrived as much then as in the 1960s. Community reaction can be seen in the stiff penalties dealt out to misdemeanour offenders, such as Kate Barry whom the *Sydney Morning Herald* of 14 January 1930 reports was imprisoned for six months for 'habitually consorting with women of ill-repute'. Maggie, a sex worker in the 1930s, reported to Perkins that one way of avoiding such consequences was to dissociate oneself from the usual methods of public prostitution and refer to oneself as a 'good time gal'. The lack of coverage in the 1930s in total contrast to the journalistic trends of the 1960s and 1980s may indicate the extent of censorship on prewar prostitution, or perhaps it was seen as less of a threat to the largely working class population of the inner city. In the 1960s though, with reactions from the Right and the new moralism to the 'sexual revolution' and feminism, as well as the spread of the middle classes into the inner city, prostitution became a key issue for the press.

THE NEW MORALISM AND POLICE PRACTICES

An important factor in changing attitudes to sex workers since the 1970s has been the danger of the spread of HIV and the need to enrol sex workers into the use of safer sexual health practices as a means of protecting 'society', clients and their families. When socially responsible behaviour from sex workers has such direct benefits and effects in the communities in which they work, the punishment and oppression they have endured in other historical periods is stopped or modified. Equally important are the resurgence of the women's movement in the 1970s and the concurrent development of international prostitutes' movements and organisations, through which prostitutes could at last have an input into the debate and the many pronouncements about their 'profession' that are so freely made by other groups and individuals in the community. Before the rise of the prostitutes' rights movement in Australia, the women themselves were largely concerned with surviving the consequences of the legal and social scapegoating and exclusion resulting from their decision to trade in sex. They had no voice. Rather there was, and still exists, a fierce determination to protect themselves through silence and anonymity. However, many men representing civic groups, chambers of commerce, parliamentary parties, residents' groups, the police, local councils and the churches felt quite free to speak out about prostitution, and their views are liberally represented in the newspapers.

The representation and coverage of *prostitutes'* views which is evident in the newspapers from the 1970s also became an effective way of checking the behaviour of other groups, such as the police, who were less likely to take advantage of the prostitutes' position by, for example, demanding money to prevent arrest — previously a commonplace occurrence. The police in the 1960s were encouraged by the community, the church and the government to eradicate prostitution, but Jeanette, who bears a scar on each breast from a policeman's cigarette burns, says that rather than drive her from business they preferred to profit by her earnings. 'There's a lot of cops' wives whom I've helped put fur coats on their backs and a lot of cops' kids whom I've helped educate', she said. Most interviewees who had worked prior to 1979 spoke of police corruption. 'The majority of cops were on the take then', says Lee. 'But it was the odd one on each shift who wasn't on the take who would do most of the arrests. "Weighing in" was part of the way things ran in those days.' Patti was among the few who did not 'weigh in'. 'I refused to pay the $40 to the cops to prevent arrest … so I had to cop the shit.' She was among the handful of defiant sex workers who made up the annual police statistics of over 10,000 arrests for prostitution in the 1960s:

> Officially they reckoned I was arrested 325 times, but in reality it was considerably much more… You'd just come back from court having paid five pounds [$10] bail and begin working to recover this and the Vice Squad would nab you, or the 21 Division would come down and bust you. You'd be back on the street in a couple of hours and then the Special Branch would pinch you. You'd get done three times a night. You'd often be working until four in the morning to catch up. You'd think: 'Oh, fuck it, I might as well stay here to earn as much as I can, go home, have a shower, get fresh-ened up and go to court in the morning'. Some of the magistrates would only fine you ten bob, five bob, whatever. They were lovely old blokes. The only reason I used to get such low fines from them was because they were clients of mine.

Workers like Patti who refused to pay the police suffered the consequences. The police also refused to take money from some women whom they disliked, probably as a means of keeping arrest statistics at an acceptable level for the department. The media of the time certainly did not delve into this kind of corruption and it was not officially recognised until the parliamentary report of the New South Wales Select Committee Upon Prostitution appeared in 1986 (Parliament of New South Wales 1986, pp 224–8). But, from the 1970s onward when issues such as police harassment, legal reform, sexual practices in brothels or incidences of inequity on the part of local councils arose that the media were able to approach key fig-ures or organisations like the Australian Prostitutes' Collective and report their perspective.

COMMUNITY CLEAN-UP CAMPAIGNS

The ethical 'problematisation' of prostitution reveals itself not least in the language used to push for greater control. There is a remarkable consistency in the use of descriptive phrases over the years. As recently as May 1993, 'clean-ups' were being called for in areas such as the 'open sewer' of Kings Cross which was a 'national disgrace' and a 'cantankerous sore' (Sydney's *Telegraph Mirror*, 17 May 1993). In the *Sydney Morning Herald* of 24 October 1974, it was reported that Fred Nile, director of the Festival of Light movement, brought a home movie showing the 'moral pollution' of Los Angeles to a seminar on prostitution held in the Law School of the University of New South Wales. The images used in arguments for or against the practice of prostitution are often laden with implicit and explicit moral judgements and conjure up disease, filth and excrement to convey the writer's disgust.

As is so often the case, genuine concern for the plight of some visibly drug-affected sex workers along 'that 200 metre strip of Darlinghurst Road between Bayswater Road and Roslyn Street' becomes an unhelpful overreaction demanding closure of the clubs and driving of the drug dealers out of business because 'everybody knows the prostitutes are on drugs'. Wild generalisations about the drug habits of Kings Cross prostitutes are based on observing a few street workers. Yet in 1985–86 Perkins (1991, p 305) surveyed 128 Sydney prostitutes and found that only 19 percent had ever used heroin, 20 percent had ever used cocaine and 33 percent had ever used amphetamines — and that only 9 percent had commenced prostitution to support a drug habit.

The real danger of making assumptions like those about prostitutes and drugs is that it can quickly escalate into a crusading battlecry. Its associated rhetoric surfaces periodically in the press. For example, a resident mobilisation against sex workers in the early 1980s was dubbed the 'battle of Darlo', with references to 'fighting' and 'battle lines' (*Sun Herald*, Sydney, 9 January 1983). The women, working near a school at night, 'invaded' and 'plagued' it, despite the fact that it was presumably empty at the time. Workers were presented as a moral threat, a contagion, or diminished as a 'mini-skirted army' who must by implication be opposed as the enemy of decency, while not really being taken seriously. Even the story of one resident who took pot shots at the girls with an airgun and died during a police enquiry was referred to by the *Sun Herald* of 20 February 1983 as the 'death of a crusader'. The dailies were quick to sympathise with residents in their 'war' and did not report the Molotov cocktails with which the girls were bombarded beneath high rise apartment dwellings. Nor did the following disturbing incident, described by brothel prostitute Allison, ever get into the newspapers: 'One day the residents held a street barbecue and hung a dummy from a tree, lynched with a noose around its neck'. During this heated campaign to remove street workers and, when that was successful, to move to eliminate brothels in East Sydney, Allison, reasonably responding to a 'Riley Street For Residents' sign, commented: 'I am a resident too' and 'the protesters came here knowing the area has had prostitutes for years'. If it had not been for Perkins recording the women's side of the story historians of the future would have no other source than the contemporary media's partisan view.

In contrast to the 'clean-up' by the Riley Street resident group, Karen talks about community attitudes in East Sydney in the 1960s. She remembers 'women in the neighbourhood cooking meals and selling these to the girls and that's the way they made a little extra cash. Others would do our washing for us at a price. In those days everyone helped everyone else in the area and nobody cared whether you were a prostitute or not'. However, Alderman F. Moran (Labor) cared. He saw political mileage out of warning about the 'spread of vice in homes' in the *Sydney Morning Herald* of 5 September 1967. With connotations of an advertisement about the need for pest control, he said: 'We eradicated vice — or at least part of it — from Kings Cross, only to find it flourishing in private homes'. It eventuated that he 'knows of two homes in the Darlinghurst and Centennial Park areas which were used for prostitution'. Unwittingly, he was commenting on the ineffectuality of zealous Vice-Eradicators in actually achieving their stated purpose. What in fact tends to occur, when suppression of activity is called for in an offending area, is that the women move elsewhere or the form of work changes to adapt to the new conditions or regulations. If streets are off limits then back lanes are used where, in the 1960s, as Lisa notes, 'the price of sex was only two pounds' but 'there was much more business and the conditions were better'. But, when she observes that 'I was there only six months when the elections closed the lanes. They were always clamping down on prostitution before an election in those days regardless of whether it was Labor or Liberal', she reveals that the stated purpose of the Vice-Eradicator is rarely the 'real' or entire purpose .

PIMPS, CUSTOMERS AND THE COMMUNITY

Other references to sex work at this earlier time introduce the idea of predator and victim, with either the Vice Squad as hunters on a 'vice prowl' or the prostitutes themselves 'preying on young fellows' on bikes who were, in all probability, sexually curious boys with little money and of no interest to the women as clients. In the 1990s there is an emphasis on the women as the victims — of low self-esteem and of parental and drug abuse. However, in the *Sydney Morning Herald* of 29 November 1966, according to one Vice Squad detective, 'the saddest thing about it' is not that the women are victims of their fate but that they have made a clear and autonomous choice — and have opted for prostitution. This detective, however, is sorry and surprised that 'these young women appear to have gone into this with their eyes open. They know what they are doing'. Indeed, back in the 1950s Lisa's disillusion with marriage and subsequent choice of prostitution was conscious and unapologetic, suggesting that sympathy is misplaced in her case:

> My marriage should never have happened. We only lasted 19 months. At 20, after this breakup, I started working as a prostitute on the corner of College and Stanley Streets. I had met a few girls who were prostitutes and thought I would try it, and once I got pinched three times the first night I thought I might as well keep going. I only intended to go six months, but I liked the money. I wasn't starving or anything; I chose to be a prostitute. Maybe I was meant to be one, for I've made a career of it now for 20 years. I could have got a straight job then, but I preferred to be a prostitute.

Although Jeanette, another interviewee, was introduced to prostitution by her abusive husband in the late 1960s, she found in sex work a way to financial independence and escape from her marriage:

> Prostitution was proposed to me by my husband. If I didn't do it he put it to me that he would bring all his friends from the hotel

around to rape me, and he went away to give me one hour to think about this. I was 16 and pregnant at the time. I'll never forget it, I was so gullible, and you know what I thought: 'It would be a terrible thing for him to have to do to me'. And that's exactly how I started. I was taken down to a corner and offloaded 200 yards from the CIB, where no girl had ever worked before. Consequently, I was arrested the first night. I remember going to court the next morning, cold and hard, with my back up, defensive, and I remember thinking: 'Right, if this is going to be my lot, I'm going to make something out of it and he's going to get nothing. You're going to have to work for a living, you're not going to get my money'. Afterwards the CIB told me, 'Look, if you want to work, this is where you go', and they pointed to where the other girls were working at the time.

Whether the women were victims or mistresses of their fate, commentators' phrases echo each other across the decades. Thus the 'blot of prostitution in our fair city' in the *Sydney Morning Herald* of 10 June 1968 becomes prostitution as the 'sordid side of our beautiful city' in the *Telegraph Mirror* of 17 May 1993.

While it is convenient, the 'problem' with prostitution cannot be located in prostitutes; only in prevailing attitudes to sexuality and sex work. The outrage or the 'nudge, nudge, wink, wink' attitude of some of the media expresses its own disgust or titillation at the sexual services that workers perform. It is increasingly unacceptable to prostitutes to be dumped with the media's and society's prejudices and with damaging and hasty notions about sex, sex work and sex workers. It is difficult enough having to deal with some clients' projections or their fear or ignorance about women's sexuality. As it is, prostitutes offer sexual initiation to many young men for which there is no other cultural provision, as well as offering a sexual outlet to men who would otherwise lack the intimacy of sex with another person. Many sex workers make a valuable contribution by participating in what is repressed elsewhere in society — or, as one Kings Cross sex worker put it in 1983, 'people have got to realise that prostitution is a community service because it provides a definite service for a lot of men who wouldn't have that outlet for their fantasies otherwise'. However, some older workers have found it hard to adapt to changes in services that may reflect gender stresses and conflicts. Karen, active in the 1950s and 1960s and still working in the 1980s, tells us about new forms of 'kinky sex' that she encountered late in her career:

> Last year I managed a parlour for someone and that's where you meet some of the weird ones. I could hardly believe it; some of the things the clients wanted I'd never heard of before. There were highly intelligent guys wanting to be dressed as babies and put in a playpen, others wanted to be whipped and these were business-men, or wanted the girl to dress up as a schoolgirl, or wanted lessons on how to dress as a woman. There were a lot of guys who were gay and couldn't admit it and would go to the parlour to dress in women's clothes.

Margaret, another of our contributors, adds that no one wants 'just a straight fuck' any more. The more conservative attitudes to sexual practices contrast with the post-'sexual revolution' genera-tion's attitudes towards sex. Such comparisons can provide a rich resource for social scientists interested in, for example, the way soci-etal power relations are manifested symbolically within sexuality.

PROSTITUTES AS SOURCES OF THEIR OWN HISTORY

In gathering this information the oral historian gains access to lively personal accounts that provide a human dimension and fresh insight into events that contribute to the history of prostitution. In conducting ethical research of this nature it is important to remem-ber that the 'whore' stigma continues to carry such negative conno-tations for its bearer that disclosure can lead to social catastrophes such as family alienation, sexual discrimination and harassment, community ostracism and violence. This has implications for the procedures used by the historian. When a sex worker agrees to be interviewed, it is the interviewer's responsibility to establish with her the boundaries of anonymity. Most prostitute interviewees will not only want their real name not to be disclosed but also their 'working name'. The reason for this is to avoid being identified by colleagues who may resent them making a particular comment, expressing a viewpoint or revealing some pertinent information about the industry. For the same reason interviewees may ask that their workplace (or brothel) not be identified either. Some workers will go as far as requesting that details of particular incidents in their lives be altered in any publication. Of course, there are legal implications as well. For instance, where certain activities associated with sex work are illegal a worker's admission to performing them could lead to her arrest. In any interview concern for her children and other members of her family are foremost in her mind. The social repercussions from public identification of a mother or daughter or spouse as a prostitute can result in enduring negative consequences for those closely involved with the interviewee. The woman's lover, for example, may be assumed to be a pimp, bringing with it the weight of the law as well as social stigma.

So, unlike other subjects of personal histories, the prostitute must often alter certain aspects of her background or avoid mentioning it altogether in order to protect her identity. Accepting this is not historical misrepresentation but proper ethical conduct in protecting the lives entrusted to the historian. Otherwise there would be no one to tell prostitutes' histories from their perspective, and this would maintain a silence that has for too long led to biased histories drawn by conventional historians from the inadequacies of police files, court records and media stories.

The opportunity to approach prostitutes not as deviants or victims but as ordinary women involved in the commercial sex industry, who have unique stories to tell about their experiences, has been squandered by the media because of its moral bias, its propensity to sensationalise and its lopsided reporting. As a result, state governments are able persistently to ignore the facts in favour of political expedience. In Queensland recently some misguided intention to give sex workers 'independence' led the Goss Government to limit (by law) active prostitution to women working alone. The tragic consequences of this were noted by us on a recent visit to the Gold Coast. Forced to work alone, one woman has apparently been murdered and other private workers are now hiring armed guards to protect themselves. It is ironical that the law has forced these women to employ violent men to save them from other violent men. Meanwhile the target of the government action, the supposed gangsters who run the brothels, are either operating clandestinely to the detriment of the women's freedom and health or, in the case of one well-known Gold Coast brothel owner, have shifted their operations across the border. Shortly afterwards, in Brisbane, Jakobsen received reports that the police are able to intimidate sex workers seeking HIV education at their local representative organisation because workers are discouraged from meeting in groups. While prostitutes we talked to have clear views about the social and emotional effects of the legislation, such as the isolation and fear it generates, these views are not reported in the newspapers. We must conclude that one of the main problems for sex workers who enjoy what they do, or who find it difficult to walk away from the financial benefits and invaluable flexibility of work conditions that would not otherwise be available to them, is having to deal with the far-reaching consequences of their 'bad press' and distorted history.

3

PROSTITUTION LAWS IN AUSTRALIA — PAST HISTORY AND CURRENT TRENDS

Marcia Neave

The purpose of this chapter is to describe the laws dealing with prostitution in Australia, placing particular emphasis on recent developments. In Australia there has been a demand for prostitution since the earliest days of colonial settlement, but the women who have met that demand have been stigmatised and punished (Arnot 1988). Tasmania, South Australia and Western Australia continue to criminalise most forms of prostitution, although in Western Australia prostitution offences are dealt with selectively under an official policy of 'toleration and containment'. Queensland recently responded to the Fitzgerald Inquiry's findings of police corruption associated with prostitution by enacting harsher prostitution laws, despite contrary recommendations by the Criminal Justice Commission. The history of the policy of criminalisation and the current provisions which apply to prostitution-related activities in these jurisdictions are discussed in the second part of this chapter.

Although most activities associated with prostitution have been punished in Australia since the late nineteenth century, the

past two decades have seen a retreat from the view that the prostitution 'problem' will be resolved by creating new offences and
imposing harsher penalties. Four jurisdictions, Victoria, New
South Wales, Northern Territory and the Australian Capital
Territory have reformed their prostitution laws. The reforms range
from regulating brothels in Victoria and escort agencies in the
Northern Territory, to removing criminal penalties for street prostitution in New South Wales and for escort agency and brothel
prostitution in the Australian Capital Territory. The third part of
this chapter discusses these reforms. Of all Australian states,
Tasmania is the only one which does not appear to have considered prostitution law reform.

Prostitution laws cannot be understood in isolation from the
context in which they are interpreted and enforced (Arnot 1988,
p 55). The history of prostitution shows that laws apparently
designed to suppress prostitution have often been used as a form
of de facto regulation. Criminal sanctions do not eradicate or
reduce the extent of prostitution, but determine the structure of
the sex industry, and the conditions under which sexual services
are sold (Daniels 1984, p 335). The adoption of a policy of 'toleration and containment' which has occurred in Australia, both
informally and at an official level, accommodates the interest of
men who buy sexual services. Sometimes prostitution is seen as a
'necessary evil' which provides an outlet for uncontrollable male
sexuality, thus protecting 'respectable women' and children from
seduction or rape. Alternatively prostitution may be seen as undesirable but inevitable. Since eradication is impossible, toleration
and containment is regarded as preferable to futile and expensive
law enforcement measures. Historically both these views about
prostitution could be accommodated by maintaining laws which
prohibited prostitution-related activities but enforcing such laws
selectively.

In the nineteenth century, concern about prostitution focused
on its threat to public order and morality and on the perception
that women prostitutes were vectors of sexually transmitted diseases (Walkowitz 1980; Daniels 1984, pp 58–80; Davidson 1984,
pp 175–86). In the latter part of the twentieth century, pressure for
government action on prostitution is more likely to focus on its

effect on 'quality of life' or property values. Greater toleration of sex outside marriage and some relaxation of the double standard applicable to men and women has led to questioning of the view that the sale of sex is inherently wrong. The notion that criminal law should be the instrument for enforcement of sexual morality has been abandoned by the majority of the community, including the mainstream churches. Although feminists are divided in their views about prostitution (Freeman 1989, p 75; Cheney 1988), feminist critiques have made it difficult to justify criminal laws which punish the seller but not the buyer of sexual services. Criticism of the effects of criminalisation has led some jurisdictions to introduce more formal systems of controlling prostitution, rather than the informal processes of toleration and containment which applied in the past. Informal systems of toleration and containment stigmatised and controlled prostitutes (who were usually women) while ensuring that men had access to their services. Just as criminal law sanctions disempowered prostitutes, controls imposed on the prostitution industry may increase the power of brothel and escort agency operators, without improving the conditions under which prostitutes work or protecting them from abuse or exploitation by employers, customers or police. This chapter is written from a feminist perspective. It seeks to assess the extent to which recent prostitution law reforms will improve the situation of people working in the sex industry, the majority of whom are women.

CRIMINALISATION OF PROSTITUTION — HISTORY AND CURRENT PROVISIONS

Until the recent law reforms in New South Wales, Victoria, the Australian Capital Territory and the Northern Territory, all Australian jurisdictions had prostitution-specific offences punishing activities such as soliciting, brothel-keeping and living on the earnings of prostitution. These offences, which were largely modelled on English legislation,[1] were introduced in most states during the middle to late nineteenth century. Before that time the behaviour of women prostitutes and their associates was regulated by selective enforcement of vagrancy and public order legislation (Daniels 1984, pp 45, 75; Arnot 1985, pp 3ff; Allen 1984, pp 199–204; Allen 1990, pp 20–2; Evans 1984, p 146). Often such legislation permitted prosecution of common prostitutes or reputed prostitutes for 'riotous or disorderly behaviour'[2] thus symbolising their stigmatisation and segregation from 'respectable' women (Mills 1984, p 299). Similarly, brothel-keepers who came to police attention could be prosecuted for public order offences or under statutory provisions designed to prevent licensed premises and shops selling food or drinks from being used as fronts for prostitution (Arnot 1985, pp 6ff; Horan 1984, p 90). In Victoria the ancient common law offence of keeping a bawdy house was sometimes used to prosecute brothel-keepers whose premises created a nuisance to their neighbours (Arnot 1985, p 9).

Selective enforcement of vagrancy laws allowed police to move prostitutes from one area to another or to charge women whose behaviour was blatantly offensive. Allen's work has shown that older, poorer prostitutes were more likely to be police targets (Allen 1990, p 25). Police powers could also be used to force women into brothels, where prostitution was less visible and to force brothel-owners to move out of desirable residential areas.

From the middle to late ninteenth century all states began to increase surveillance and control of prostitutes by criminalising a wider range of activities. Historians have suggested that harsher attitudes to prostitutes were consistent with decreasing social tolerance for public manifestations of deviance and disorder and with the desire to control and civilise the urban poor (Arnot 1988, p 52). Extension of the criminal law was also supported by abolitionists who regarded prostitutes as 'more sinned against than sinning', and sought harsher penalties against the brothel-keepers and 'bludgers' who exploited women and children. Medical debate about the role of prostitutes in spreading sexually transmitted disease contributed to acceptance of the policy of criminalisation. In Tasmania (Daniels 1984, pp 58ff) and Queensland (Evans 1984, pp 141ff) legislation modelled on English contagious diseases legislation was introduced to permit compulsory detention and treatment of women suspected of infection with venereal diseases.[3] In some states police campaigned for extension of offences to make it easier to obtain convictions of prostitutes and brothel-keepers (Allen 1990, pp 73ff).

THE CRIMINAL LAW IN WESTERN AUSTRALIA, TASMANIA AND SOUTH AUSTRALIA

The offences introduced in all states around the end of the nineteenth century remain part of the criminal law in Western Australia, South Australia and Tasmania, although they have been refined and expanded. Queensland has recently enacted a number of new prostitution offences which are discussed in more detail below. Prostitution-specific offences fall into two main groups. The first group primarily concerns pimps, brothel-keepers and those who own premises used for the purposes of prostitution. Part A of Table 3.1 sets out offences falling into the first group. The second group, which is set out in Part A of Table 3.2, is intended to cover prostitutes. (Section numbers which appear on the tables are not footnoted.) In Western Australia, Tasmania and South Australia procuring a person for the purposes of prostitution (ie inducing a person to sell sexual services) is an offence, as are brothel-keeping and living on the earnings of prostitution. It should be noted that the procuring offence is not directed at clients of prostitutes, but at brothel-keepers and pimps. It is rarely prosecuted.

Although the 'keeping or managing a brothel' offence was originally intended to apply to brothel owners it is frequently used to prosecute women answering the telephone in brothels or acting as receptionists. Western Australia and Tasmania have also retained provisions making it an offence to be an occupier of a house frequented by prostitutes or to 'harbour' a prostitute. Such offences were originally directed at owners of property used as brothels, but could also be used against women working as prostitutes.

Activities which are not forbidden by the criminal law are lawful. Even the states which have continued to support the policy of criminalisation have not gone so far as to make the act of prostitution illegal. In 1957 the English Wolfenden Committee argued that the role of the criminal law should be to prevent harm to the community, rather than to enforce morality. Thus prostitution-related activities should be subject to criminal law sanctions only to the extent necessary to protect the public from nuisance and to protect prostitutes (especially women) from exploitation. In England, consistently with this distinction, brothel-keeping offences did not apply to 'freelance' prostitutes who used their own premises (*Singleton v Ellison* [1895]

1 QB 607; *Strath v Foxon* [1956] 1 QB 67. Cf *Donovan v Gavin* [1965] 2 QB 648; *Abbott v Smith* [1965] 2 QB 662).

The failure to punish prostitution itself made it possible for sex workers to find ways of selling sex without breaking the law. Prostitutes (but not their clients) can be punished for soliciting or loitering in a public place for the purposes of prostitution in Western Australia, Tasmania[4] and South Australia. (Western Australia also retains an archaic offence directed at disorderly behaviour by 'common prostitutes'.) However, in Western Australia and Tasmania premises used by a single prostitute are not defined as brothels, so that freelance workers cannot be convicted of brothel-keeping offences. In these states women can also work for escort agencies without committing a criminal offence, though their employers may be charged with living on their earnings. Much of the prostitution in Tasmania is arranged through escort agencies.

By contrast, in South Australia the definition of brothel was expanded to catch single prostitutes, ensuring that virtually all forms of prostitution were criminalised.[5] The South Australian policy of punishing prostitutes working on their own behalf dates back to Section 3 of the *Suppression of Brothels Act* 1907 which defined a brothel to include premises used by a *woman* (singular) 'who is accustomed to receive men ... for sexual purposes'. The current provision makes it an offence 'to receive any money paid in a brothel in respect of prostitution'. The provision was intended to make it easier to obtain convictions of sex workers by dispensing with the requirement that sexual services had actually been provided. In *McDonald v Samoilenko* (1989) 51 SASR 119 the Supreme Court of South Australia held that the offences of brothel-keeping and receiving money in a brothel applied to single prostitutes using their own premises.

In South Australia the reach of the criminal law was further expanded by the 1972 decision of the High Court in *Samuels v Bosch* (1972) 127 CLR 517, which held that premises where men went to engage a prostitute came within the definition of a brothel, for the purposes of the South Australian legislation, even though sexual services were not provided on those premises (Goode 1991, pp 15–25). This meant that the brothel-keeping offences could apply to escort agencies, though their application could be avoided by making telephone bookings, rather than allowing men to come to the premises to select their 'escorts'. The effect of the provisions discussed above is that in South Australia most forms of prostitution are criminalised.

Despite the policy of criminalisation which existed in all Australian states until recently, prostitution laws have always been selectively enforced. Offences such as loitering for the purposes of prostitution allow police considerable discretion. They may ignore the offence, force prostitutes to move on, charge them on a regular timetable, charge them only if they commit other offences, or charge them for loitering. Even greater scope for discretion exists in the case of prostitution conducted discreetly through escort agencies or brothels, where there is usually less community pressure for action. Policing of prostitution has historically been associated with corruption but, even when this is not the case, police may reach an accommodation with brothel operators to make their work easier. Selective enforcement may be used to keep prostitution invisible, to move brothels from desirable residential locations to industrial or working class residential areas, and to force prostitutes to undergo examination and treatment for sexually transmitted diseases.

DE FACTO REGULATION IN WESTERN AUSTRALIA

Both Western Australia and Queensland have had de facto systems of regulation for most of this century. By 1910 Kalgoorlie police and the local council had collaborated to confine brothels to a 'red-light' area in Hay Street, where they remain today (Davidson 1984, p 162). Prostitutes in Kalgoorlie must still live in the brothels, cannot have partners or children in town and are not permitted to visit public places such as hotel bars and the local swimming pool. They are also required to have regular health checks (Western Australian Community Panel on Prostitution 1990:8). From early this century Perth police also controlled the location and number of brothels. In 1990 ten brothels, one massage parlour and two escort agencies were permitted to operate in Perth. Police requirements for these brothels and escort agencies include a 'registration of all workers, no alcohol or drugs to be consumed on the premises, regular health checks and no juvenile involvement' (Western Australian Community Panel on Prostitution 1990, p 8). Brothel and escort agency operators not included in the list of thirteen 'approved' establishments are prosecuted. In 1982 the Western Australian Ombudsman, who had been asked to report on corruption allegations relating to the Western Australian Police Force, referred to a letter of the Commissioner of Police containing an official statement of the policy of 'containment and toleration'. The Commissioner's letter stated that the aims of the policy were to 'contain the number of operators of such premises to an acceptable and manageable level, whilst achieving a maximum level in standards of conduct and health with minimum public inconvenience or nuisance'. The policy was based on recognition that prostitution was 'inevitable' in any society and that it was preferable to contain and regulate, rather than suppress it (Dixon 1982, p 16).

The Community Panel established in 1990 by the Western Australian Government to consider prostitution law reforms recommended that prostitution-related offences, other than those applying to street soliciting, should be repealed and that the de facto system of regulated prostitution should be replaced by controls on the location of brothels through zoning and by registration of premises used for the purposes of prostitution (including premises used by freelance prostitutes). These proposals have not been implemented.

HARSHER PROSTITUTION LAWS IN QUEENSLAND

Until recently a policy of containment and toleration applied to brothels and escort agencies in Queensland. The 1987 Fitzgerald Inquiry found that selective enforcement of prostitution laws was associated with widespread police corruption and raised the question whether it would be preferable to control and regulate prostitution rather than to attempt to suppress it. Following the Fitzgerald Inquiry the Criminal Justice Commission conducted a review of prostitution laws and their enforcement. The Commission recommended abandonment of the policy of criminalisation, except for street prostitution, and the introduction of a system of regulation of brothels and escort agencies. The Commission proposed that offences should be introduced to protect children and disadvantaged groups and to punish coercion and/or intimidation of adult prostitutes. Explicit and offensive advertising of prostitution services should be prohibited. Self-employed prostitutes should be permitted to operate from their own homes, subject to local planning provisions.

The Criminal Justice Commission's recommendations proved controversial. The majority of the Parliamentary Criminal Justice Committee did not support regulation of prostitution and Premier Goss indicated his personal unwillingness to consider this approach. The *Prostitution Laws Amendment Act* 1992 introduced sanctions for prostitution-related activities which are now the harshest in Australia. The Act reflects the traditional 'abolitionist' view that the target of prostitution laws should be those who organise or profit from prostitution rather than prostitutes and that prostitution can be reduced by creating new offences with harsher penalties. Thus freelance prostitution is not criminalised, except where it involves soliciting or loitering. In response to the criticism that prostitution laws are gender-biased because they punish the provider but not the seller of sexual services, the Act introduces new offences directed at clients.

The legislation may include a wider range of activities within the definition of prostitution than has been the case in the past. Prostitution is defined as engaging 'in a sexual act with another person under an arrangement of a commercial character'.[6] The definition of sexual act is not limited to sexual intercourse, masturbation or other physical acts. An act which is 'sexual' can come within the definition even if it does not involve physical contact.[7] Thus voyeurism and activities such as stripping and tabletop dancing where a dancer titillates men without permitting them to touch her could possibly be prosecuted under the legislation.

The Act retains the offence of procuring a person to engage in prostitution and creates additional offences relating to sexual exploitation of children and procuring sexual acts by intimidation on false pretences. It makes it an offence for a person with an interest in premises (for example an owner, landlord, tenant or occupier) to knowingly allow the premises to be used for the purposes of prostitution by two or more prostitutes. Provision is made for police to warn a person with an interest in premises that the place is being used for prostitution, and evidence of this warning is admissible in a prosecution for this offence. The exclusion of premises used by a single prostitute allows a person who rents premises to a freelance sex worker to escape prosecution.[8]

In addition to these offences, the *Prostitution Laws Amendment Act* introduces new offences which have no equivalents in other Australian states. It is an offence to 'knowingly participate, directly or indirectly in the provision of prostitution by another person'. The offence is clearly applicable to brothel and escort agency operators but it could also apply to a taxi driver who gives the name of a prostitute to a passenger, a person who drives a prostitute to a client's house in return for a fee, a newspaper employee who accepts an advertisement knowing that it is for prostitution, or a person who is paid to answer the telephone for a brothel. The offence applies to those providing these services to a freelance prostitute (the exemption in favour of an individual prostitute is not applicable in this context). The old 'living on the earnings' offence was theoretically applicable to the situations set out above, but it was generally used to prosecute only brothel and escort agency owners and the male partners of sex workers. A client of a prostitute 'knowingly participates in the provision of prostitution by another person' and could presumably be charged with this offence.

Historically it has been difficult to obtain convictions against brothels and escort agency operators. In most states convictions of prostitutes outnumber convictions of those involved in the organisation of prostitution. Section 229L creates an 'unlawful presence' offence permitting punishment of a person found in, or leaving, a place suspected on reasonable grounds of being used for the purposes of prostitution by two or more prostitutes. The provision is presumably intended to make it easier to obtain convictions of brothel owners or managers, but could also be used to prosecute prostitutes who work in brothels and their clients. A defendant who is prosecuted for this offence can apply to the court for a certificate of discharge and an order prohibiting publication of identifying information. To obtain a discharge for the unlawful presence offence the defendant must give evidence and be cross-examined on all matters relevant to the offence and on the commission by other persons of an offence against the legislation.[9] Presumably it was hoped that this provision would make it easier to obtain evidence against those involved in the organisation of prostitution. It seems unlikely that the provision will be any more successful against brothel operators than the rather similar provision originally contained in the South Australian *Suppression of Brothels Act* 1907.

In the light of Fitzgerald's findings of police corruption it is ironic that the Queensland 'reforms' expand police powers. Where a police officer finds a person committing, or reasonably suspected of committing, an offence under the legislation, or believes on reasonable grounds that the name, address or age of the person is required to enforce the legislation, the person may be required to state their name, address and age.[10] Use of a premises for the purposes of prostitution can be inferred from evidence of the condition of the place, material found at the place and other relevant factors and circumstances.[11] Presumably this is intended to overcome the need to use entrapment to obtain convictions.

Public health authorities have argued that criminalising prostitution is counterproductive because it forces sex workers underground, and makes it more difficult for them to seek information and treatment. Lip service is paid to this concern by the provision that evidence of condoms or materials on safer sex practices is not admissible in prosecuting prostitution offences.[12] The fact that a prostitute or client has undergone a sexual health check within three months before committing an offence can also be taken into account in mitigation of sentence.[13]

By refining prostitution offences, providing a weapon to force prostitutes to give evidence against their employers and expanding police powers the *Prostitution Amendment Act* 1992 attempts to suppress the demand for and the sale of sex in Queensland. In the short term sex workers may leave Queensland for jurisdictions with less oppressive laws. In the long term, the history of prostitution in Australia and elsewhere suggests that the legislation is more likely to force prostitution further underground, to make prostitutes vulnerable to coercion by brothel owners and police and to expand the opportunities for extortion and corruption.

PROSTITUTION LAW REFORM — THE LAST TWO DECADES

Over the past decade and a half in the states of New South Wales and Victoria and both territories some effort has been made at reforming laws, but with varying success.

Decriminalisation of Prostitution — Advance and Retreat in New South Wales

Until 1979, New South Wales prostitution laws were similar to those in other Australian states. There was also a strong link between prostitution law enforcement and police corruption (Parliament of New South Wales 1986, pp 224–8). According to Allen (1990, pp 73ff), the effect of criminalising prostitution in New South Wales was to force women out of freelance work and to make them more vulnerable to coercion by pimps, brothel owners and the police.

In 1979 the New South Wales Government repealed the *Summary Offences Act*, including the provisions penalising street prostitution. According to the second reading speech of the Attorney-General, Frank Walker, the offences created by the Prostitution Bill 1979 reflected the view that the purpose of the criminal law should be to punish those who organised, promoted or profited from prostitution (New South Wales Parliamentary Debates 23 April 1979: 4917). While soliciting and loitering offences were repealed because they discriminated against prostitutes as compared to their customers, sanctions were retained for procuring,[14] living on the earnings of prostitution[15] and using premises 'held out' as available for use for massage parlours, sauna baths, photographic studios etc. for prostitution.[16] It was an offence to advertise that premises were used or that a person was available for prostitution.[17] The Act did not repeal the *Disorderly Houses Act* 1943, which enabled police to apply to the Supreme Court for a declaration that premises were 'a disorderly house' so that thereafter persons found on the premises were guilty of an offence. The *Offences in Public Places Act* 1979, which was enacted as part of the same legislative package, was intended to prevent outrageous and offensive behaviour. The Act made it an offence for a person in, near or within view or hearing of a public place or school to 'behave in such a manner as would cause reasonable persons justifiably in all the circumstances to be seriously alarmed or seriously affronted'.[18]

Not surprisingly, the retention of provisions directed at brothels, coupled with the ban on advertising and the decriminalisation of street prostitution, led to an increase in street prostitution. Virtually every interest group was critical of the legislation. Sex workers argued that the legislation did not go far enough and that the *Offences in Public Places Act* provisions were being applied arbitrarily by the police. Police campaigned against the legislation, advertising in the *Daily Telegraph* that they could no longer guarantee safety on the streets. The legislation was criticised by some members of the judiciary (Johnston 1985, p 269). Local residents claimed that street soliciting had increased dramatically in the Darlinghurst area and that their quality of life was threatened by kerb-crawling, traffic problems and the behaviour of customers and voyeurs.

In response to these criticisms the *Prostitution Act* and the *Offences in Public Places Act* were amended in 1983. The new section 8A of the *Prostitution Act* made it an offence to solicit in a public street 'near' a dwelling, church, school or hospital, or in a school, church or hospital. According to the Attorney-General, the purpose of the amendment was to ensure that residents were not subjected to the 'flagrant and unseemly aspects of prostitution... The effect of creating an offence of soliciting ... will be to redirect what is essentially a commercial activity back into commercial and industrial areas' (NSW Parliamentary Debates 29 March 1983: 5243). But the imprecision of the word 'near' considerably expanded the powers of police. Amendments to section 5 of the *Offences in Public Places Act* 1979 removed the requirement of serious alarm or affront and replaced it with a provision making it an offence to behave near or within a public place or school in a manner that would be regarded by a reasonable person as offensive. In 1986 the New South Wales Select Committee Upon Prostitution reported that the offensive behaviour provision either was not being enforced or was being selectively enforced against prostitutes rather than their clients (Parliament of New South Wales 1986, p 268).

The Select Committee was established to investigate the public health, criminal, social and community welfare aspects of prostitution. The Committee estimated that in New South Wales, in July 1985 in the case of street prostitution, and in September 1984 in the case of other types of prostitution, there were a minimum of between 7000 and 9600 customers using prostitution services in any one day. On one day during these months it was estimated that customers spent between $171,000 and $720,000. It concluded that criminalising prostitution simply drove 'that activity underground beyond the reach of normal commercial regulation which would ensure neighbourhood amenity and minimum conditions of health and safety' (Parliament of New South Wales 1986, p 236). The Committee proposed that criminal sanctions against prostitution-related activities should be repealed, that discreet advertising of brothels in the print media should be permitted and that controls should be introduced on the location and ownership of brothels. The Committee opposed reintroduction of soliciting and loitering offences, but recommended changes to the *Prostitution Act* to clarify the meaning of the offence of soliciting 'near' certain premises.

Unfortunately these recommendations were not implemented. In 1988 the Liberal Government of Nick Greiner repealed the *Prostitution Act* and the *Offences in Public Places Act*, replacing it with a new *Summary Offences Act*. The legislation did not reintroduce the offence of soliciting or loitering for the purposes of prostitution, but created a new offence of behaving 'in an offensive manner in or near, or within view or hearing from a public place or school'. The section leaves it to police officers to determine what is offensive, by removing the previous requirement that the conduct be such 'as would be regarded by *reasonable persons* ... in all circumstances, as offensive'. It is also an offence to 'take part in an act of prostitution' in or within view of a school, church, hospital or public place or within view of a dwelling. The offence applies to 'each of the persons taking part in an act of prostitution', so that it theoretically applies to both prostitutes and their clients. Because of their breadth and uncertainty the provisions increase the scope for selective enforcement and police corruption.

Like the 1979 reforms, the *Summary Offences Act* 1988 left brothel and escort agency prostitution in a legal 'grey area'. The offences of living on the earnings and holding out premises were retained. The Act also created a new offence of publishing an advertisement for a prostitute, which is presumably intended to prevent brothels recruiting new workers.

The history of New South Wales prostitution legislation provides some valuable lessons for reformers. Decriminalisation of street prostitution, combined with retention of some offences relating to brothels, made prostitution more visible. In turn this increased the likelihood of confrontation between residents and street workers. In conflicts between 'respectable citizens' and prostitutes, who are members of a highly stigmatised group, the views of prostitutes are unlikely to carry much political weight. The problem is one about competing uses of public space. Neither removal of criminal law sanctions nor return to a policy of criminalisation is likely to solve the problem. In order to prevent a backlash of the kind which occurred in New South Wales, which may disadvantage prostitutes even more than selective enforcement of criminal law penalties, some means must be found of reconciling this conflict.

DECRIMINALISATION WITH CONTROLS — VICTORIA

Victoria was the first Australian state to adopt a formal policy of controlling prostitution rather than suppressing it. Pressure for a new approach to prostitution first emerged in the 1970s, when massage parlours (a concept imported from California) appeared in Melbourne (and other capital cities) for the first time. In an attempt to control their location the Melbourne Metropolitan Planning Scheme, which controlled land use in Melbourne, was amended in 1975 to permit premises to be used as massage parlours in certain areas (usually industrial and commercial zones) with the consent of the relevant council. In a triumph of hypocrisy over reality, massage parlours were defined as premises 'used for the purpose of body massage by a person other than a person registered [as a physiotherapist] whether or not it is used solely for that purpose'.[19] Permits were often granted subject to the condition that prostitution did not occur, but council officers complained that this condition was virtually impossible to enforce. In the Melbourne metropolitan area, 28 'massage parlours' had obtained planning permits prior to 1 July 1984, and two massage parlour permits had been granted in Geelong under the similar provisions of the Geelong Regional Planning Scheme (Victorian Government 1985, p 152).

This attempt to use planning laws to control location of massage parlours (in reality, brothels) was unsuccessful. Councils were reluctant to grant permits and most brothel operators had to appeal to the Town Planning Appeals Board. Councils had insufficient powers to close down massage parlours operating without permits. In South Melbourne and St Kilda residents objected to the clustering of massage parlours and the disturbance caused by the men who visited them. Around the same time the gentrification of St Kilda, where street prostitution had existed since the First World War, led to residents pressuring the local council, police and the State Government to 'clean up' the area by getting rid of prostitutes (Daniels 1984, pp 338–59).

In 1984 the Labor Government established a Working Party to examine controls on the location of brothels and to recommend how planning controls could be made more effective. Although the Working Party was not primarily concerned with street prostitution, it was felt that street soliciting in St Kilda might be reduced if prostitution in brothels ceased to be illegal.

The Working Party's report was the origin of the Victorian approach under which brothel location is controlled through town planning laws. The Report recommended *inter alia* that brothels should be treated as legitimate land uses for town planning purposes and that the offences of living on the earnings of prostitution, keeping or managing a brothel or using premises for prostitution should not apply to brothels with planning permits. By removing criminal penalties relating to brothels with permits but retaining them for brothels which operated illegally, the Working Party attempted to provide an incentive for brothel operators to move out of residential areas. These recommendations were implemented in the *Planning (Brothels) Act* 1984. The Act also contained provisions, introduced by the Opposition and accepted by the government, which were intended to exclude persons convicted of drug or other serious criminal offences from obtaining or continuing to hold brothel permits. The Opposition was critical of many aspects of the legislation, and the government obtained its passage by promising to establish a broader inquiry into the social, economic, legal and health aspects of prostitution.

The 1985 Report of the Inquiry (often called the 'Neave Report') estimated that between 3000 and 4000 men, women and transsexuals worked on a reasonably regular basis in Victoria. Only about 150 of these worked as street prostitutes — the most visible form of prostitution — and the vast majority were women. The Inquiry estimated conservatively that prostitutes and clients had about 45,000 sexual contacts per week (although this did not necessarily represent 45,000 men). It also suggested that the criminal law had been relatively ineffective in suppressing prostitution in Victoria. Of the 115 people who participated in a structured interview less than half (43%) had been charged with prostitution-related offences (Victorian Government 1985, p 79).

The Inquiry's recommendations for law reform fell into three main categories. First, the Report recommended repeal of specific offences for most prostitution-related activities, including the use of premises for habitual prostitution (an offence which permitted prosecution of individual prostitutes using their own premises), the ownership, management or use of brothels, living on the earnings of prostitution and procuring of adult prostitutes. It proposed introduction of new offences relating to prostitution of minors and assault or intimidation of adult prostitutes. Soliciting and loitering offences should not be repealed, the Report said, but councils should have the power to 'opt out' of street soliciting laws and permit soliciting to occur in designated areas.

Second, the Report supported the application of planning laws to brothels employing two or more people. It recommended that brothels should not be confined to 'red-light areas' and that planning laws should apply to brothels in the same way as they applied to other businesses. However, in recognition of community concern about location of brothels close to homes and schools, local authorities should be required to take certain factors into account in deciding whether to grant a brothel permit, including the nature and size of the brothel, its proposed hours of operation, its proximity to buildings used for residential purposes and the desirability of preventing clustering of brothels. To ensure that these planning controls were effective Magistrates Courts were to be given powers to close down brothels operating without permits. Planning controls were not to apply to unattached dwellings used by individual prostitutes. This last recommendation was intended to give sex workers the freedom to choose between working in a larger brothel and being self-employed. With hindsight the recommendation applying to premises used by a single prostitute seems too restrictive.

The recommendations of the Inquiry differed from those of the Working Party. The Working Party recommendations that prostitution-specific offences should continue to apply to brothels without planning permits produced the anomalous result that a brothel owner living on the earnings of 60 prostitutes was not guilty of the offence of living on the earnings if his brothel had a planning permit, but the unemployed husband of a freelance prostitute who did not have a permit could be prosecuted. The Neave Report took the view that if the arguments in favour of repeal of criminal offences were accepted it made little sense to retain these offences for brothels without planning permits. Control of location of brothels could be more effectively achieved through enforcement of planning laws.

Third, the Report rejected the view that sex workers should be registered or otherwise regulated, on the grounds that this would legitimise prostitution and stigmatise prostitutes, making it difficult for them to move out of prostitution. Instead the Report recommended that brothel operators and managers should be licensed. The effect of the proposal was that the location of brothels was to be regulated by planning law and the management of brothels by the Licensing Board. Licensing requirements were not to apply to small brothels defined as brothels employing fewer than three workers. Like the exclusion of premises used by an individual sex worker from the planning laws, this was intended to allow prostitutes to work on a freelance basis.

The aim of this legislative package was to provide some protection for people working in the sex industry without legitimising or encouraging prostitution. The removal of criminal sanctions was based on the recognition that a policy of criminalisation does more harm than good, while controls on location of brothels were intended to prevent the backlash which occurred in New South Wales in response to the 1979 changes.

Although the Victorian Government proposed to implement almost all of the Inquiry's recommendations, the Prostitution Regulation Bill 1986 was extensively amended in the Legislative Council. The amendments removed the distinction between small-scale 'freelance' prostitution and larger brothels, making it necessary for all 'brothels', even those involving only a single worker, to obtain licences and planning permits.[20] Rejection of this distinction reflected the view of the Legislative Council that it was necessary to impose strict controls on all forms of prostitution. The amendments retained the offence of living on the earnings of prostitution and made it an indictable rather than a summary offence, increasing the penalty of imprisonment for four years.[21] Illogically, retention of the offence was defended on the grounds that it discouraged pimps and bludgers. Apparently businessmen who owned large brothels were not regarded as falling into this category, since the offence was inapplicable to brothel operators with planning permits and licences.

The Report of the Inquiry recommended that local councils should not have the right to veto brothels. The recommendation recognised the reluctance of councils to be seen to approve prostitution even where they had turned a blind eye to brothels in their municipality in the past. Based on the approach taken to massage parlour permits, it was felt that giving councils the right of veto would have forced most brothels to continue to operate illegally. Amendments to the legislation gave councils such a right, subject to a ministerial power to override it.[22]

In response to these amendments, which effectually undermined the strategy recommended by the Neave Inquiry, the Labor Government did not proclaim many parts of the *Prostitution Regulation Act*.[23] The result is that prostitution laws in Victoria remain an irrational patchwork. In Victoria the *Vagrancy Act* offences of living on the earnings of prostitution, brothel-keeping and managing and using premises for habitual prostitution continue to apply to brothels without permits, and harsher penalties can now be imposed for soliciting and loitering. The provisions requiring licensing of brothel operators were not proclaimed. Councils have been reluctant to grant permits, so that most applicants have had to appeal. The lengthy and expensive process of obtaining a permit has discouraged smaller operators from satisfying planning requirements. The Prostitutes' Collective argues that there has been a shift from smaller to larger-scale brothels, and that women working in legal brothels are subjected to harsher working conditions than was the case prior to the legislative changes. The number of escort agencies seems to have increased, exposing prostitutes to greater dangers from clients than they face in brothels. The police have alleged growing criminal involvement in prostitution, although the evidence on which this view is based is equivocal.

For these reasons the Victorian legislation is sometimes regarded as a 'failed experiment'. It would be fairer to say that the approach recommended by the Neave Inquiry was never really tried. It is also misleading to suggest that current legislation has created greater social harms than the earlier policy of suppressing prostitution and punishing sex workers. Removal of criminal penalties for those who work in brothels is a step towards decriminalisation. Use of planning laws to control location of brothels is a more effective way of dealing with concerns about public nuisance than the old criminal law provisions. As Goode has commented:

> While there are defects in the present Victorian legislative structure, many, if not most, of these can be learned from and addressed, and ... no-one involved in Victoria in implementing and working with the reforms which took place in 1986 would want to return to a policy of criminalisation. (Goode 1991, p 60)

Shortly after its election in 1992 the Kennett Government announced a further review of prostitution laws. In the meantime a moratorium has been imposed on the granting of new brothel permits (Victoria, Parliamentary Debates, 17 March 1993: 290). By artificially limiting the number of legal brothels the government has forced some brothels to remain 'underground', increased the value of existing legal brothels and created the conditions for escalating conflicts between brothel owners.

Regulated Prostitution — Northern Territory

Until recently Northern Territory prostitution laws were similar to those in force in other jurisdictions. However, a de facto system of regulation applied to escort agencies. This system was described by the Attorney-General, Daryl Manzie, in a Ministerial Statement announcing a review of prostitution laws:

> It is ... public knowledge that the Northern Territory police have come to an arrangement with the escort agencies in order to monitor the industry and to ensure that problems such as abuse and/or trafficking of drugs, organised crime and involvement of under-age girls do not occur.
>
> This arrangement operates in the following manner. First, before the operator of an escort agency agrees to act on behalf of a woman, that woman is required to attend the Berrimah Police

Centre or any appropriate police station in the area. At the police station, she is interviewed by 2 members of the Bureau of Criminal Intelligence. During the interview, the police inform her of the laws relating to prostitution in the Territory. The interview itself is recorded in its entirety and towards its conclusion the woman is photographed. The photographs give the police a positive record of the woman's identity, regardless of the number of names she may use. A check of the woman's criminal record is also conducted. If any serious convictions are revealed, particularly drug-related convictions, sufficient information is referred to the operator to convince him or her of the woman's unsuitability. The operator ordinarily then declines to act for her (Northern Territory Parliamentary Record, 31 August 1989: 7180).

The impetus for prostitution law reform in the Northern Territory appears to have been the views expressed by Fitzgerald QC in relation to police corruption in Queensland. In his Ministerial Statement the Attorney-General referred to the relationship between discretionary enforcement and police corruption, and the lack of police power to compel women to submit to the 'weighing in' process described above (Northern Territory Parliamentary Record, 31 August 1989: 7184). Further impetus for the legislation was provided by advice given to the Government by Mulholland QC. The Mulholland Inquiry was not concerned with prostitution but with police investigations of drug dealing. However, one of the witnesses was an escort agency worker called Rhonda, who had been a police informant and had had an affair with a police officer. Although Mulholland's advice found no evidence of institutionalised corruption in the Northern Territory police force, it criticised the lack of a statutory basis for police regulation of escort agencies (Northern Territory Parliamentary Record, 18 November 1991: 3305).

The *Prostitution Regulation Act*, which criminalised brothels but established a system of regulation for escort agencies, became law in 1992. The Act retained penalties for soliciting and loitering for the purposes of prostitution (the offence was also applied to clients), keeping or managing a brothel and allowing premises to be used as a brothel. It was originally proposed that premises used by an individual prostitute should be excluded from the definition of a brothel but this exclusion was not retained in the Act. A brothel does not include a hotel room used for the provision of sexual services when the arrangements for provision of those services are made elsewhere. Thus hotel-keepers cannot be prosecuted for brothel-keeping if their rooms are used by escort agency workers, but freelance prostitutes who take clients to their own premises are guilty of an offence.[24] The offences of living on the earnings of prostitution and procuring have been repealed (although new offences cover coercion of adult prostitutes and living on the earnings of child prostitutes). The Act makes it an offence to advertise to induce persons to seek employment as prostitutes and places some controls on advertising prostitution services.

The operator or manager of an escort agency must obtain a licence from the Escort Agency Licensing Board. The Board has power to grant, renew and cancel licences and to request the Commissioner of Police to investigate complaints about the management of escort agencies.[25] Operators of escort agencies must obtain licences and renew them annually, but prostitutes who work as freelance escorts are not required to obtain licences.[26] Persons convicted of specified offences within the preceding ten years are not eligible to hold licences.[27] Provision is made for registration of details of escort agency licences. Licences for agencies employing more than three prostitutes are recorded in a register accessible to the public, while agencies employing fewer than three prostitutes are recorded in a private register which can only be inspected by police authorised to do so by the Commissioner.[28]

The legislation formalises the 'weighing in' process which existed prior to its enactment, although it does not formally provide for the establishment of a register of prostitutes. Before a prostitute is employed by an escort agency the operator or manager of the agency must apply for a certificate in respect of that person from the Commissioner of Police, or ensure that a certificate relating to the person has already been issued to another agency. It is an offence for an escort agency operator to employ a person without having obtained this certificate. Certificates cannot be issued in respect of people who have been convicted of 'violent offences' or specified drug offences in the preceding ten years.[29] Thus men or women with convictions for these offences cannot work for escort agencies employing others, although they can work as escorts on an individual basis.

Historically, systems of regulated prostitution have required compulsory medical examination of prostitutes but not of their clients. In his Tabling Statement the Attorney-General acknowledged that implementation of a mandatory system of testing for sexually transmitted diseases would discourage sex workers from cooperating with health authorities and encourage clients to avoid taking precautions to protect themselves against infection (Northern Territory Parliamentary Record, 6 December 1990: 132). In recognition of the need to discourage clients from believing that medical examinations of prostitutes provide a guarantee that the sex worker is free from infection, the Act requires licensees to take reasonable steps to ensure that the fact that a prostitute has been medically examined is not used to induce clients to believe that she is not infected with a sexually transmitted disease.[30]

The Northern Territory legislation regulates escort agency prostitution while continuing to punish sex workers who work in brothels or as street prostitutes. Because prostitutes can only work legally as escorts, agency operators have considerable control over their employees. Although the Escort Agency Licensing Board is independent of the police, police involvement in certification gives them information about and power over prostitutes, which may be abused.

The *Prostitution Regulation Act* 1992 ensures that the sexual needs of male tourists and Territory residents who can afford to rent a hotel room are met, but does not improve the situation of women at the lower end of the 'marketability' scale whose appearance, lack of education or drug addiction makes it unlikely that escort agencies will employ them. By permitting escort agencies but continuing to criminalise brothels the Act meets the community demand that prostitution should be kept 'out of sight and out of mind', but forces prostitutes to provide sexual services in a way which makes them more vulnerable to injury or death at the hands of clients.

RADICAL REFORM —
DECRIMINALISATION IN THE AUSTRALIAN CAPITAL TERRITORY

Although prostitution was criminalised in the A.C.T. until 1992, a de facto system of regulation applied to brothels. Between 1970 and 1990 the prosecution of offences relating to brothels required the consent of the Attorney-General or his delegate (No such restriction was imposed in relation to offences of soliciting and living on the earnings.) In 1984 the Director of Public Prosecutions adopted prosecution guidelines with the consent of the Attorney-General. Under this policy brothel-keeping offences were not prosecuted except where there were 'aggravating circumstances'. Factors taken into account in determining whether prosecution would be in the public interest included: the location of the premises; whether there had been complaints from the public about the premises; whether drugs were being used on or distributed from the premises; whether there was evidence that juveniles were being employed; and whether the premises presented a threat to public health (Australian Capital Territory 1991, pp 13–15).

Seven brothels operated in Canberra, six of them in Fyshwick, a light-industrial area, which was considered by the police to be an appropriate location. Police visited these brothels every two or three weeks and records were kept relating to the conduct of each brothel. They also maintained records of prostitutes in a manual card index. A number of escort agencies also operated in the A.C.T. but police did not appear to monitor them as closely as they did brothels.

In 1991 the Australian Capital Territory Legislative Assembly established a Select Committee on HIV, Illegal Drugs and Prostitution. The Committee recommended the establishment of a brothel and escort agency licensing board along the lines of the Northern Territory model, although it did not support the certification process applied to prostitutes working for escort agencies in the Northern Territory. This recommendation was rejected by the Australian Capital Territory parliament, in favour of the more radical approach of decriminalisation. The prostitution laws in force in the Australian Capital Territory are now the least repressive in Australia.

The *Prostitution Act* 1992, which started its life as a private member's Bill, retains penalties for soliciting or loitering but repeals the criminal offences relating to brothel-keeping, living on the earnings of prostitution and procuring. The owners and managers of escort agencies and brothels are not required to obtain a licence but simply to register the business. Persons opening brothels or escort agencies must notify the Registrar of Brothels within seven days.[31] The register may be inspected by specified persons, but the address of an individual prostitute is available only to a specified group of people including police officers.[32]

The Act creates offences which are designed to protect prostitutes from intimidation and coercion and to prevent children from becoming involved in prostitution. It is an offence for the operator of a brothel or escort agency to permit a child to be on the premises without reasonable excuse. The Act also makes it an offence to operate a brothel outside a prescribed location, but this provision does not apply to premises used by a single prostitute. Two areas of the A.C.T., Fyshwick and Mitchell, have been prescribed, thus allowing existing brothels to continue to operate.[33]

The provisions of the Act relating to sexually transmitted diseases are unique in Australia, and probably in the world. The objects of the legislation include safeguarding public health and promoting welfare and occupational health and safety of prostitutes.[34] Operators of brothels or escort agencies are to take reasonable steps to ensure that sexual services are not provided by prostitutes infected with sexually transmitted diseases. It is an offence for a person to 'provide or receive commercial sexual services' if that person knows or should know that he or she is infected with a sexually transmitted disease. Operators of brothels or escort agencies are to take reasonable steps to ensure that condoms are used, and it is an offence to 'provide or receive commercial services that involve vaginal, oral or anal penetration' without the use of a condom. Presumably this provision was included for its educative effect, despite the practical impossibility of enforcing it. As in the Northern Territory, operators of brothels or escort agencies and prostitutes are required to ensure that the fact that a sex worker has had a medical examination is not used for the purposes of inducing a person to believe that the prostitute is not infected with a sexually transmitted disease. An attempt is made to reduce police involvement in the control of prostitution: a provision in the Act limits police power to enter a brothel or escort agency without a warrant to occasions on which the officer believes on reasonable grounds that offences relating to children are being, or are likely to be, committed on the premises and that entry is necessary to prevent the commission or repetition of the events.[35]

To some extent the *Prostitution Act* reflects the influence of minority parties in the Australian Capital Territory legislature and the demographic peculiarities of Canberra. But it is interesting to speculate about why both the Liberal Party and the Residents Rally party supported removal of the licensing provisions, thus going further than the recommendations of the Select Committee. Perhaps the planning controls which exist in the Territory, the location of existing brothels in a light-industrial area and the consequent lack of conflict between residents and brothel owners made enactment of the legislation possible.

CONCLUSION

In the past two decades New South Wales, Victoria, the Northern Territory and the Australian Capital Territory have retreated from the policy of criminalising prostitution and have repealed some prostitution-specific offences. A similar approach has been unsuccessfully advocated by law reformers in Queensland, South Australia and Western Australia. There are now considerable differences between prostitution laws in the various Australian jurisdictions, giving future reformers the opportunity to learn from and improve upon the approaches adopted elsewhere. To the extent that any pattern in prostitution law reform is discernible it is in the direction of regulation of the sex industry, through controls imposed on brothel and escort agency operators, rather than on sex workers.

Historically, stigmatisation and punishment of prostitutes deprived them of any voice in the policies adopted towards prostitution. Instead such policies were influenced by myths and stereotypes about prostitution, by the experience of the male 'consumers' of prostitution services and by the enforcement practices of police. In recent years sex workers' voices have ceased to be silenced. Prostitutes' collectives now exist in all States (though the extent to which they are representative is debatable) and government inquiries and law reform bodies have been increasingly prepared to seek their views.[36] Despite discouragement and harassment by brothel owners and sometimes by the police, prostitutes are now actively involved in lobbying for law reform.

Nevertheless there is a danger that the controls imposed on prostitution in the future will reflect the interests of the buyers rather than the sellers of sexual services. The current movement towards escort agency prostitution is an example of this trend. Because it makes prostitution less visible it is seen by the majority of the community as less problematical than other forms of prostitution, but women working as escorts run a high risk of death and physical injury. Similarly, the purpose of regulating prostitution may be to meet concerns about its 'nuisance' aspects, rather than to protect sex workers from injury and exploitation by clients, police and brothel owners.

If this is the case the removal of prostitution-specific offences, such as living on the earnings of prostitution, which at least forced brothel and escort agency operators to avoid conviction by maintaining some distance from their employees, may be to make sex workers more rather than less powerless.

Table 3.1
Prostitution Laws in Australia — Past History and Current Trends
Laws Criminalising Prostitution-related Activities

Part A — Jurisdictions Retaining the Policy of Criminalisation

State	Living on earnings	Brothel-keeping	Procuring
Western Australia *Police Act* 1892 Criminal Code	An offence; *Police Act* 1892 s 76G	Keeping or managing a brothel; *Police Act* 1892 s 76F Keeping a place for prostitution; Criminal Code ss 209, 213	An offence; Criminal Code s 191
South Australia *Summary Offences Act* 1953 *Criminal Law Consolidation Act* 1935	An offence; *Summary Offences Act* 1953 s 26	Keeping or managing a brothel; *Summary Offences Act* 1953 s 28(1)(a) See also *Criminal Law Consolidation Act* 1935 s 270	An offence; *Criminal Law Consolidation Act* 1935 s 6
Tasmania *Police Offences Act* 1935 Criminal Code	An offence; *Police Offences Act* 1935 s 8	Keeping a bawdy house; Criminal Code s 143	An offence; Criminal Code s 128
Queensland *Prostitution Laws Amendment Act* 1992 amending the Criminal Code and the *Vagrancy, Gaming and Other Offences Act* 1931 Note: Wide definition of prostitution, Criminal Code s 229E)	An offence included in wider provision contained in Criminal Code s 229H, 'knowingly participating in prostitution'	An offence included in wider provision contained in Criminal Code s 229K 'having an interest in premises used for the purposes of prostitution'	An offence; Criminal Code s 229G See also s 217 (procuring young person for carnal knowledge) and s 218 (procuring sexual acts by coercion)

mitting premises to used for prostitution	Advertising	Other
ant, lessee or occupier permits premises to be l for prostitution, landlord knows premises used; e Act 1892 s 76F		Occupier of a house frequented by prostitutes; *Police Act* 1892 s 65 Permitting prostitutes to assemble in places of public resort; *Police Act* 1892 s 84
or sublets premises wing to be used as a hel; or permits use of nises as a brothel; mary Offences Act 1953 s		Consorting with prostitutes; *Summary Offences Act* 1953 s 13 Occupier of premises frequented by prostitutes; *Summary Offences Act* 1953 s 84
ng a house knowing it is e used as a brothel; *Police nces Act* 1935 s 11		Consorting with prostitutes; *Police Offences Act* 1935 s 6 Occupying a house and harbouring prostitutes; *Police Offences Act* 1935 s 10(1)(b) Lodging or entertaining a prostitute to the annoyance of the inhabitants; *Police Offences Act* 1935 s 10(i)(d)
ffence; Criminal Code s <	An offence to 'knowingly advertise prostitution' (includes advertising availability of services and advertisement for a sex worker); *Vagrancy, Gaming and Other Offences Act* 1931 s 18B	Permitting a child or an intellectually impaired person to be at a place used for prostitution by two or more prostitutes; Criminal Code s 229L Unlawful presence offence; s 229I, s 229J

State	Living on earnings	Brothel-keeping	Procuring

Part B — Jurisdictions Which Have Enacted Reforms

State	Living on earnings	Brothel-keeping	Procuring
New South Wales *Summary Offences Act 1988* *Crimes Act 1900* *Disorderly Houses Act 1943*	An offence; *Summary Offences Act 1988 s 15*	Owner, occupier or manager, or person assisting in management allowing premises held out as available for other purposes, to be used for prostitution; *Summary Offences Act 1988 s 17*	An offence; *Crimes Act 1900 ss 91AA, 91B* See also s 91D which pro hibits promoting or enga ing in child prostitution
Victoria *Prostitution Regulation Act 1986* *Vagrancy Act 1966*	An offence, except where premises have a planning permit; *Vagrancy Act 1966 s 10*	An offence except when premises have a permit; *Vagrancy Act 1966 s 10*	An offence to force a per son into or to remain in prostitution or to provide financial support out of prostitution; *Prostitution Regulation Act 1986 ss 10,11* Offences relating to chil dren; *Prostitution Regulati Act 1986 6–8*
Northern Territory *Prostitution Regulation Act 1992*	Not an offence unless a child is involved or adult is forced to pro vide financial support by intimidation or supply of drug of dependence; *Prostitution Regulation Act 1992 ss 12, 15*	An offence; *Prostitution Regulation Act 1992 s 4*	Not an offence unless a child is involved or adult subject to force or coerci *Prostitution Regulation Act 1992: ss 13,14,* causing, inducing or allowing a child to take part in pros titution; s 16, entering int agreement in respect of prostitution services pro vided by an infant; s 11, forcing adult to become remain a prostitute
Australian Capital Territory *Prostitution Act 1992*	Not an offence unless the payment is derived from com mercial sexual services provided by a child; *Prostitution Act 1992 s 12*	Not an offence	Only an offence where a person is induced to pro vide sexual services by intimidation, supply of a drug of dependence or fraud; *Prostitution Act 19 s 8;* or a child is caused induced to provide com mercial services; *Prostitution Act 1992 s 1*

mitting premises to used for prostitution	Advertising	Other
pearing, acting or behaving having management of a orderly house which is itually used for the pur- es of prostitution; orderly Houses Act 1943 8, 8, 9 (applies to owners occupiers)	Advertising premises are used or a person is available for prostitution, *Summary Offences Act 1988* s 18A Advertising for a prostitute; *Summary Offences Act 1988* s 18A	
ant, lessee or occupier o permits premises to be d is guilty of an offence ept where premises have a n planning permit; rancy Act 1966 s 12 ilarly for landlords	An offence if contravenes regu- lations or is intended to induce a person to seek employment; *Prostitution Regulation Act 1986* s 14	Owning or managing an escort agency without a licence; *Prostitution Regulation Act 1986* s 6 (does not apply to single operator) Arranging provision of prostitution services by a person without a police certificate; *Prostitution Regulation Act 1992* s 9
ner, landlord or occupier o allows premises to be d as a brothel; *Prostitution ulation Act 1992* s 5	An offence if (i) contravenes regulations, (ii) is intended to induce a person to obtain employment as a prostitute; *Prostitution Regulation Act 1992* s 19	Failing to take reasonable steps to ensure a medical certificate is not used to induce a person to believe that a prostitute is not infected with a sexually transmitted disease; *Prostitution Regulation Act 1992* s 20
an offence	Form of advertisements may be prescribed, *Prostitution Act 1992* s 22	An offence to operate a brothel out- side a prescribed location; *Prostitution Act 1992* s 9 An offence to permit a child to be on the premises without reasonable excuse; *Prostitution Act 1992* s 14 Offences relating to sexually trans- mitted diseases: providing or receiv- ing paid sex if infected, *Prostitution Act 1992* s 16; using fact of medical examination to induce belief that a person is free from infection, *Prostitution Act 1992* s 17; provision or receipt of commercial sexual ser- vices without use of a condom, *Prostitution Act 1992* s 18

Table 3.2
Prostitution Laws in Australia — Past History and Current Trends
Laws Punishing Prostitutes and Clients

State/Territory	Street Work

Part A — Jurisdictions Retaining the Policy of Criminalisation

State/Territory	Street Work
Western Australia *Police Act 1892*	Common prostitute who solicits, importunes or loiters, s 59 wandering in streets or highways or being in a place of publ resort or behaving in a riotous or indecent manner, s 65(8), s 76G
South Australia *Summary Offences Act 1953*	Accosting, soliciting or loitering for the purposes of prostitution in a public place, or within view or hearing of public place; s 25
Tasmania *Police Offences Act 1935*	Common prostitute who solicits or importunes in a public place or within view or hearing of a public place, or loiters f such a purpose; s 8(1)(c)
Queensland *Prostitution Laws Amendment Act 1992* amending Criminal Code and the *Vagrancy, Gaming and Other Offences Act 1931* Note: Wide definition of prostitution, criminal code s 229E	Publicly soliciting for the purposes of prostitution (this includes loitering in a public place or in a place that is in view of a public place); *Vagrancy, Gaming and Other Offences Act 1931* s 18A Nuisance associated with prostitution; *Vagrancy, Gaming and Other Offences Act 1931* s 18C

Part B – Jurisdictions Which Have Enacted Reforms

State/Territory	Street Work
New South Wales *Summary Offences Act 1988*	Soliciting near or within view of a dwelling, school, church (hospital, or in a school, church or hospital; s 19(1)(2) Soliciting another person in, near or within view of a school church or hospital or public place in a manner that harasses or distresses that person; s 19(3). Taking part in an act of prostitution in or within view of a school, church, hospital or public place, or within view of a dwelling; s 20 Conducting him or her self in an offensive manner within view or hearing from a public place or school; s 4
Victoria *Prostitution Regulation Act 1986* *Vagrancy Act 1966*	Soliciting, accosting or loitering in a public place for prostitution; *Prostitution Regulation Act 1986* s 5
Northern Territory *Prostitution Regulation Act 1992*	Accosting, soliciting or loitering in a public place; *Prostitution Regulation Act 1992* s 10
Australian Capital Territory *Prostitution Act 1992*	Accosting, soliciting or loitering in a public place; *Prostitution Act 1992* s 10

...othel Work	Escort agency work	Clients
...ould be prosecuted if occupier ...rmits premises to be used as a ...othel; s 76F. Occupier of a house ...quented by prostitutes; s 76(7) ...ne-person brothel not an offence	Not an offence	No specific offences
...ceiving money paid in a brothel ... respect of prostitution; s 28(1)(b) ...ne-person brothel included	Depends on organisation of escort agency	No specific offences
...ot an offence	Not an offence	No specific offences
...wner, landlord, tenant or user of ...emises who allows premises to be ...ed for prostitution by two or ...ore prostitutes; Criminal Code ...229K ...ing found in a place reasonably ...spected of being used for prosti-...tion, s 229I, s 229J ...ne-person brothel not an offence	Not an offence	Being found in a place reasonably suspected of being used for prostitution; Criminal Code s 229I, s 229J Knowingly participating in the provision of prostitution by another person; s 229H Publicly soliciting for the purposes of prostitution; *Vagrancy, Gaming and Other Offences Act* 1931 s 18A (applies to clients) Nuisance associated with prostitution; *Vagrancy, Gaming and Other Offences Act* 1931 s 18C
...ot an offence unless premises are ...ld out as available for massage, ...una, photographs etc; s 16	Not an offence	*Summary Offences Act* 1988 ss 4, 19, 20 apply to clients
...n offence except where premises ...ve a town planning permit; ...grancy Act 1966 s 11 ...ne-person brothel included	Not an offence	*Prostitution Regulation Act* 1986 s 5 applies to clients
...ne-person brothel included; ...ostitution Regulation Act 1992 s 3 ...ould be charged with management ...fence	Not an offence, but cannot work without a police certificate	*Prostitution Regulation Act* 1992 s 10 applies to clients
...ot an offence	Not an offence	*Prostitution Act* 1992 s 10 applies to clients

...urce: The original source was Neave, 'Changing prostitution laws — the strategy for change'. Paper given at 1st National Sex Industry ...nference, 25 October 1988. It was later adapted for the purposes of Department of Community Services and Health, *Report of Working ...nel on Discrimination and Other Legal Issues* 1989, pp 29-32 and has since been updated by the author.

4

ON A STREET BEAT WITH THE POLICE
Mike Lazarus

Since 1978 I have been a member of the New South Wales Police Service. For my entire service I have worked in the inner Sydney area with over 13 years of service in the Kings Cross area. This area has a worldwide reputation as being the vice market of Sydney and possibly of Australia. Its reputation nurtures a substantial and lucrative market for those involved in all forms of prostitution in Kings Cross and the surrounding areas.

From 1978 until 1990 my only contact with street prostitutes was either when they were arrested by the Vice Squad or when I was called upon to investigate a police matter in which a prostitute was involved as a victim, a witness or an offender. In the early years of my career vice-related matters were policed by the Vice Squad. Then, with the Commissionership of John Avery, these matters were devolved to patrol level and were of particular relevance to beat police. Thus it was only after 1990 and the advent of the new community policing strategy adopted by the Service under the leadership of John Avery that I began to liaise on a regular basis with street prostitutes, following the creation of the Kings Cross Beat Unit.

Working on foot as a beat police supervisor I saw my role as not only coordinating the Beat Unit but also as being primarily a problem solver and catalyst for social change who maximised police-community interaction, ascertained 'policing factors' and created and implemented strategies which positively impacted upon these factors. I acted and will always continue to, in a thoroughly professional manner. My concept of the term 'community' includes any person who permanently or temporarily inhabits the area in question, in this case Kings Cross and the surrounding areas. Therefore street prostitutes are members of the community — however, they are also a major policing factor for the Kings Cross Police Patrol.

Between 1990 and 1993 I became privileged to know and, in some cases, befriended a large number of street prostitutes in the Kings Cross Police Patrol area. On many occasions during the daily peak hour in Darlinghurst Road or at night in that wind tunnel of a street named William Street, I and other beat police would stop or be stopped to chat with the male and female prostitutes. I found many to be caring, sincere human beings. But the fact that deeply disturbs me to this day is that very few ply their trade by choice. In virtually all cases it is because of economic necessity created either by drug addiction or by a need to provide for relatives or acquaintances (usually children), or just in order to provide for an adequate lifestyle. I consider this a very poor indictment of our society as I feel that the real issues relating to prostitution have never been adequately resolved.

I would now like to relate to you my knowledge of the street prostitute in the Kings Cross Patrol area and the relationship and liaison that were created between the Police Service and the street prostitutes, their organisations and the support agencies who work so tirelessly in this area. Before I proceed I would like to dedicate this chapter to the street prostitutes whose story and way of life are unknown to the average Australian — at least, in some cases, until the frightening reality is borne home when a member of one's family joins the profession.

PROFILE OF PERSONS INVOLVED IN STREET PROSTITUTION, KINGS CROSS

Adult females: The vast majority of adult females prostituting themselves in the Kings Cross area are between 18 and 30 years of age, over 95 percent are heroin addicts; and the majority live in the inner city or eastern suburbs, with 20 percent residing within the area. Adult female street prostitutes can number between 50 and 100 at any one time on an average Friday or Saturday evening, with the majority soliciting in the vicinity of William Street, East Sydney.

Transsexuals: The transsexuals prostituting themselves on the street are considerably older than their female counterparts and are usually aged over 30. The majority live in the area and, although many are drug users, compared with their female counterparts far fewer are heroin addicts. The majority solicit in the William Street area during the hours of darkness, and during peak periods of trade would number between 20 and 40.

Adult males: The majority of adult male street prostitutes are younger than their counterparts and their age range is between 18 and 26. The vast majority live in the area and are drug users. However, fewer are heroin users than their female counterparts. The two areas where most male prostitution occurs are Fitzroy Gardens, Kings Cross, and the area surrounding Green Park, Darlinghurst, including the most heavily used area known as 'The Wall'. The latter is in close proximity to the gay entertainment area centred on Oxford Street, Darlinghurst. There are far more adult male prostitutes offering their services from park seats and from within the confines of the reserves than there are female or transsexual prostitutes.

Juveniles: There are approximately 50 juvenile persons (under the age of 16 years) who inhabit or reside in the area on a permanent basis. There are at least another 50 who inhabit the area on a semi-permanent though regular basis, such as on weekends. The majority of these juveniles prostitute themselves, many doing so in public places. There are also a significant number of juveniles aged between 16 and 18 years who prostitute themselves on the street in the same locations as the adult prostitutes. Because of their mode of dress and their physical maturity it is extremely difficult to differentiate between these juvenile prostitutes and the adults.

The vast majority of juvenile prostitutes are drug users and very few, once permanently residing in the area, do not use intravenous drugs such as heroin. Most street juvenile prostitution occurs during the hours of darkness and the locations used most frequently are Fitzroy Gardens and 'The Wall' in Darlinghurst. It is estimated that over 50 percent of adult street prostitutes initially enter the profession as juveniles.

COMMON CHARACTERISTICS OF ON-STREET SEX WORK

The street prostitute, after finalising negotiations with the client, will often accompany the client to a nearby room where the service is performed. However, in order to avoid the cost of maintaining accommodation it is becoming increasingly common for the service to be provided in the client's motor vehicle, at the client's address if nearby or at any relatively secluded nearby location, whether private or public.

The debatable advantages of the prostitute plying her/his trade on the street are that there are minimal overhead costs, unlike escort or brothel work. The street offers a last resort for prostitutes who are too old, and is used by juveniles and drug-addicted workers. It also offers prostitutes 'more freedom'. They are their 'own boss', and some consider it less competitive than brothel work. The frightening disadvantages are that the prostitutes are in very real danger of being sexually assaulted, otherwise assaulted, robbed or even kidnapped and, in extreme cases, murdered.

Health Factors: Because of the nature of their work and their working conditions a good deal of general ill-health occurs in what is, by and large, a very youthful population of prostitutes. Poor eating habits, lack of sleep, emotional and physical distress, inadequate housing and drug abuse are conditions commonly affecting those involved in the profession. Also, many have had a traumatic adolescence or childhood which compounds their health problems.

Drug Factors: Over 95 percent of street prostitutes use drugs of addiction and it has been estimated that as many as 80 percent in Sydney are heroin-dependent. Therefore there is a very strong link between heroin usage and street prostitution. The majority of street prostitutes have informed me that they earn up to $500 a shift soliciting, and some earn more. However, there appears little doubt that the length of the shift depends in the main on the amount of money earned, the target being that needed to purchase sufficient drugs to satisfy their addiction.

Besides heroin, other illegal hard drugs are commonly used by prostitutes, such as 'black market' methadone, cocaine, LSD and 'speed' — in fact virtually every illegal drug which is readily available. For these prostitutes their profession is an economic necessity which leads to a swift deterioration in health and, for many, a premature death.

Many of the street prostitutes supplement their income through acting as drug suppliers. As their bodies deteriorate with drug use and their clientele decreases, many are forced to replace prostitution with supplying drugs as their main, and sometimes only, source of income. As well, drugs replace monetary payment for services rendered by the prostitute. And the practice of managers or owners of casual accommodation supplying drugs to street prostitutes at the commencement of their shifts is common. This practice means that the prostitute is continually working to repay money owing for drugs supplied by these premises, and is therefore securely 'locked into' the profession.

Thus street prostitutes are providing a very lucrative marketplace for the illegal drug trade. Not only are they purchasing illegal drugs but they are also being used as on-street outlets for the suppliers' products, hence decreasing the prospect of detection by members of the Police Service.

COMMUNITY CONCERNS AND PERCEPTIONS

The prostitutes who solicit in public places, like the business and commercial areas, such as Darlinghurst Road and William Street, are very seldom, if ever, a cause for community complaint. But, invariably, when prostitutes solicit on the street in residential areas complaints increase dramatically. Their positioning creates noise pollution from increased motor traffic consisting of potential customers, sightseers or people harassing the prostitutes both verbally and physically. The prostitutes themselves cause noise pollution through territorial disputes and through verbal altercation with passing vehicle and pedestrian traffic.

Contrary to a commonly held belief, 'pimps' are not a major factor. Very few male persons act as 'pimps' in the traditional sense for a number of street prostitutes. Virtually all male persons observed remaining in the vicinity of the prostitutes are boyfriends, who, like the prostitutes, are heroin-dependent and who remain in the vicinity to ensure their girlfriends' safety. Prostitutes who provide their services in motor vehicles face added safety risks and the boyfriends are used to record registration numbers of customers' vehicles. It is not unknown for a boyfriend to report the fact to police that his girlfriend's return is overdue.

The prostitutes who perform services in motor vehicles, and in some cases in darkened streets and reserves, cause particular community concern. Besides the noise factor the discarding of condoms and other debris, often on private property, is of major community concern. Furthermore, the increased pedestrian traffic causes problems such as persons urinating or vomiting, and increased drug activity in affected areas results in an increase in discarded syringes and associated debris.

THE COMMUNITY ON-STREET PROSTITUTION COMMITTEE

In 1991 it was obvious to me that the policing strategies relating to prostitution were reactive rather than based on long-term planning and consideration of community needs. After conferring with the Patrol Commander of Kings Cross Police Patrol it was decided to create an On-street Prostitution Committee comprising street prostitutes, their representative organisations, members of the community, council and judicial representatives, and members of support organisations in fields such as health and youth support.

This committee was formed and positive response from all members of the community was immediate. One of the first policing initiatives, which was introduced as a result of the committee meetings, was the designating of specific areas in which street prostitution was legal under the current legislation. Members of the Police Service themselves had had differing opinions as to which streets and positions were legal under the legislation, so it was not surprising that the prostitutes were totally confused and frustrated at the uncoordinated policing of their profession.

Members of the service from the Vice Squad, the Kings Cross Patrol and the Police Legal unit, together with the prostitutes themselves and representatives from their organisations, made a thorough examination of the Kings Cross Patrol area. As a result of this, and with the support of the judiciary and the Police Service administration, a number of legally designated areas were agreed upon. The street prostitutes were informed of these areas and maps illustrating the designated areas were distributed by police and committee representatives. The response from the prostitutes was good and most made a genuine attempt to remain within the areas.

The establishing of designated areas also created advantages for the support organisations (such as health, welfare and community organisations) as the prostitutes could be more readily located and offered assistance. The consistency that these areas established in policing of prostitution led to what I believe was increased trust in the policing service on the part of the other members of the committee, especially the prostitutes themselves.

The advantage in having so many groups and representatives with so many differing viewpoints was that, after a number of meetings, it was obvious that not only was trust and understanding in the Police Service growing on the one hand, but also that friction between the prostitutes and their representatives and community organisations (such as Neighbourhood Watch and local council representatives) on the other was decreasing. There was a reduction in community complaints relating to prostitution as the prostitutes themselves and the local residents and their representatives began to better understand the relevant laws and the concerns of the various parties.

Other initiatives of the committee included giving total support for the increased funding and relocation to larger premises of the Kirketon Road Centre, which has been virtually solely responsible for servicing the health and welfare needs of the prostitutes. The Centre's submission for authorisation to begin a complete methadone program was also strongly supported. There have been only a limited number of places available on the public health methadone program and, although the situation has improved, it appears that the government is subsidising and assisting private programs, which are more expensive for the user of the service. The waiting time to be admitted to the program has usually been months, and for such a program not to be readily available to all persons who desire to participate is totally illogical. Regrettably, it reflects a society in which a disproportionate amount is spent on policing drug enforcement as compared with rehabilitation services such as the methadone program.

In 1986 recommendations were made in the report from the New South Wales Select Committee on prostitution to continue to monitor the scale of the heroin addiction problem and if necessary to continue the expansion of a range of methadone treatment programs so as to ensure the availability of treatment for all those diagnosed as suitable for it. The report also recommended that the assessment of heroin addicts be streamlined and expedited in order to undercut the heroin market and absorb addicts into suitable treatment programs.

Unfortunately, these recommendations have not been implemented efficiently and effectively considering the gravity of the situation in the Kings Cross Patrol area. The majority of crime reported to the Police Service in New South Wales is drug-related and past intelligence analysis has revealed that the percentage is higher in the Kings Cross area. The main on-street drug distribution network is centred on using prostitutes Therefore the rehabilitation of these people should be one, if not the major, priority of the community and its elected representatives.

The advantages are logical and in my opinion irrefutable. Firstly, once a prostitute is undergoing methadone treatment there is some chance of rehabilitation, but to refuse treatment is to offer virtually no hope of rehabilitation and to delay treatment is to dramatically reduce any hope of rehabilitation. Once the person enters the program he or she is accessible to counselling and other rehabilitation services. The Kirketon Road Centre has the facilities to offer transitional assistance on housing, education and employment matters to encourage and enable prostitutes to support themselves without relying on prostitution.

The On-street Prostitution Committee also fully supported the need for increased funding and resource allocation for the Kings Cross Adolescent Unit, a government-funded section of the Department of Youth and Community Services.

The need to address the problem of juvenile prostitution is a very important factor in any viable long-term strategy dealing with street prostitution. Many forget that these young people are the human beings who will be corrupted and recruited by unscrupulous individuals to be 'educated' in drug use and prostitution, usually in that order, and to continue the chain of generations of drug-addicted prostitutes and drug distributors who participate in these and associated criminal activities. The need to detect these young people, to rapidly remove them from the street environment and to assist them in regard to rehabilitation, accommodation and other welfare services is a major determining factor in the success of any long-term strategic plan of the Kings Cross Patrol.

The Kings Cross Adolescent Unit has provided an excellent service in the area. However, it is understaffed and underfunded, which in my opinion is a tragedy. Unless a concerted and coordinated community effort is made to break the cycle the major policing factors in the Kings Cross area will be far more difficult for the Police Service to deal with.

The committee's efforts led to substantially increased liaison between the Police Service and all other members of the committee, especially the prostitutes and their representative organisations. The Kings Cross Patrol created liaison officers to work with sex workers and their representatives and in a short time a bond of trust was established, as any complaints from the sex workers regarding the Police Service were promptly dealt with. An enormous amount of intelligence and reports of serious offences involving sex workers were reported to the liaison officers — which led to a number of arrests, including one for 'demanding money with menaces', relating to an offender standing over male prostitutes at 'The Wall' and demanding regular monetary payments.

During the period of my service in the Kings Cross Patrol there were genuine attempts at internal reallocation of resources, with the creation of a drug unit at the Patrol and teams of personnel specifically examining the major policing factors including drugs, juveniles and prostitution. The drug unit targeted the higher strata of the drug supply channels and worked cooperatively with health organisations such as Kirketon Road and Langton Clinic on drug users' problems.

CONCLUSION

The New South Wales Police Service is forced to prioritise or target certain demographic factors and certain offences, and this has become an integral part of the strategic planning process. There is no doubt in my mind that, whether consciously or unconsciously, both police personnel and the judiciary have recognised the fact that the use of drugs, although still an offence in this state, is rarely dealt with successfully by punitive penalty. It appears totally contradictory to me that the use of prohibited drugs is still an offence here when the implements to inject these drugs are freely distributed by State Government bodies through the needle exchange program.

This program is an exercise in commonsense as it recognises the fact that drug use is common and that to prevent the spread of contagious diseases syringes must be freely and readily available to users. The State Government also recognises that drug use is a significant social problem: it funds both State and private bodies as rehabilitation and welfare agencies.

However, you have a situation in which members of the Police Service in Kings Cross are virtually competing with welfare workers. The latter are attempting to locate drug users and offer assistance, while police officers are bound by law to arrest and charge any person who can be proved to have used, or be using, prohibited drugs. I am of the opinion that New South Wales needs to have clear strategic aims with all agencies working together towards a common goal.

I have no doubt that in the next decade the question of legality of usage of various drugs will become perhaps the most controversial political topic. The supply of prohibited drugs and the massive profits resulting from their sale have been recognised by police agencies, the judiciary and governments as their major priority. The success or otherwise of their strategies relating to the illegal drug trade could well shape our future social structure; the various problems experienced by street prostitutes in the Kings Cross Patrol area are nearly all related to this industry of death and misery.

At the same time I have no doubt that the Police Service in areas such as Kings Cross must target those persons, businesses and organisations who supply illegal drugs to sex workers and who lure young people into a life of drug abuse and prostitution. And the Police Service must continue to liaise with welfare agencies, the community, the prostitutes themselves and their organisations in order to succeed.

When I joined the Police Service in 1978 there were over 50 female street prostitutes working in Darlinghurst Road who were not drug users. These women were proud of their profession and many were financially secure. Now there are less than a handful of non-drug-using street workers in the area — the rest having moved into brothels, moved interstate or retired. I have spoken to numerous sex workers who are drug users and I am yet to meet one who would be working except for the financial need to provide for their addiction. I found it noteworthy that it was common for these workers to inform police of the location of young people who had recently been lured into the profession, not because of the increased competition but because of genuine concern for the young people and knowledge of the life which awaited them — perhaps one lasting for years before an untimely death at a youthful age.

Hopefully street sex workers might in future be able, through the efforts of the New South Wales Police Service and other government and privately supported organisations, to ply their profession by choice and not through necessity.

PART II

INSIDE VIEWS

INSIDE VIEWS

5

A FEMALE
SEX WORKER'S VIEW
Roxy Blain

I began working in the sex industry in Adelaide ten years ago, when I was in my early twenties. I first became aware of prostitution on a personal level because a friend of mine was involved in the sex industry. She was able to dispel many of the misconceptions I'd been brought up to believe by telling me the realities of working as a prostitute. Even so, I only considered trying prostitution myself when I became unemployed and financially desperate.

My friend was able to put me in touch with parlour owners which made getting a job easier. I would never have known how to seek out sex employment without my friend's help nor would I have had the courage to turn up to work the first time without her support. Prior to working as a prostitute my biggest fear about sex work was that, when the crunch came, I wouldn't be able to go through with it. I wasn't very sexually experienced and I didn't think I would be able to handle having sex with a complete stranger, whether money was involved or not.

My only sexual experience had been one relationship for a

couple of years and one date rape after terminating the relationship. Interestingly, it was probably the rape that most put me in a state of mind in which I was able to consider prostitution for me. The rape gave me a whole new perspective on sex which I had previously experienced only with love and in a relationship. After the rape I realised that something that had felt so nice (sex) could also feel so horrible, and probably varying degrees of good and bad between those two extremes. I also knew for certain now that sex and love were two different things that sometimes went together, and that men were equally able to enjoy sex with and without love. In fact, I saw nothing wrong with loveless sex as long as the woman consented and was compensated for her lack of enjoyment.

From that point on I found it difficult to be judgemental about sex for money as it seemed consensual and compensatory.

Even so, it was not easy to face the act of prostitution for the first time. I remember being so nervous that first time that I was literally shaking when I entered the room. Luckily for me, my first client was experienced and didn't try to make the session personal at all. He didn't even try to kiss me or fondle me. I began by massaging his back with oil while we chatted superficially. After about five minutes he turned over and I rolled on the condom and lube. I hopped on, he said nothing, touched little, came quickly and it was over. I cleaned up the room as he showered and thought to myself, 'that's the easiest $35 I've ever made'.

And the sex felt nothing like any sex I'd ever had before. It was too clinical for me to associate with sex in relationships and too polite and comfortable to be compared with the date rape. It felt more like a cross between a gyno visit and a serviced massage with me in control. From then on it was hard to think of prostitution as anything other than a job, and any moral conflicts I'd had about doing it vanished.

The first parlour I worked in was located in a small house in the back streets of Adelaide. Its setup included two 'work' rooms, the girl's room/kitchen, a lounge, a bathroom for the girls and a communal bathroom for the clients. As I had never worked before I was given a rundown by one of the girls. I was told that prostitution was illegal in South Australia and that I had to be wary of policemen pretending to be clients. If I didn't follow the correct procedures and there was a problem I would be the one arrested, so it was in my best interests to get it right. I was told to use condoms but nothing about STDs or how to check clients for them.

The parlour ran with two girls on each eight-hour shift, sometimes with a sitter, sometimes alone. We took turns answering the door and seeing the clients. Occasionally the client would ask to meet both girls so he could pick one, and we would oblige. When it was my turn and the client rang the doorbell I would open only the front door, keeping the security screen locked. Before allowing entry it was up to me to establish whether this was another client or the police. If the police were at the door it was my job to stall them for as long as possible while sounding the 'vice' bell to warn the others.

Mostly it would be a client at the door and this would be my opportunity to make money. I would take the client into one of the work rooms and ask him to undress completely before I described any of the prices and services available. (Undressing the client was supposed to screen out police as even undercover cops were not supposed to remove their underpants on the job.) The prices ranged from $35 for topless massage and hand relief to $65 for full sex with the works of which I paid $20 per client to the 'house'. Mostly the difference between each service was the time allocated to the job; top dollar bought half an hour while the lesser paid sessions lasted as little as ten minutes.

The client would make a decision and offer a certain amount of money which I would ask him to leave on the table. I would not touch the money until the service was completed as touching the cash was the equivalent of accepting money for sex and thus illegal. Waiting till after the service to collect the money saved you from arrest if a police raid occurred during the job — and it often did.

There was one occasion in that parlour when a police raid occurred just as I was finishing a service and getting dressed. The vice bell went and I grabbed the cash off the table and gave it back to my client, saying: 'Take your money back and remember you haven't *paid* me for sex — both you and I have done nothing illegal. Get dressed quickly'. No sooner had I spoken when the police started banging on the door. I let the officers in and they separated me from the client immediately. The client was interrogated but as

I had returned his money he could not truly say he had paid me for sex and the police were unable to arrest me.

The parlour I stayed at the longest during my time in South Australia was run by an ex-prostitute who seemed to have invested a lot of money both in furnishings and in legal advice. At this establishment, the clients paid $70 for 30 minutes use of the spa, sauna and massage — no sex included. I had a massage therapist's certificate, as did all the girls, and I was paid $35 (50 percent of the total price paid by the client) to provide a massage.

Halfway through a service I would say something like, 'I wouldn't normally do this, but you're so cute would you mind if I hop into bed with you?' — to which the client would respond with 'yes'. Thus we avoided arrest by propositioning every client with sex which was offered free of charge to those who had paid to use the premises. But even this foolproof method eventually came unstuck when the police started targeting the parlour seven days a week, placing bugs, going undercover, threatening and hassling prostitutes and clients alike as they left the premises and, of course, arresting the prostitutes whenever they could.

In the ten months I worked in South Australia, I was forced to move from parlour to parlour several times as the police closed them down. The parlours never stayed closed for long. Mostly they reopened in different locations with different routines to avoid arrest, like date agency memberships or escorts, but the police were unrelenting. I could never understand why the police and judiciary of South Australia spent so much time and money prosecuting prostitution when it was only a $60 fine with criminal conviction for a guilty plea.

The constant stress of the police raids, with their insults and confiscation of money and condoms and the general unfairness of the situation, soon tired me. I finally left town, disillusioned by the legal system but not by the sex industry.

Twelve months later I was in New South Wales, unemployed and again short of cash. I knew little of the difference in the laws governing the sex industry in New South Wales but it wasn't long before I found the benefits of working in a partially decriminalised system. The first difference I noticed was how much easier it was to find a job. In fact I was able to choose from a selection of parlours and agencies, all of which advertised quite clearly what they were in a magazine. I rang one of the vacancy ads, got an interview straight away and started the next day. I'd never had an interview in South Australia; employment was all by word of mouth.

I went to work in a parlour in Kings Cross. The whole attitude in the parlour was different from what I'd been accustomed to. Here no one worried about the police. When I asked what to do in case of a police raid I was laughed at. The other girls told me they had never seen the police except when there was a problem with one of the clients, in which case the police were called to assist us.

As far as what you did in the rooms goes, it was all upfront. The client still paid $70 for half an hour but this time it was for massage, part-French and sex (and some clients even paid for an hour or more which rarely happened in South Australia). The house still retained 50 percent of my earnings, and it was up to me to sort out my own taxes (which I declared and paid as a self-employed person).

I was told the use of condoms was optional and I took that to mean optional for me — if I wanted to go without I could. In fact, it was optional for the client. I never had much trouble getting a client to use a condom, particularly as I was happy to do something else of interest to compensate for the 'lack of sensitivity', such as using a vibrator on him. If all else failed I would willingly miss out on a job if I knew that a man was a no-condom client, but the bottom line was that if you couldn't work it out with the client then you could lose your job over refusing to provide a service (this was the sex industry prior to AIDS).

The parlour operated with receptionists to let in the clients, take their money and be responsible if there were any problems. We usually met the clients in a line-up, either individually or all at once. The first thing that struck me about working by line-up was the variety of girls the clients picked. I usually did well even though I wasn't the most beautiful girl on shift. I was particularly surprised by how often the 'big' girls got picked, since women's magazines had led me to believe that men preferred their women skinny. (Over the years I have come to realise that women's magazines know little about what men prefer.)

Sydney was the first time I was able to work free from the threat of arrest and this lowered the stress levels I had previously associated with prostitution work. With the lowering of work-related stress came a change in my attitude towards working as a prostitute. In South Australia the sex industry was a place to make money but to get out of as quickly as possible, preferably before gaining a record. In New South Wales, with the partial decriminalisation of the sex industry, I was able to consider prostitution as a career for the first time. I realised that by working fewer days a week I could enjoy my work more when I was actually doing it and still make a reasonable income. Best of all, I could work for years at it without burning out (and I have).

As time passed I became more interested in the fantasy/B & D (bondage and discipline) side of the industry. Straight sex services had become boring to me and the few fantasy clients I did do were much more fun than the usual sessions — and I was good at it. As usual, I turned to the Situations Vacant column of the local sex paper and rang one of the big B & D houses for an interview. I was told that B & D was a specialised field and that I would need to serve an apprenticeship of sorts to become a Mistress (Dominatrix). The apprenticeship involved assisting experienced Mistresses in their sessions until I knew enough to conduct sessions on my own. Only then would I be able to charge the client for my appearance in the session.

I began working two or three days a week at the B & D house for next to nothing (just the occasional tip) and two days a week at the regular parlour to support myself. After about three months the manageress put me on the roster at the B & D house as a fully fledged Mistress and I quit at the parlour. The shifts at the B & D house were long — twelve hours minimum — during which you generally saw two or three clients. The sessions were structured differently from the straight parlour in that the clients were charged for what they did, not for how long they stayed. Consequently, you had to discuss in detail what the clients wanted to do just to set the price of the session. It was not uncommon to spend half an hour talking before starting the session.

Fantasies ranged from castration and baby fantasies to complete confinement and corporal punishment — and everything in between, with the exception of intercourse. Straight sex was not provided at all and clients wanting parlour services were sent on their way. Sessions generally lasted an hour to an hour and a half and ended when the client climaxed. Clients would climax from doing the most amazing things.

Most clients were looking for B & D but we catered to all kinds of tastes. One client I knew had a foot fetish. He loved licking legs and feet in high-heeled shoes. He liked to be stepped on all over and he would come when you stepped on his neck and face with full body weight. I thought he was amazing because he didn't even have to masturbate with his hand, it just happened when you stepped on those parts of his body. Although I found that spankings were popular, especially after an election, and that the full moon often brought out the cross-dressers (transvestites), there was no real pattern to who came in and when.

Mistressing was always interesting and I really enjoyed playing the different roles that each client required. It was like being director, scriptwriter and actress all in one.

After a few years I decided to try working privately. By then I had become very good at dealing with clients and I felt that handing over 50 percent of my money was too high a price when so many of my clients were regulars (that is, they regularly saw and booked me). I decided on working from my own home and converted one room into a dungeon/playroom. I advertised my services as private and worked by appointment only, giving my address only to clients I knew or had spoken to a number of times.

Working for yourself has a lot to offer in terms of work conditions and control, but there can be problems too if you aren't careful. I tried to keep a low profile in the neighbourhood to avoid problems with the council, police or other residents of the area. None of my neighbours ever complained about me; in fact I doubt they even knew I was working from home since I only saw four to six clients a week. The biggest drawback was the large number of appointments that didn't show. Probably only one in every ten bookings actually turned up at the door, leaving me somewhat concerned about the growing number of men with my address. I only ever had one guy turn up without an appointment — he'd obviously got my address previously and I gave him such a roasting that he never came back.

The more intimate surroundings seemed to put clients more at ease than the big B & D house did, and I found some of the more unusual clients coming out of the woodwork. Men who wanted to be forced to eat dog food and be locked in a backyard for days; men who wanted to be treated like the Christmas tree fairy and told to fly away — even men who wanted to be given enemas and to be bound in plastic wrap when they released them.

I learned to be very non-judgemental but would offer to participate only if I felt sufficiently comfortable with what they wanted to do. My trademark was that I never did anything I didn't want to do and if possible I tried to enjoy doing what they wanted to do.

As the sex industry offers nothing in the way of sickness or holiday pay prostitutes take little time off and generally work nearly 52 weeks a year, every year. I was no exception and after working from home for two years and in B & D for almost five years I felt like I needed a break. I also felt that I had done the fantasy scene to death and I wanted to get back to the straight sex scene with its relaxing monotony.

I decided to combine my return to straight sex with a change of environment. This time I checked the laws regarding prostitution in the different states to see if moving state was even viable. I decided on Western Australia because, although organised prostitution was illegal, being a prostitute was not. I figured that this would be as good for me as decriminalisation was in New South Wales, since I was planning on being a prostitute not organising the work. I couldn't have been more wrong. What Western Australia lacks in prostitution legislation it makes up for in police discretionary powers, regardless of the abuse of human rights and civil liberties that they might entail.

I rented a house in Perth and set up a room for clients. I checked the laws and made sure that home occupation prostitution was not illegal. I noticed that the sex industry advertised in the personals section of the *West Australian*, so I put in an ad. This involved both providing the newsagent with an ID to prove who I was and being at home for the *West Australian* to verify my work number by calling me.

The next day I had about forty calls from clients and was happily taking bookings when the Vice police rang me up. They told me I had to come in and register if I intended to work in 'their' town.

I decided to ring some of the other private operators advertising in the paper to find out what the story was with Vice. What I heard horrified me. Even though I wasn't breaking the law I had to register or Vice would come around in marked cars to take me in for questioning, making sure my whole neighbourhood became aware of my presence. (This would usually lead to eviction by the landlord or problems with the council.) Sometimes, I was told, Vice would send thugs around to pretend to be clients and bash you. When you rang the police for help you would be asked if you were registered and if you were not no assistance would be given.

Needless to say, I decided to register. This involved making an appointment with Vice police for an interview during which I was photographed and required to verify my identity with a photo ID. The police then politely explained that I had to keep them informed of my address should it change, who I lived with and where I worked. They said that I was not allowed to see clients privately if I was working for one of the 'containment' parlours (the police seemed unduly interested in protecting the 'containment' parlours from 'ruthless' prostitutes who might make a little on the side by seeing regular clients at home).

I told the police what they wanted to know under the assurance that all the information I gave them was strictly confidential and would not be released to anyone outside Vice, not even other police. Two days later I received a phone call from the Special Tax Audit section of the Australian Taxation Office (Western Australian branch). The man identified himself as a taxation officer and told me that he'd got my number from Vice and that Special Tax Audit would need to interview me. So much for police confidentiality.

I asked the tax officer why he needed to interview me as my taxes were in order and up to date. He told me that Special Tax Audit dealt specifically with the sex industry to make sure, by meeting prostitutes individually to discuss their financial situation, that they complied with their income tax obligations. He said that only by meeting me could he be sure that my taxes were in order. When I disputed this he explained how beneficial it was for the officers to meet the prostitutes in person, to see what they looked like, as knowing their appearance helped the officers to gauge if their correct income was being declared.

I was furious. I told him that I had always paid my taxes, but without declaring myself to be employed as a prostitute and I was not about to begin that now since it was not a requirement of the Taxation Act. As far as judging my income by my looks was concerned I refused to allow such an invasion of my privacy. Besides which, in my experience of the sex industry, looks rarely gave any insight into anyone's expected income. I gave the tax officer my accountant's name and address and suggested that in future they contact him regarding my taxes.

Certain threats were then made about auditing my income for the last five years, but I stood my ground and refused to arrange an appointment at the tax office. A few days later the tax boys turned up at my door unannounced and, although I refused to answer their questions, they got what they wanted — to look at my face and body.

The police and tax experiences unsettled me. Perth was a small town and all this official attention made me feel conspicuous, a feeling I didn't like. I became very unsure about working at home alone and the laws precluded my hiring someone, even for security. To top it off I felt very isolated as I didn't really know anyone in Perth. I would have gone back to Sydney at that point but I'd spent all my savings coming to Perth, so I needed to earn the money to leave. Also I didn't like the idea of being run out of town within four weeks.

I decided to go and work in one of the 'containment' parlours. The police obviously condoned their operations (even though they were illegal) so I figured that the parlours would be hassle-free. It was worth paying them 50 percent for a feeling of security. The parlours all advertised in the *West Australian* so I looked them up and made some phone calls. The madams seemed keen to interview some new blood and I was keen to see what the parlours were like. What I saw and heard horrified me.

All the parlours I visited required police registration and allowed the Special Tax Audit boys to interview you in your work clothes (lingerie) in the parlour. They required weekly medical appointment cards (to prove you had weekly STD scans) and your real name, address and tax file number (I hate giving the kind of people who run parlours my personal details — in Sydney a first name and phone number will usually do). In return the parlour madams decided what shifts you'd work, how many shifts you'd work, what you'd wear, what services you'd offer in the room — and if there were any disputes you were fired. The atmosphere in the parlours was tense and repressive, even at the interview. A bit like what the Adelaide parlours were like during a police raid.

The prices at some parlours started as low as $20 for ten minutes of full sex in premises that had no showers and that had locks on the front door to keep the girls in. No personal phone calls were allowed, even in the case of an emergency. The split was less than 50 percent because the madams deducted their version of the tax out of your half of the money before you received it. The madams also decided what income to declare you earned (and therefore what to tax you on) based largely on how much income their business was declaring. For all the interest Special Tax Audit people gave the sex industry, the tax rates deducted by different parlours were hardly standard. Rates varied from 49 cents in the dollar (commonly charged) to an amount on a sliding scale of never less than 20 percent based on the Daily Tax Schedule provided by Special Tax Audit for 'seasonal workers'.

Although I was less than impressed by the parlours I needed to work with people at that stage, so I took a job at the parlour with the best atmosphere and where the staff seemed happiest.

The prices at this parlour ranged from $35 to $160 depending on what the client wanted. I had to pay a $200 bond upfront just to start work. I had to pay a $20 shift fee from my 50 percent share of what the client paid. Then tax was calculated and deducted by management out of what remained of my 50 percent, and I received whatever was left — once a week, on payday. I was never sure how much of the money deducted as tax actually made it to the tax department. No one seemed to check that and the records the girls were given never stated our true income or deductions and never equalled the actual cash we received. It was so confusing that all I know is that I usually made about 25–30 percent of what the client paid. I felt this type of arrangement tempted the girls to do extras in the room for a bit more money (for example, oral sex without a condom).

I wasn't prepared to risk my health and future livelihood on providing any unsafe services, no matter what amount of money was offered (and there were always men offering extra money; that never stops). It was easy to become depressed working under these conditions and hard to watch most of the money you made disappear into the hands of others.

The police-approved parlours were the worst I'd ever worked in. Police approval gave the parlour madams a stranglehold over the sex industry. If you left on bad terms with one madam, you could be blackbanned in all the other parlours too. It was a nightmare.

I saved my money and later left town feeling that the police should never be allowed to 'run' prostitution as they do in Western Australia. I know the people of Perth thought the cops did a good job but 'containment', much like legalisation, leaves the people with the smallest vested interest in health and safety standards in charge (eg the parlour owners, police and tax department). The prostitutes themselves have virtually no power under this system and they are the ones whose health (and livelihood) are on the line, as parlour owners can always replace sick workers but prostitutes cannot replace their bodies.

I returned to Sydney and I now work in a small collective parlour. We share expenses and shifts to minimise the costs of running the parlour and maximise our earning capacity. I am happy to be able to work without harassment, in safety and without having to put my health on the line. The best advice I can give anyone interested in trying prostitution is to never do anything sexually that you don't want to do. It's never worth the extra cash, and if the client doesn't understand let him see someone else.

Overall, I would have to say that there is almost nothing I regret about the choices I've made in my life as a prostitute (except the Perth stint, maybe). Mostly I feel that sex work has given me more confidence, financial security, independence and a better understanding of both men and women. I am happy and secure in myself and in the relationships I have outside work.

That is not to say that there aren't negatives to sex work. Probably the worst thing is living with the huge public stigma that society places on prostitutes — forcing us to lie to parents, friends, relatives, banks, doctors, landlords, etc. I can tell you I learnt that the hard way by telling people whom I thought were open-minded to what I did only to find myself disowned by longstanding friends and relatives. When people close to you treat you that way, why risk telling anyone else?

It often feels as though people think that prostitutes come from Mars, or that we have some strange disposition to sex work (other than financial). We don't. In fact I remember asking all the girls on shift one night if any of them had thought they could cope with prostitution before they'd tried it. We all said no.

6

A MALE
SEX WORKER'S VIEW
Steven Goodley

I had my first boyfriend at the age of 17. I wasn't aware of all the intricacies of gay life or gay sex at that time, but I had known about my sexuality since I was twelve. The boy I began seeing when I was 17 was 22 and, even though we lived in the suburbs, he introduced me to a lot of other gay people. One of the gay guys I met through him was a beautiful blond boy who occasionally worked 'The Wall' and I learnt about Sydney's hustling scene through him. After talking with him I decided that I wanted to do the same.

I wasn't attracted so much by the amount of money that could be made. It was more to do with the fact that the money could be made easily and that there was a certain 'glamour' in being a male prostitute. It seemed to me that I could not express my sexuality in a better way: the thought of having men gloat over my body and then pay to be next to it was definitely appealing.

What prevented me from entering prostitution at that stage was that I already had a well-paid job and was making far more than any other 17-year-old I knew. Also, the idea of venturing into the inner city, a place for which the suburban lifestyle I was used to had not really prepared me, and the fact that I would have to begin a new lifestyle and become involved with people about whom I knew very little scared me enough to not even explore the possibility of doing it part time.

Nonetheless, I knew I wanted to become a male prostitute and that desire stayed with me until I finally decided to take the step and do it. I continued with my job until I was 24 and during those years I gradually became more familiar with the gay lifestyle and with the inner city and Oxford Street gay scene. I then moved through a few jobs until I actually made the decision to try my hand at prostitution as I had wanted for so long.

I had an argument with my boyfriend and went to stay with my mother for a couple of days. I took some gay magazines with me and that was when I began my preparations. With a pad and pen I systematically worked my way through all the agencies listed and called them to make appointments. When I returned home I broke the news to my boyfriend. He had worked before and he vehemently tried to discourage me from getting involved with prostitution. That was the end of our relationship.

The next day I visited four agencies. The reception I received was very warm in all cases. One agency seemed to be very efficient and organised the interview very well, and the premises made me feel that it would be a high class place to work. When they accepted me I agreed. I took the name 'Brian' and began work immediately.

When beginning in a new position there is always some uncertainty and anxiety: you ask yourself why you're there, what's expected of you, who are the other people around you, and whether you fit in. In the past I had always had great confidence in myself but this was different. There was no position as such: I was just there and my only way to make money came with a buzz on the door or a ring on the phone. Retainers are non-existent and I had to get clients in order to have an income. Not only was that hanging over my head but the whole situation was competitive. It was a selling game and you had to sell yourself in any way possible.

My attributes were a nice body and being naturally smooth. Some of the others had fabulous bodies and would show it in any way possible, or they had huge cocks and wore the tightest lycra shorts possible to show it off.

Each time I had to meet a potential client it became easier to round the corner and do the introduction but there was always a feeling of uneasiness. The thought usually ran through my mind: 'Am I good enough to be here?'. I felt that I was good enough but I wasn't getting the work at first. Even regular clients who would always see the new boys didn't take me. I finally realised that it was all to do with self-confidence and making yourself look good — selling yourself. From that point things turned around and I began to get the clients and enjoy the work.

By the time I had it all 'figured out' and began to get enough work to make my being there worthwhile, I discovered that the clients were quite ordinary and human. I had always heard how the working girls were treated badly, as though they were just a 'hole to fill', were generally roughed up and were called horrible names — treated as filth. That certainly was not my experience with the clients I saw. My clients certainly did not make me feel as though I was just a 'hole to fill' — even if that was what they wanted they did not make me feel that way. They were usually in their late thirties to late fifties, well-kept, clean and friendly. Usually, they were married men who just needed a young man to fill a particular gap in their lives.

Overall, though, there was a broad spectrum of clients. They ranged in age from as young as 18 upwards. Some of them were men who were not really sure of their sexual preference and just wanted to see if it was what they really wanted. Others just wanted to try sex with another man to experiment with it. And there were others again who clearly knew that their sexual preference was for men but were not brave enough to go to a gay venue such as a sauna or a gay pub. Some of these men were unsure about what to do and did not know where they could start and so they came to a working boy as a way to deal with that situation.

One young client like this used to come in during the day. He said he was about 18 but I could have believed him if he'd said he was 17 or even 16. He was very good looking with blond hair and blue eyes. He selected me and when we went into the room he absolutely mauled me. Under other circumstances I would have thought of him as a really good sex partner and I would have taken him home without question. After the sex we talked a while and he has since been back a couple of times.

Another client who used to come to see me regularly was a man in his fifties. He was incredible for his age. He worked out in a gym and had a fantastic body of which most workers would be proud. The first time he came in was after a gay dance party. We had great sex. He told me that he was a highly respected barrister. He had been married earlier in his life and had a tribe of children. He explained that he had only married because in those days being gay was not an acceptable lifestyle, particularly for someone in his position. He had divorced his wife a few years earlier so that he could be free to live his life as he really wanted. He told me that he had a fantasy of hiring me for the whole night of Mardi Gras so that he could seduce me in the middle of the dance floor, surrounded by 10,000 people.

This particular client was unusual. The most common situation is that a client will see a boy once or twice, then move on to someone else, and so on. But occasionally a client will develop a special affection for a particular worker. This client was like that: he continued to come into the agency where I worked but stayed faithful to me and, when I stopped working at that agency, he stopped coming in.

Most often, the typical client just wants affection. If he does want penetration it is usually that he wants to be penetrated by the boy. I found some difficulty coming to terms with this at first because some boys with a ten-inch dick, quite capable of penetrating clients, had lots of clients and made very good money, even though they weren't particularly good looking. Overall, though, it is the basically good looking boys who can show a lot of affection who get the repeat business.

The monetary rewards for coping with being a male sex worker are not all that good compared to what working girls can make. The average boy at peak times would make between $400 and $1000 per week, depending on how often he works and how 'average' he is. Fortunately, at least in the places I worked in, the earnings were not dependent on who you slept with.

Agency work is only one of several ways a boy can ply his trade. My boyfriend, who has had experience of working at agencies and working privately, pointed out to me that working in an agency means that all the expenses are taken care of, from the advertising to the condoms and the lube. The security of an agency also means that 'mugs' (a term for clients) do not know your phone number or where you live. A mobile phone can take care of at least some of that problem but the typical client, being married, often cannot explain mobile phone numbers. And clients often are unwilling to give their own number to a private worker because they fear being called at home, whereas they may trust the confidentiality of an agency more.

Also, working privately can attract a less desirable clientele. This is because, the rates being cheaper, a private worker often sees clients who cannot afford an agency. These clients are often not as clean and are more demanding. They sometimes turn up unannounced and are often not as interested in the affection as in getting whatever sex it is that they want.

Workers in an agency are not permitted to work the streets, and agency staff sometimes pass by 'The Wall' to make sure that none of their own workers is there. I have had a lot of contact with workers from the streets, but the ones that I have most to do with are those who simply choose to work there rather than from an agency or from home. They seem to do quite well, but are always on the lookout for thugs and bashers, as well as those who demand 'protection money'.

There is another group of boys working the street scene. These are the street kids, some under 18, many drug-dependent. They usually cannot make it in an agency or would not be allowed in an agency (either because they are too young or because of their drug problem). They are generally runaways and they do not have a place in the Oxford Street gay scene, so they find a place in the street hustling scene.

One of the most rewarding aspects of sex work is the people you meet. I have been fortunate enough to meet perhaps a couple of hundred working boys. They come from all sorts of backgrounds and have different stories. There are straight boys who work — in fact there are a surprising number of them! Some do it out of sheer desperation and last a day or two to a couple of months. Many of them are surprisingly good at their work, even if only for a short time. The experience of sex work often opens their eyes to a whole new life and they meet people they probably never would have met otherwise. A few straight boys make sex work a fairly comfortable way of earning a living and stay for several months, but they usually maintain that they are straight and manage to do that satisfactorily. For the most part these boys manage to fit into the scene and the clients would be very unlikely to realise that they were straight. There are very rarely any complaints about these boys.

However, most of the boys who are working are gay and mix in the Oxford Street gay scene, and most of the managers of the agencies are also gay. The boys in male prostitution are generally openly gay and aged between 19 and 25. They are usually out and about in the gay party scene. Some have other jobs but most of those working for agencies are fairly dependent on prostitution, at least for a while. Typically, workers in an agency last from a few months to a year or more. They usually make the parlour a fun place to work in and usually know each other out in the gay scene. They all know people who know each other, but they do not go about telling their friends that 'so-and-so is a sex worker'. Even so, no matter how much someone might want to keep it a secret, a lot of people generally know about it. Secrets like this are hard to keep in the gay scene.

On the other hand, it is usually considered that working as a prostitute involves a stigma and that people would want to keep it a secret if they were doing sex work. I have not found this to be the case as a male prostitute. I have never really felt stigmatised by other gay people as a result of my working. Except for a few who try to keep certain nocturnal activities a secret, it's no big deal to be known as a male prostitute. While secrets may be hard to keep in the gay scene, the scene is itself protective of sex workers thanks to the simple fact that most people do not mind what someone else does. This makes being a sex worker a viable career in the gay scene.

7

A BROTHEL OWNER'S VIEW

Caroline Barlow

I was born in the southern suburbs of Sydney in 1954. My father was a taxi driver who developed polio and died at the age of 29 years. My mother was left emotionally bereft after this. She had two children, me at three and my brother at six years of age, and no visible means of support. She eventually got a job as a hairdresser, but her meagre wage hardly supported us all. She eventually remarried when I was about seven years of age. My stepfather had fled his homeland in Europe after the communists had confiscated his family's extensive landholdings. My strongest memory of this time is that of pretending I was asleep while my mother and new stepfather argued continually about money. We moved to the western suburbs, living in a fibro house on a dirt road some distance from the nearest town, and purchased a local milk-run as a means of supporting the family. But I enjoyed the benefits of a semi-rural environment. There were acres of natural bushland, numerous creeks to swim in, horses to ride, dogs to play with and many adventures to be had. As a child I always felt that I would have preferred to be a boy, as they seemed to have more active, exciting lives than we girls did at that time. I was not particularly interested in school and little was expected of me scholastically. My specialty was watching TV many hours a day. I did virtually no school work, cooked dinner during TV commercials, and did all the household shopping every Saturday morning with my trusty four-wheel trolley.

For a few years my life seemed to be drifting nowhere, until I began to reassess my choices towards the end of my fourth year in high school. I realised I needed to be in a different environment to give myself some kind of opportunity. I opted to go to boarding school and we selected the least expensive school we could find, which happened to be on the beautiful north coast of New South Wales. Boarding school was a gradual revelation and taught me the value of self-discipline, despite my having no outstanding attributes. I eventually finished with three level A's in humanities and proceeded to university on a teacher's scholarship. About this time I remember my stepfather driving me to Central Station at the end of my school holidays, and while he was driving he asked me if I knew what my mother had been doing lately. I said I didn't know. Then he told me that they had run into financial difficulties and that she had been working as a prostitute to help out. Thus in her early forties she had begun to work on the streets of East Sydney to clear our debts. But he seemed to want to turn me against her. I responded to him by saying that if that was so she was obviously doing it to help us. He dropped the subject immediately after that and never brought it up again. But my mother was picked up and charged by the police for soliciting. In those days (the early 1970s) the women on the streets were constantly harassed by the police. It put an end to her career as a prostitute since the threat of fines and legal fees made our financial situation worse.

I stayed at university for two years without showing any real interest in my studies or having a clue as to what I really wanted. I also got tired of living on Vita Wheat crisps and peanut butter. At the end of my second year I discontinued my tertiary life and began a varied career ranging from cleaner to waitress. Because of my mother's experience I viewed prostitution as an economic necessity, but at this stage I never considered working in the sex industry myself. Instead I met an interesting group of people living in a large inner city commune and eagerly moved in with them. But I was incredibly naive and sexually inexperienced. I fell pregnant but did not want to have a baby. In the 1970s it was virtually impossible to obtain an abortion without a psychiatrist's recommendation. By the time I eventually got a psychiatrist's report my pregnancy was over 12 weeks and I was told it was too late for an abortion. I was determined to find another way. Fortunately there was an experimental program using postglandins to help women over 12 weeks. So I ended up in a hospital vomiting and miscarrying. After that I resolved to change my attitude and take control of my own destiny.

Not long after this I came into contact with a number of prostitutes while working as a waitress. I now felt independence was important and as a female my choices were limited without specialist training. Shortly afterwards I was offered the use of a city apartment by a woman who worked there privately. I took the opportunity without knowing what to expect. But everything went well and I was surprised to find how nice the clients were, and I made a lot of money. After a few months I became lonely working by myself and longed for the company of other women. Then I met a young woman who mentioned that she earned good money at the parlour known as 'A Touch of Class'. I applied for a job there and although I did not fit the male owner's stereotype of large-breasted, slender-waisted women I started soon afterwards. The place had many attractive women working there and at first it was a little intimidating. However, I was determined to do well and worked hard to build up a regular clientele. My efforts were successful and I felt a sense of satisfaction in doing a good job, as well as earning excellent money. Soon I had the financial independence I aimed for and before long owned my own apartment. Eventually I decided to work for myself and not just earn money for other people. I also wanted the freedom to make my own decisions.

I worked hard at this goal and in a couple of years felt I was ready to begin my own business. I decided to renovate the property I owned as I couldn't afford anything else at the time. I continued saving every dollar I earned. Then I met a 'local identity' who sternly informed me that he 'owned the street' where I lived and intended to start my business. Luckily, though, by the time I was ready to start operating he had a lot more important problems to worry about. I moved into the top floor of my terrace house and organised the lower sections for business. I contacted a couple of women with whom I had previously worked and invited them to work for me. But within three months the local council took me to court because I did not have a development consent. Of course, the irony is that no one in this business can get a legitimate consent under the current zoning laws unless it is under some other guise. The council eventually withdrew its action when I proved that I had existing-use rights thanks to the place having a previous history as a brothel. But this was the most difficult time of my life: physically, emotionally and financially. Initially I merely paid the bills from any spare cash and gave the greater portion of my profits back to the women as an incentive to stay with me. For the first couple of years any spare money went back into the business. I managed to keep my head above water and survived for a few years. I eventually bought a larger place in the inner city, and as this business grew I purchased another parlour in the suburbs.

The sex industry has changed dramatically since I started owning my own business over a decade ago, due to various internal and external factors. External factors affecting business have included changes in laws, police attitudes and council's attitudes and, of course, the threat of AIDS. Internal factors have included the type of women working for you, their treatment of their clients and the type of men who are attracted to parlours — as well as the need for continual repairs and maintenance of the premises and the need to change the decor from time to time to upgrade the business. The women who work for me differ between my inner city parlour and the one in the suburbs. In my suburban business the women are older, quieter, less temperamental and more stable; while those in the inner city tend to be young, often between 18 and 25, who seem to have less specific goals than the older women other than to pay the rent and to buy clothes and other immediate needs. A common attitude among the younger women is that sex work is not a 'proper job' and they have a casual attitude towards it, turning up to work when they feel like it and generally being much less reliable than the older women. Some of them also have many problems. Their biggest problem is having to hide what they do from their parents and other relatives and friends. For this reason they come from the outer suburbs, or even further, to work in my inner city parlour. Susie is a 20-year-old with an extremely religious mother who wanted to visit her at work. I was able to provide a convincing cover for her as an office worker with some friends of mine. Similar problems occur when the women need a reference for accommodation or purchases on credit. I have often provided a verbal reference for my workers under various guises.

Long irregular working hours dealing with many men of various personality types leaves some of the women physically and emotionally drained. It is difficult for them to maintain a full emotional or sexual relationship in their private lives. Some women put their private lives 'on hold' while they concentrate on their work, but others persevere with a boyfriend. Boyfriend problems are quite common among many of my workers. Young attractive Nikki constantly has problems with her temperamental Lebanese boyfriend, who has beaten her on numerous occasions. Recently she fled from him leaving her clothes and other belongings behind and changing her working name. Ironically, she has become increasingly irrational and unreliable, and since leaving him has lost her motivation to work now that he is not around to make financial and emotional demands on her. On a number of occasions I have helped other women move their clothes and belongings when their boyfriends weren't at home to stop us, only to find the women moving back shortly afterwards.

Another problem only too common among the younger women is alcohol and drug abuse. After work it is not uncommon for them to go out on a rage in the many bars and clubs of the inner city. Although I have liquor on the premises, in order to offer customers a complimentary drink, I have to be vigilant in watching that some of the girls do not overindulge at work. Recreational drugs, such as pills, might be consumed outside before commencing work, and more rarely you find the occasional worker using intravenous drugs before coming to work. Anyone who is found intoxicated with drugs or alcohol while at work is sent home immediately. Justine is a young woman with a drug problem who made a lot of money one night. During her revelry after work she fell asleep with too much alcohol and too many pills, only to wake and find her entire earnings and other belongings stolen.

It is still possible to make a very attractive living from the sex industry, despite a recent drastic decline in turnover. But although many women earn excellent incomes, they continue to have financial problems due to their standard of living. Expensive clothing, jewellery, nice apartments, cars, overseas travel and demanding boyfriends become commonplace. Unfortunately, little provision is made for a future time when their source of income from sex work has to stop for some reason. Many women become tired of the constant demands of the job and leave, but others remain in the industry and as they get older they find their income dwindles when they become less in demand from clients. The more organised women have a financial plan, with the help of a good accountant. But too many leave the sex industry with little to show for it but a tired body and an uncertain future. Judy is an extremely attractive woman in her early thirties with 16 years in the business and virtually nothing to show for all her hard work. Health problems are also commonplace due to long hours, lack of proper sleep, too many pills, too much alcohol, too many cigarettes, too much coffee, inadequate diet and being generally rundown. Elena, on the other hand, a beautiful South American blonde, exercises regularly with the help of a personal trainer who ensures that she maintains a healthy lifestyle.

Many people think that we parlour owners live off the fat of the land, so to speak. They do not realise the enormous expense involved in running a sex business. As with any commercial premises there is a lot of wear and tear which needs constant attention, from normal wear to breakages caused by clumsy or tipsy clients. Carpets and rugs wear out much more quickly than in ordinary households because of the amount of traffic going through the place; high heels, spilt drinks and cigarette butts all take their toll. Linen needs to be laundered daily and replaced because of excessive use. Curtains and other furnishings have to be cleaned regularly, all of which is very expensive. Spa bath motors, air conditioning and electrical wiring require constant maintenance, not to mention the continual replacement of broken glasses, coffee tables, lamps and other items. TV sets sometimes get broken with so many hands twirling the dials, and are occasionally stolen. Fantasy outfits need renewing to cater for changing demands by clients. Music equipment, video units and microwaves need ongoing maintenance. As I run a 24–hour service I have to have the rooms professionally cleaned every day, and frequent renovations are necessary to prevent the place becoming shabby. And you can imagine what the electric light bill is in a three-storey house of 20 rooms, a dozen TVs, air conditioning in every room, and lights which are never turned off. And that is only the start.

Apart from unreliable staff, unpredicable clients and everyday maintenance there are many other problems, not least of which are sexually transmissible diseases — AIDS, hepatitis B, herpes — and every other ailment which can keep staff off work for a week or infect a client who may threaten to sue or take some other action, none of which is good for business. Therefore condoms are a must, another expense borne by the house. These days my girls offer clients safe sex with a sensual massage and hand relief, rather than full sexual contact, first. Also, with the sex business in decline and more and more women working in private flats all over Sydney, I have had to advertise for 'masseuses' to attract staff. Massage work is less emotionally, if not physically, draining but it can get you arrested if girls offer sex as well.

Local councils are another ongoing problem. Although the law is the same throughout New South Wales different councils choose to enforce it in their own way. Some councils will not legally pursue an establishment if no trouble is being created. This is an extremely intelligent approach as they understand that we provide a valuable service to our clients. Other councils continually harass and persecute us. Private detectives are sometimes sent in at the ratepayer's expense to collect evidence for a court case. Huge amounts of time and money are expended on closing a business which doesn't hurt anyone and actually provides a community service. Ironically, because we cannot get development consents approved the normal health and building requirements of any conventional business are not checked by the council as we are not meant to really exist.

Over the years the police have had various policies regarding enforcement of the prostitution laws. Recently the Vice Squad was disbanded, so that enforcement is left to local police — who also have differing attitudes to enforcing the law. But the laws are antiquated and contradictory. Although there is no illegality in a woman selling sexual services, as an owner of a business where a woman can work I can be charged with 'living off her earnings'. She might not want to work in a private situation or escort agency with a risk of client violence, but might choose to work in my establishment where she is safer and has the advantage of a serviced room with everything provided. Yet I run the risk of arrest for providing her with a safe, clean environment. It makes little sense.

The parlour is an undeniable aspect of modern life. Like any business it has a good as well as a bad side. Not only have the women who work in this business changed over the years — they tend to be younger, less professional, and more prone to drug and alcohol consumption — but so have the clients. They too are becoming younger, with fewer of the old-style wealthy businessmen visiting us. The modern client is more demanding, wanting to pay less, looking for kinkier sex and, I believe, more likely to turn to violence. But the parlour industry goes on in the face of all these changes and the many difficulties, and it will continue to do so until it is finally acknowledged by the government and the community. We will always exist in some form or other, so why not legislate with this in mind? Why not give us similar responsibilities and requirements to those applying to operators in any other field of business?

PART III

SOCIAL
AND HEALTH
PERSPECTIVES

8

FEMALE PROSTITUTION
Roberta Perkins

The 'oldest profession' is at least as old as written history and probably considerably older, if reports of its existence in pre-literate societies are to be believed (see, for instance, Burley and Symanski 1981; although Decker 1979, pp 28–9 would argue against the existence of prostitution in tribal societies). Prostitution is frequently recorded in the Old Testament and given prominence in the observations of the fifth century BC historian Herodotus. In many ancient Near Eastern civilisations female prostitution occurred in temples as a sacred duty (Henriques 1962; Bullough 1967; Simons 1975). But since classical times female sex work has taken place in public places (streets, taverns, etc.) and in brothels (bordellos, seraglios, bagnios, stews, etc.), and with the invention of the telephone there has emerged the phenomenon of the private prostitute (or 'call girl'). These forms of female prostitution were introduced to Australia with the First Fleet (see Chapter 1) and through subsequent interventions by Western culture.

The present chapter describes these forms of female prostitution in Australia as it exists today. Much of it will be viewed from the perspective of the sex workers, including insights into their private life. But most of it is the result of empirical investigation. It is hoped that the findings presented in this chapter will bring to a wide audience a clearer understanding of the role of the modern-day sex worker and demonstrate that her background and social life beyond prostitution are little different from that of other women.

The empirical evidence derives from four separate studies: (1) a comprehensive survey in 1985–86 of 128 female prostitutes in Sydney, which will be identified throughout as *Sex Workers 1986*, compared with two similar-size control samples of health workers and tertiary students identified respectively as *Health Workers* and *Students* (from Perkins 1991); (2) a health survey in 1990 of 280 female prostitutes across New South Wales and the Australian Capital Territory, identified as *Sex Workers 1990,* compared with a control sample of 436 women from a *Cleo* (1991) survey, identified as *Cleo Women* (from Lovejoy et al. 1991, Pt 1); (3) a survey in the next year of 322 female prostitutes providing information on their clients, identified as *Sex Workers 1991* (from Lovejoy et al. 1991, Pt 2); and, (4) surveys in 1993 of 78 private prostitutes, identified as *Private Workers*, and 124 brothel workers, identified as *Brothel Workers* (from Perkins 1994).

LITERATURE ON FEMALE PROSTITUTION

A great body of literature exists on prostitution. Bullough et al. (1977) claimed that some 5500 works on prostitution had been published between 1539 and 1977, more than a third of it being devoted to issues of public health and legislation, over a quarter of it in the disciplines of the social sciences and humanities, and less than 1 percent of it on male prostitution, clients and pimps. There are likely to have been as many as this number of works published since 1977. What such a quantity of literature attests to is the enormous interest in prostitution, as much a response to curiosity and fascination as to public and official concerns over contamination and morality. The literature can be divided into a number of categories, including autobiographical material (eg Madeleine 1919; Adler 1953; Hollander et al. 1972; French and Lee 1989) and biographies (eg Randall 1969; Longstreet 1970; Blaikie 1980) by women in the sex industry and by professional biographers, which represents nearly 5 percent of the works in Bullough's list. Although many events described in these works should not be taken too seriously, they do provide excellent insights into a much misunderstood industry and in some cases are the only source of historical references of a bygone era.

Perhaps greater reliance can be placed on the qualitative material of social researchers, but unfortunately most of these works are relatively recent and limited as historical sources. One exception is the extraordinary account of early twentieth century American prostitution given by the 'father' of symbolic interactionism, William Isaac Thomas (1923) — a sympathetic view of mostly young migrant women turning to prostitution in New York in order to survive, and demonstrating for the first time that sex workers are neither permanently trapped in prostitution nor damaged by it, as many later become successful wives and mothers or easily adjusted to other occupations. In recent years qualitative research has become a necessary and dynamic part of studies about prostitutes (eg Millett 1971; Jaget 1980; Perkins and Bennett 1985; Delacoste and Alexander 1987; Jordan 1992).

Quantitative studies on female prostitution have been carried out since early in the nineteenth century (Parent-Duchatelet 1857; Sanger 1858), but most have been interested in the prostitute only as a phenomenon in medicine, criminology, psychiatry or psychology (eg Lombroso and Ferrero 1895; Agoston 1945; Glover 1953; Greenwald 1970; Gibbens 1971). These works fail to recognise prostitutes as ordinary women who happen to choose sex work as an economic option, but seek to understand them as deviant women. Their often conflicting theories on causality indicate how fragile this line of enquiry has been, but many investigators still persist in pursuing a theory of predestination for prostitution in the psychological or socio-psychological backgrounds of their female subjects. Two empiricists, psychologist Charles Winick and sociologist Paul Kinsie (1971), were among the first to investigate female prostitutes in social deviance theory which inclined towards social, rather than idiosyncratic, causation. A decade later Eileen McLeod (1982) viewed prostitution from the prostitute's perspective and described the sex industry as a practical means of acquiring an income for unskilled and low-skilled women in the workforce. There has been very little social research on female prostitution in Australia, and those studies which have occurred incline towards sensationalism (Winter 1976) or fail to sufficiently explore prostitutes' social backgrounds (Filla 1975).

STREETS, BROTHELS AND PRIVATE PLACES

The numbers of women working in the sex industry across Australia at a given time is impossible to estimate with any real degree of accuracy. Certainly the numbers have declined in the past decade with a general decrease in sex business due to the unstable Australian economy, a change in tax laws which disallows 'entertainment' tax deductions, and the impact of AIDS, especially with the introduction of mandatory safe sex in most areas of sex work. In 1986 the New South Wales Parliamentary Select Committee Upon Prostitution estimated that between 1500 and 2000 female and male prostitutes worked across the state on any single day (NSW Parliament 1986, p 68). A year earlier the Victorian Inquiry Into Prostitution claimed as many as 4000 prostitutes of both sexes in its state (Victorian Government 1985, p 46). Concentrating on the three major types of professional prostitution — street work, brothel work and private ('call girl') prostitution — I estimated that no more than 1000 females did sex work in Sydney in a single week of 1986 (Perkins 1991, p 17). Later my colleagues and I made a 'head count' across New South Wales and concluded that just over 1500 female prostitutes worked in the state each week (Lovejoy et al. 1991, Pt 1 p 5). Estimates for other states include: 250 in South Australia, 330 in Western Australia, 500 in Queensland, 100 in Tasmania and 50 in the Australian Capital Territory (Perkins 1991, pp 17, 64–5). Juggling with all of these figures for a national estimate, we find that the percentage of Australian women in sex work ranges from 0.03 percent (the South Australian estimate) to 0.16 percent (the Victorian estimate). From this, we may conclude that with a projected 1994 total female population in Australia of approximately 5,800,000 between the ages of 15 and 64 (ABS 1992), the population of prostitute women in the country lies somewhere between 1700 and 9500. Perhaps the latter figure is closer to the truth.

The major forms of professional prostitution[1] and various pseudo-prostitution, non-professional and casual commercial sex transactions of amateurs, are all represented in Australia. This chapter will deal only with professional prostitution. Street prostitution involves soliciting male pedestrians and cruising motorists and negotiating a price for various sexual services, usually 'French' (fellatio) or 'Sex' (coitus) or 'short-time' (5 to 15 minutes). Brothel work refers to employment in a house of prostitution where fixed prices are established for basic services (French and Sex) within certain periods (half-hour, one hour, etc.). Fixed prices also exist for more complex and exotic services, such as doubles (two workers), lesbian acts (performed by two workers), anal sex, fantasy scenarios and bondage; even kissing can require extra payment. Brothels, usually referred to as 'parlours' in the argot of the sex trade, range from large bordellos with lavish interiors, 15 to 20 workers to a shift and auxiliary staff, to small two to four bedroom houses with between two and six workers per shift and a receptionist. Private prostitutes, sometimes known by the American colloquialism, 'call girls', usually work in a residential apartment rented by between one and four women, whose clandestine operations depend on arousing client interest with advertisements in local newspapers and making appointments by telephone contact. Some brothel workers and private prostitutes, as well as those women working for escort agencies, will agree to visit clients in their own home or hotel.

In Sydney streetwalking takes place in the inner city and outer suburbs. Street workers in the commercial areas of Kings Cross and on William Street do not contravene existing prostitution laws, but those on outer suburban streets are usually 'within view from dwellings' and consequently in breach of current soliciting laws. My data in the sample *Sex Workers 1986* indicates that many street workers are substance abusers and are attracted to the streets where the highest incomes from sex work are expected. Violence is a serious issue in streetwalking, especially when prostitutes work in clients' cars rather than taking them to a hotel or specially provided house. In the past few years a handful of street workers have disappeared and now and again the murdered remains of one of them are discovered.

In Melbourne streetwalking occurs in the back streets of St Kilda because of the present legal prohibition on soliciting. Drug abuse and violence are also prevalent here. Streetwalking occurs with some frequency in Brisbane's Fortitude Valley, but on a much smaller scale than in Sydney or Melbourne, and it is dominated by males and transsexuals. Elsewhere street prostitution is almost non-existent, although it occurs periodically in Newcastle and Port Kembla in a small way.

About 70 brothels operate across the Sydney metropolitan area. The larger bordellos are found in the inner city, while smaller houses exist in nearly every major suburb. A few old-style 'red-light houses' continue to flourish in East Sydney, where workers stand in open doorways inviting passers-by to discuss terms and services. They are the last of the traditional brothel trade which once flourished in the lanes and streets of the area in the 1950s and 1960s and earlier, before the upmarket parlour trade began squeezing them out of business. 'Asian' parlours, in which workers from Southeast Asia predominate, operate in areas with a large Asian population but fluctuate in size and number depending on how active the federal police are in rounding up illegal immigrants. About 20 brothels also exist in major towns across New South Wales, with the largest concentrations in Newcastle and Wollongong. Working in brothels in New South Wales does not contravene any laws, but owners and auxiliary staff are in breach of laws on pimping and brothelkeeping.

In Melbourne there are about 60 legalised brothels operating under Victorian legislation in place since 1984. Brothel prostitution also occurs in all capital cities except Hobart. In Canberra brothels are legal but are confined to the city's industrial zones. In Brisbane and Adelaide they are clandestine because of prohibitive laws, but operate as pseudo massage parlours or escort agencies. In Perth and Kalgoorlie brothels operate openly under police sufferance and close scrutiny in the so-called 'containment policy', which requires workers to register as prostitutes at local police stations and brothel owners to abide by strict rules established by the police.

Private prostitution can be found in all suburbs of Sydney, although most frequently in the eastern suburbs and on the North Shore, where a predominantly middle class exists. These workers are not contravening prostitution legislation but may be in breach of local government by-laws on planning and environment. This is another area of prostitution in which, according to my data from the sample of *Private Workers,* there is a high level of violence, especially for women on escorts and home visits. The women in this end of the business tend to be older than the street or brothel prostitutes and are usually experienced sex workers who have moved into this more independent form of prostitution after years of brothel work. Their clients tend to be middle-aged to elderly businessmen who prefer the pretence of having a mistress to the more blatantly mercenary approach of street and brothel workers. Private prostitution exists in some country centres across New South Wales but it is not as widespread or as prevalent as are brothels.

In Canberra private prostitution is more often of the escort kind, but most escort work and home visits are organised by the brothels. In Melbourne, private prostitutes are probably more prevalent than in Sydney due to Victoria's legal limitations on brothels. In Tasmania private prostitution is the only form of prostitution in operation. In Perth and Adelaide private workers run the risk of contravening existing environmental laws as well as criminal laws, and in Western Australia they are also likely to arouse the wrath of the police who usually only tolerate controlled brothels. In the Northern Territory escort work is the only sex work that is legal. In Queensland the private sex workers working alone is the only form of prostitution allowed by law. But this mode of operation places workers at great risk and some serious incidents of violence against the women have taken place in Brisbane and on the Gold Coast.

SEX WORKERS' SOCIAL BACKGROUNDS

The popular image of a prostitute is that of a teenager or very young woman. Table 8.1, indicating the age groups of four samples of sex workers, dispels that fallacy.

Another popular assumption is that prostitutes come from deprived poverty-stricken backgrounds. This is not always the case. Table 8.2 indicates the occupations of prostitutes' fathers, showing quite clearly that female sex workers come from diverse socioeconomic backgrounds.

Table 8.1

Ages of Female Prostitutes

Age Group	Sex Workers 1986		Sex Workers 1990		Private Workers		Brothel Workers	
	(n=128)	%	(n=280)	%	(n=78)	%	(n=124)	%
Under 18	3	2.3	9	3.2	–	–	1	0.8
18–20	24	18.8	40	14.3	4	5.1	11	8.9
21–25	46	35.9	72	25.7	15	19.2	38	30.6
26–30	25	19.5	90	28.6	11	14.1	31	25.0
31–35	15	11.7	35	12.5	18	23.1	25	20.2
36–40	12	9.4	21	7.5	10	12.8	7	5.6
over 40	2	1.6	23	8.2	20	25.7	11	8.9

Table 8.2

Occupations of Female Prostitutes' Fathers

Occupation	Sex Workers 1986		Sex Workers 1990		Private Workers		Brothel Workers	
	(n=128)	%	(n=280)	%	(n=78)	%	(n=124)	%
Managerial	16	13.3	38	13.5	6	7.6	12	9.7
Professional	16	13.3	68	24.2	13	16.7	8	6.5
Self-employed	28	21.9	0	0	17	21.8	26	21.0
Farmer	4	3.1	17	6.0	3	3.8	7	5.6
Clerical	5	3.9	14	5.0	–	–	3	2.4
Skilled Labourer	22	17.2	56	20.0	14	17.9	25	20.2
Unskilled Labourer	5	3.9	17	6.0	10	12.9	18	14.5
Transport	14	10.9	19	6.7	7	9.0	4	3.2
Unemployed	4	3.1	6	2.1	2	2.6	0	0
Other	11	8.6	38	13.5	4	5.1	12	9.7

Some female prostitutes had distant, competitive or even violent relationships with their mothers.

> We have nothing in common and just don't get along at all. We are very different in terms of personality … we simply don't like each other. (June, parlour worker, Sydney's North Shore)

I can't ever remember my mother coming to visit me at my grand-parents' farm, where I lived, until this one time when I was about ten... She sat on the verandah and painted her nails red and fixed her hair up because she was going out with one of my cousins that night who was as much a floozy as my mother was supposed to be. I was just fascinated... I never lost this fascination for her, which I think had a lot to do with the fact that I never really knew her. (Jeanette, brothel worker, East Sydney)

As a child I was close to my grandmother, whereas I felt very competitive with my mother, who was very young, and I think because my grandmother took the mothering role it relieved her of that responsibility. (Maggie, private worker, Sydney's North Shore)

Our mother was drunk all the time. She was very cruel to me, and used to beat me a lot. Once she nearly chopped off my finger. (Sharleen, brothel worker, East Sydney)

While some female prostitutes had distant relationships with their fathers, others were close.

My childhood was such a hell... My mother left me when I was four and so I was with my father a lot of the time... I had one small room with my father and I would wait in there for him to come home from work or from dancing. I had no one else, just him. So I would wait for him to come home; constantly I waited for him. (Fatale, bondage mistress, Kings Cross)

I spend a lot of time with my father. I go on annual holidays with him; we go away every year. We are very close but we don't talk about sexual things or very personal things. (Martine, bondage mistress, Kings Cross)

The pattern of religious upbringing of female prostitutes varies only slightly from that of other Australians, which is 24 percent Anglicans, 26 percent Catholics, 16 percent other Protestants, 7 percent other Christians, 2 percent other religious believers and 13 percent non-believers (Australian Bureau of Statistics 1986) — as can be seen from their inherited religions in Table 8.3. Their current beliefs are shown for comparison. Their pronounced retreat from orthodox religions is understandable in view of these religions' position on prostitution.

Female prostitutes' educational levels are quite varied and higher at both extremes than those for other Australian women in 1991, which were 46 percent below highest school level, 14 percent with highest school level, 3 percent with trade qualifications, 25 percent with a diploma or certificate and 7 percent with a degree (Australian Bureau of Statistics 1992, p 147). The prostitutes covered in Table 8.4 are compared with the control group of *Health Workers*.

Table 8.3

Systems of Beliefs of Female Prostitutes

System of Belief	Sex Workers 1986 % of 128		Sex Workers 1990 % of 280		Private Workers % of 78		Brothel Workers % of 124	
	IR*	CB	IR*	CB	IR*	CB	IR*	CB
Church of England	36.6	10.2	41.0	12.8	30.8	9.0	35.5	16.1
Catholic	42.9	20.3	41.7	16.0	33.3	19.2	35.5	22.6
Other Protestant	9.9	5.5	9.1	1.4	6.4	1.3	3.2	–
Other Christian	7.8	4.7	8.5	4.6	6.4	3.8	6.4	11.3
Islam	1.4	–	–	–	1.3	–	0.8	2.4
Jewish	0.7	1.6	1.8	0.7	3.8	2.6	0.8	0.8
Buddhism	–	2.3	1.8	3.2	3.8	3.8	3.2	6.5
Hinduism	0.7	–	–	0.4	1.3	2.6	–	–
Other Religion	–	9.4	7.1	13.1	3.8	10.3	3.2	6.5
Agnosticism	–	39.1	–	27.5	2.6	25.6	2.4	16.1
Atheism	–	7.0	–	18.2	2.6	17.9	6.5	13.7

IR=Inherited religion (*multiple responses, as some parents had different religions)
CB=Current belief

Most female prostitutes have worked in occupations other than sex work. These can be seen in Table 8.5, as well as work other than health carried out by the *Health Worker* controls. The high proportion of low income occupations among the prostitutes might partly explain why sex work may appear an attractive alternative to many of these women. What is surprising is the similarity between the prostitute responses and those of the *Health Workers*.

Table 8.4
Educational Levels of Female Prostitutes and Health Workers

Education Level	Sex Workers 1986 (n=128)	%	Private Workers (n=78)	%	Brothel Workers (n=124)	%	Health Workers (n=133)	%
Below School Cert.	44	34.4	19	24.4	31	25.0	2	1.5
School Certificate	34	26.6	20	25.6	34	27.4	12	9.0
Higher School Cert.	18	14.1	10	12.8	29	23.4	20	15.0
Matriculation	10	7.8	4	5.1	8	6.5	18	14.3
Diploma/Trade Cert.	18	13.9	7	9.0	9	7.2	44	33.1
Degree	4	3.1	18	23.1	13	10.5	36	27.1

Table 8.5
Female Prostitutes and Health Workers' Past Occupations

Occupation	Sex Workers 1986 (n=128)	%	Private Workers (n=78)	%	Brothel Workers (n=124)	%	Health Workers (n=115)	%
Administrative	14	10.9	14	17.9	16	12.9	15	13.0
Office Work	60	46.9	26	33.3	47	37.9	40	34.8
Welfare/Health	9	7.0	11	14.1	7	5.6		
Nursing	19	14.8	10	12.8	13	10.5		
Teaching	7	5.5	7	9.0	6	4.8	18	15.7
Other Professions	4	3.1	2	2.6	1	0.8	3	2.6
Sales Work	63	49.2	27	34.6	49	39.5	37	32.2
Service Industry	61	47.7	24	30.8	29	23.4	42	36.5
Stripping	9	7.0	15	19.2	11	8.9	2	1.7
Domestic Work	37	28.9	9	11.5	25	20.2	28	24.4
Transit Industry	6	4.7	3	3.8	5	4.0	3	2.6
Factory Work	41	32.0	12	15.4	22	17.7	21	18.3

Multiple responses from all four sample groups

Many female prostitutes are married and in many cases their husbands are aware of their sex work. A fifth of the the *Sex Workers 1986* were married, as also were 16 percent of the sample of the *Sex Workers 1990*, 21 percent of the *Private Workers* and 14 percent of the *Brothel Workers*. Men who marry prostitutes are not necessarily pimps, for many have their own income. But it takes an extraordinary understanding on the part of these husbands to appreciate their wives' sex with other men as merely work. Most men would be unable to tolerate their wives earning an income through sex because they usually consider their regular sex partners as their possession. They would fear that their wives might enjoy sex with other men, they would feel like a cuckold, and the wives would no longer be their sole property.

Many more prostitute women have children than are married. Indeed, single motherhood is often a key factor in a woman's decision to be a prostitute. Nearly half of the *Sex Workers 1986* had children, a third of the sample of the *Sex Workers 1990*, 41 percent of the sample of *Private Workers* and 51 percent of the *Brothel Workers*. Unlike husbands of prostitutes, the children almost never know about their mothers' sex work. Fear of losing their children's respect, and constant anxiety over authorities removing their children from them, forces female prostitutes to keep their occupation a secret from their children, as well as from neighbours, friends and relatives.

> My oldest son will be 13 this year and I don't want to be at work much after that. He will soon be at a stage where he will be ... venturing into the Cross. I wouldn't like to be working at a time when he is likely to ... spot me on the street. (Kelly, street worker, Kings Cross)

In this section we have seen that the social backgrounds of female prostitutes are little different from those of other women. Many of them come from financially secure homes, and while some have had stormy or negative relationships with their parents others have had close, warm relations. While many more prostitutes have had negligible education as compared with other women, just as many have been better educated. Their other jobs, however, have been remarkably similar to those of a high status group of women like health workers. According to the findings from the sex worker samples discussed above about half of them have children, which is not very different from other women similar in age. Many fewer of them are married, though this is due less to their aspirations for married life than it is to the fact that most men avoid wedlock with a sex worker. In summary, it seems true to say that female prostitutes are no different from other women in all but their occupation.

SEXUALITY

Probably no aspect of the social lives of female prostitutes is subject to so much misconception as their sexuality. Given that sexuality continues to be a major mechanism for socially controlling women this is, perhaps, not too surprising. Sex workers are seen as the most extreme example of female defiance of sexual mores guiding socially appropriate behaviour for women. Like most other myths about sex workers, popular assumptions about their sex lives are far from the truth. To begin with, many prostitutes are lesbians. This may seem incongruous to people who assume that heterosexual prostitution is as much a reflection of the sex worker's sexual preference as her client's. But, as lesbian sex workers point out, working in heterosexual prostitution creates less emotional problems for them than it does for 'straight' workers, as they can more easily separate their work practices from their private sex lives.

Some psychoanalysts, such as Frank Caprio (Caprio and Brenner 1961), have claimed that lesbians are more likely to become prostitutes than are other women due to a psychological defence against suppressed homosexual desires. But that is simply untrue, for I have known many lesbians in prostitution who have satisfying relationships exclusively with women, beyond work. Table 8.6 indicates the sexuality of the prostitutes in my samples. By comparison, 22 percent of the *Health Workers* indicated that they were lesbians, 3 percent of the *Cleo Women* claimed to be lesbians and 5 percent bisexuals, and in the Kinsey survey of American women 3 percent were exclusively homosexual and 20 percent had had some lesbian experiences (Kinsey et al. 1953, p 488).

Table 8.6

Sexuality of Female Prostitutes

Sexuality	Sex Workers 1986		Sex Workers 1990		Private Workers		Brothel Workers	
	(n=128)	%	(n=280)	%	(n=78)	%	(n=124)	%
Heterosexual	86	67.2	224	80.0	61	78.0	94	75.8
Homosexual	12	9.4	15	5.3	1	1.3	6	4.8
Bisexual	27	21.1	35	12.5	12	15.4	21	16.9
Other/Uncertain	3	2.3	6	2.1	4	5.2	3	2.4

The childhood sexual experience of most female prostitutes seems not to have been extraordinary and was as varied as other women's experiences.

> I was six and with this little girl across the road we used to play lovers, pretend we were adult lovers and kiss and cuddle. I used to think that was really dirty, and that's why we did it. (Caroline, parlour worker, Kings Cross)

> Sex was never a big deal in our family. My family walked around in the nude in front of one another. We were quite sexually educated, so when it happened we never made a big thing of it, but it was part of what we were doing, such as playing around with other kids, fingering one another, playing doctors and nurses, mothers and fathers, things like that. (Marie, bondage mistress, Kings Cross)

> My childhood was very lonely because I could never get to know any of the children at school. I had to hurry straight home after school and wasn't allowed to go out by myself... On a couple of occasions they let me go to kids' parties on condition that the parents of the girl whose party it was picked me up and dropped me home again. My foster brother used to babysit me when the rest of the family was out. When I was eight he sat in the lounge room with just a towel wrapped around him. He started masturbating and made me sit there and watch. I was scared of them all so I did as he asked. (Kelly, street worker, Kings Cross)

> My mother's lover was living in our house since I was 11 and he used to give us cuddles. In looking back now, it was sexual molestation I suppose, but my twin sister and I competed for his favours. We fell in love with him, absolutely adored him. (Zoe, parlour worker, Kings Cross)

Child molestation is often assumed to be a predetermining factor in prostitution. Indeed, child sexual assault has figured prominently in at least two American studies of prostitution aetiology. James (1977) found that 16 percent of her sample of street workers in Seattle had been incest victims, and Silbert and Pines (1982) found that 60 percent of their mostly juvenile prostitutes had suffered from child sexual abuse. However, in my much more broadly based *Sex Workers 1986* sample only 39 percent had been sexually abused as children, compared to 29 percent of the *Health Workers*. Furthermore, only 15 percent of the *Private Workers* and 14 percent of the *Brothel Workers* had incestuous relations under 16 years of age, and only 8 percent of the *Sex Workers 1986* and 3.6 percent of the *Sex Workers 1990* had ever received, under the age of 13, cash or gifts for providing sexual access.

One thing which stands out in these prostitute samples is the fact that a very high proportion of them, compared to other women, had 'lost their virginity' before the age of 16. Kinsey, for example, found that only 3 percent of American women in his survey had experienced coitus by 15 and only 20 percent by age 20 (Kinsey et al. 1953, p 288). We might expect these figures to be much higher today, although they are still likely to be considerably lower than the findings in Table 8.7.

Table 8.7

Age of Female Prostitutes and Health Workers' First Penetrative Sex

Age	Sex Workers 1986 (n=128)	%	Private Workers (n=78)	%	Brothel Workers (n=124)	%	Health Workers (n=115)	%
Under 12	10	7.8	10	12.8	20	16.2	1	0.9
12–15	53	41.4	25	32.1	44	35.5	12	10.4
16–18	46	35.9	33	42.3	50	40.3	36	31.3
19–20	12	9.4	7	9.0	9	7.3	36	31.3
21–25	3	2.3	2	2.6	1	0.8	20	17.4
Over 25	1	0.8	1	1.3	–	–	4	3.5

The fact seems inescapable: female prostitutes 'lose their virginity' much earlier than other women do. Furthermore, this initial coitus is usually a positive experience, for such negative experiences as rape and incest figured in only 16 percent of initial coitus instances in the *Sex Workers 1986* sample, 20 percent in the *Private Workers* sample and 22 percent in the *Brothel Workers* sample — compared with, say, 6 percent in the control sample of *Students*. Most prostitute women 'lost their virginity' in the context of love affairs, sexual experimentation and, in some cases, marriage.

> I was 18 and I was a virgin when I got married. So it happened after I was married. I had known him since I was seven and we had never even played doctors and nurses. I wish I had because I would have known what to expect. I remember thinking on our wedding night: 'That was it?'. (Maggie, private worker, Sydney's North Shore)

Other prostitutes, though, were sexually active long before their first coital experience.

> With lots of American girls, particularly Catholic girls, we learn to give a blow-job before intercourse. And that was about a year before my first actual intercourse at 17. (Laura, American 'call girl', Sydney's eastern suburbs)

One explanation for this phenomenon could be that prostitutes have had sexual intimacy with men for a longer period than other women have by the time they reach their late adolescence and early twenties, the age when most sex workers enter prostitution. The years of familiarity with men's sexuality and with bitter romances, as well as an economic crisis, could well have made the potential sex workers more pragmatic about sex than are other women, more able to separate sex and love and more able to appreciate sex as an economic commodity.

Another phenomenon in female prostitutes' sex lives is a high incidence of rape. In the *Sex Workers 1986* sample 47 percent of the women had been raped some time in their lives and a fifth of these victims three or more times, compared to 21 percent of the *Health Workers* and 12 percent of the *Students*. It might be assumed by many people that sex work itself would have a high incidence of rape. But only 20 percent of the sample had been raped at work. Also, only a third of the rapes had been by strangers, compared to 13 percent by husbands, 16 percent by friends and 35 percent by other men known to the women. In other words, as in the case of other female rape victims, the rapists are likely to be men with whom the victims are familiar. If this is so, then why are women who work as prostitutes singled out for sexual assault more often

than others are? I believe it is because most men who rape prostitutes (outside sex work) know they are sex workers and assume, as
most people do, that these women are sexually accessible on
demand. Prostitutes often become bored with sex after a day's work
and want nothing more than a cuddle from their lovers when they
come home — but this is often not understood by most male
lovers, whose egos find that rejection from a prostitute is particularly difficult to bear.

Once again, the evidence in this section indicates how similar
female prostitutes are to other women in their private lives. Their
sexuality runs counter to the popular misconception, and the evidence of child sexuality does not support the argument that child
sexual abuse is a major predetermining factor in entering prostitution. Even the phenomenon of early coitus, which is more a circumstance that may *condition* a woman for sex work rather than
predispose her for prostitution, is similar in its social contexts to
the initial coitus of other women. However, because of social attitudes about their work prostitute women come under much greater
social pressure and stress than other women do. A prime example
of this is, of course, the extent to which they are subjected to rape,
which is due not to any unique characteristic of prostitutes but to
the male view that sex workers are constantly 'on heat'. It may sur-
prise many people to learn that many prostitutes are asexual
beyond prostitution — only 14 percent of the *Sex Workers 1986*
sample had no sex at all outside work.

WORKING IN THE SEX INDUSTRY

Women enter prostitution as children or adolescents, as young
women or when they are middle-aged; but mostly during late adolescence and early adulthood, as Table 8.8 indicates.

The reasons for entering prostitution are many but are mostly
economic circumstances, as Table 8.9 clearly indicates. It is interesting to note that, contrary to popular opinion and impressions
given by the media, pimping and drugs have a low incidence in the
aetiology of prostitution.

Entering prostitution through inducement by pimps was much
more common prior to the legal reforms of 1979, but it still occurs
occasionally even in an atmosphere of legal relaxation.

I was living with this guy for four years and his ex-wife was a prostitute. As the years went by I found out he was having an affair with a girlfriend of mine and he started her working. Be it as it may, love is blind, and I gave him an ultimatum; if he got rid of her I would start working for him. (Kelly, street worker, Kings Cross)

Table 8.8

Age of Female Prostitutes' Entry into Sex Work

Age Group	Sex Workers 1986 (n=128)	%	Sex Workers 1990 (n=280)	%	Private Workers (n=78)	%	Brothel Workers (n=124)	%
Under 16	7	5.5	15	5.3	4	5.1	5	4.1
16–18	34	26.6	56	20.0	8	10.3	24	19.4
19–20	21	16.4	48	17.0	8	10.3	23	18.5
21–25	42	32.8	90	32.1	25	31.1	33	26.6
26–30	10	7.8	36	12.8	11	14.1	21	16.9
31–35	8	6.3	19	6.7	9	11.5	9	7.3
Over 35	5	3.9	16	5.6	13	16.7	8	6.5

Table 8.9

Reasons why Female Prostitutes Entered Sex Work

Reason*	Sex Workers 1986 (n=128)	%	Private Workers (n=78)	%	Brothel Workers (n=124)	%
Unemployed at the time	47	36.7	15	19.2	29	23.4
To support a family	24	18.7	15	19.2	26	21.0
To support another adult	7	5.5	2	2.6	7	5.6
To support a drug habit	12	9.4	2	2.6	9	7.3
To earn more money than present	57	44.5	44	56.4	58	46.8
To be more independent	5	3.9	32	41.0	25	20.2
To seek more excitement	7	5.5	6	7.7	6	4.8
Sexual enjoyment or experimenting	4	3.1	3	3.8	4	3.2
Satisfy curiosity about self	33	25.8	15	19.2	23	18.5
To seek a husband or a lover	–	–	1	1.3	–	–
For a specific purpose	20	15.6	1	1.3	8	6.5
Other	–	–	6	7.7	10	8.1

*Most of these subjects gave multiple responses

While most pimps are men, female pimps are not uncommon.

> I was 13 and had run away … it was my first time up the Cross. I met this lady of 30–something… It was for her that I worked. She had other girls working for her on the street but I felt really secure with her. I remember the first time I went out and she was saying: 'Go on, you can do it'. I was standing in Victoria Street still in my school uniform with her saying: 'It's OK, just ask them if they want a girl'. (Margaret, street worker, Kings Cross)

Working the streets involves attracting the attention of passing male motorists and pedestrians, usually requiring provocative clothing to catch the eye of a prospective customer. Street workers form territorial boundaries, which they will vigorously defend against 'claim jumpers'. Their operations usually involve a 'quickie' for a price agreed with their client. Many work in their clients' cars, a dangerous method responsible for some of the most vicious deaths of sex workers over the years. Others take their clients to the protection of a private hotel or a house rented for street prostitution. However, out on the street, the women, at the front line of the sex industry, endure constant taunts from passers-by, harassment from irate residents and continual threats of violence from dangerous young hooligans. Given such circumstances one might ask why women work on the street. The answer is income. With 'short-time' jobs and flexible hours, street workers turn over many more clients than other sex workers do and may work as often as they like.

Brothel workers work in a closed and structured environment which includes a manager and receptionist, who receive customers as they arrive at the door. Workers roster on to shifts and share their shift with between two or three and ten or more other workers depending on the size of the establishment and its location, whether it's day or night work, and the day of the week. Prices are fixed, and are based on the length of time a customer decides to spend with a worker. A client selects the worker of his choice by viewing all those on the shift in a line-up. Some establishments insist on their workers wearing cocktail or evening dresses, others prefer lingerie; while some leave the choice of clothing to the women themselves. Whatever the work attire, brothel prostitution is the most competitive type of sex work, calling for individual ingenuity in appearing more appealing than other workers. Some brothel managers encourage interstaff rivalry by running 'best whore of the week' competitions.

Brothels vary enormously in style and purpose, from bordellos with lavish decor catering to businessmen and tourists to unpretentious little bawdy houses aimed at the lower end of the market. 'Asian' parlours employ Thai and other migrant sex workers, and have oriental decor of rice-paper lanterns, Buddhist shrines, pagodas and silk-screens. They attract Chinese, Vietnamese and other Asian clients. Bondage houses have dark interiors, chains, whips and harnesses hanging from the ceiling, and other sado-masochistic objects such as racks, pillories and other torture equipment strategically placed throughout the establishment. Just as varied as the types of brothel are the variations in staff relations. In some places relations between workers are so harmonious that they even take it in turns with clients, but in others the competition is so fierce that jealousy and bitterness keep staff divided. In the latter cases tensions between workers and management may be increased by individuals courting a male boss in an effort to gain favours at the expense of their colleagues. But whatever drawbacks might exist in working in a brothel it is undoubtedly the safest form of sex work.

Private prostitutes work alone or with others. Their operations are as diverse as the number of women in this type of business, and are very different in kind from those of brothel workers. The time that private prostitutes spend with their clients is usually more flexible, more affection is often shown to customers, and each worker usually has a greater repertoire of services. For lone workers and those who do escort work and home visits there is the ever present danger of violent misogynist clients. Some of the most grisly murders of prostitutes have occurred when women work alone. Developing strategies to avoid violent confrontations plays an important part in the lone worker's modus operandi. Working alone, however, does not necessarily mean isolation, since private workers in the same area often make themselves known to each other by telephone for security, company and even sharing of clients.

The services that female prostitutes offer their clients vary a great deal. As Table 8.10 indicates, coitus ('Sex') and fellatio ('French') are offered most often, while anal sex ('Greek') is offered least. Greek has long been considered distasteful by most female prostitutes; but in recent years its association with AIDS has resulted in nearly all workers avoiding it.

Table 8.10
Services Offered by Female Prostitutes

Service	Sex Workers 1986 (n=128) %		Sex Workers 1990 (n=280) %		Private Workers (n=78) %		Brothel Workers (n=124) %	
Hand Relief	108	84.4	103	36.8	18	23.1	33	26.6
Full French	65	50.8	91	32.5	28	35.9	56	45.2
Part French & Sex	117	91.4	246	87.9	68	87.2	121	97.6
Sex Only	114	89.1	100	35.7	19	24.4	34	27.4
Greek	6	4.7	15	5.4	5	6.4	6	4.8
Fantasy Jobs	51	39.8	66	23.6	34	43.6	53	42.7
Heavy Bondage	14	10.9	46	16.4	8	10.3	16	12.9
Lesbian Acts	59	46.1	–	–	40	51.3	62	50.0

Do prostitute women receive any pleasure from sex work? Many insist that they never or rarely orgasm at work, others say that they deliberately prevent it.

> When I feel I'm coming I'll generally switch off by thinking of the $20 I've made and work-related things like that. (Jeanette, brothel worker, East Sydney)

> I orgasm more frequently outside of work. I think work is part of you, but you can't take your hormones for a walk. It all depends on the other person. (Maggie, private worker, Sydney's North Shore)

There are those, however, who do orgasm at work, sometimes even more often than in their private sex lives, either due to a relaxed attitude about sex as work or in response to a sexual fantasy.

> I actually orgasm more with work, perhaps once every 20 times. I don't know why. Out of work I orgasm very seldom, about once a year. (Laura, private worker, Sydney's eastern suburbs)

> I never had an orgasm in my life up to the day I begun to work as
> a prostitute. I probably have an orgasm in eight out of ten jobs. It's
> more easy to have an orgasm the more ugly and unattractive the
> client is. It's really made my sex life great. (Katherine, private
> worker, Sydney's eastern suburbs)

Of course, physiologically it is probably more difficult *not* to
orgasm at work, and resistance to it is obviously tied to the inter-
nalised stigma of prostitution or to morals associated with the puri-
tan work ethic.

> When I first started work, whenever I felt myself getting excited I
> would stop myself and I told myself that I was doing that because
> I would get too tired after I orgasmed. But then, the more I kept
> stopping myself the more I realised I was doing it because I felt
> guilty. I thought that if I had an orgasm it wouldn't be a job any
> more but pleasure; it would be too enjoyable and I shouldn't get
> paid for it as you get very sexually excited jumping in and out of
> sessions. Now I think if I don't orgasm it just becomes like any
> other job. (Martine, bondage mistress, Kings Cross)

CRIMINALITY

There is a general assumption that as a female prostitute is (considered to be) the archetypical 'bad girl' she is prone to criminal
behaviour. The same perception influences police attitudes, with
the result that once a woman is known to be a prostitute she comes
under closer police surveillance, making the chance of arrest for
some misdemeanour more likely than it is for most other women.
Criminals are just as influenced by this popular assumption and are
attracted to prostitutes as female counterparts of themselves, so that
prostitute women tend to find themselves in closer contact with
more 'bad guys' than most other women do. But as we can see in
Table 8.11, a list of juvenile and adult offences committed by the
Sex Workers 1986 sample, most crimes are misdemeanour offences.

Some female prostitutes may have been introduced to prostitution as a result of the juvenile justice system. Those in the 1986
sample who had entered prostitution under the age of 19 recorded
much higher incidences of broken homes and juvenile arrests. This
suggests a scenario of a stormy home life driving a girl into Kings

Cross, being identified by authorities as a 'wayward child', and acquiring a peer-based reputation of 'bad girl'. It is then only a short step to living up to this reputation through casual sex work and eventually professional prostitution. Nanette Davis (1971) refers to this process as 'the drift' into prostitution.

Table 8.11
Offences Committed by Female Prostitutes

Juvenile Offence	Sex Workers 1986 (n=128)	%	Adult Offence	Sex Workers 1986 (n=128)	%
Uncontrollable Child	15	11.7	Malicious Wounding	5	3.9
In Moral Danger	7	5.5	Offensive Behaviour	7	5.5
Theft/Shoplifting	18	13.8	Larceny/Shoplifting	16	12.4
Possession of Drugs	6	4.8	Drug Offence	16	12.4
Prostitution	8	6.2	Prostitution	22	17.0
			Fraud	5	3.9
Miscellaneous	6	4.8	Miscellaneous	4	3.3
No Offences	77	60.2	No Offences	64	50.0

The prostitution offences listed in Table 8.11 refer to arrests made prior to the law reforms of 1979 when New South Wales prostitution legislation meant that all sex workers were likely to be arrested for 'soliciting' on the streets or 'consorting' by working with other prostitutes in a brothel. In New South Wales some of the highest rates of arrest for prostitution ever recorded took place throughout the 1960s and 1970s.

> We used to get arrested every night, and once I got arrested seven times in one night. In all, I've probably been arrested about 2000 times. (Sharleen, brothel worker, East Sydney)

Older sex workers like Sharleen were not only arrested but also had to pay the police off to minimise the rate of convictions.

> The parlour was paying protection money to a police undercover guy… But the council was trying to close us because we weren't a

health studio. We began losing money because the clients were getting scared with council men snooping around, so we didn't have the pay-offs for the cops, who began putting pressure on us to pay up or get busted. (Zoe, parlour worker, Kings Cross)

They're so corrupt in Sydney. Cops pick us up and say: 'Well, it's like the old days, girls, cough up or you're going to get busted'. (Bonnie, street worker, Kings Cross)

And it wasn't always money that police demanded.

A friend of mine had drugs planted in her handbag and one detective wanted her to go down on him. (Katherine, private worker, Sydney's eastern suburbs)

Of the 56 percent of the *Sex Workers 1986* sample who accused police of malpractices, 32 percent said police planted drugs on them, 22 percent said they demanded free sex, 18 percent said they demanded money, and 32 percent said they physically maltreated them.

Another popular misconception about prostitution is that most sex workers are drug addicts. The incidence of illegal drug use by prostitute women is shown in Table 8.12.

Table 8.12
Illegal Drug Use by Female Prostitutes

Drug	Sex Workers 1986		Sex Workers 1990		Private Workers		Brothel Workers	
	(n=128)	%	(n=280)	%	(n=78)	%	(n=124)	%
Marijuana	50	39.1	110	39.3	36	46.2	74	59.7
Amphetamines	42	32.8	42	15.0	16	20.5	56	45.2
Hallucinogens	28	21.9	16	5.7	15	19.2	41	33.1
Heroin	24	18.8	26	9.3	8	10.3	30	24.2
Cocaine	25	19.5	29	10.4	17	21.8	36	29.0

Undoubtedly female prostitutes consume illegal drugs much more often than does the general female population. Like criminals generally, drug dealers are attracted to sex workers, not only because these women have a reputation for being 'on the wrong side of the law' but also because they have a lot of money. With a variety of drugs constantly offered them some prostitutes will experiment and some will become addicted. The latter, being addicts as well as prostitutes, come under even closer surveillance by police. The double stigma of 'whore' and 'junkie' makes a conviction even more likely and often results in a third stigma, that of 'criminal'.

HEALTH

Female prostitutes are often accused of spreading sexually transmissible diseases to the rest of the community. While they are infected more often with more diseases than other women are, there is no evidence that as a group they infect more men than do the rest of the female population. In fact, it can just as easily be argued that an infected prostitute might not infect as many men as an infected client might infect prostitutes and other women. Table 8.13 indicates the diseases the sex worker samples have had.

Table 8.13
Sexually Transmissible Diseases of Female Prostitutes

Disease	Sex Workers 1986 (n=128) %		Sex Workers 1990 (n=280) %		Private Workers (n=78) %		Brothel Workers (n=124) %	
Gonorrhoea	40	31.2	44	15.7	10	12.8	13	10.5
Syphilis	2	1.6	5	1.8	2	2.6	2	1.6
Chlamydia	17	13.3	55	19.6	14	17.9	29	23.4
Trichomonas	28	21.9	35	12.5	13	16.7	10	8.1
Non-spec. Urethritis	27	21.1	23	8.2	13	16.7	7	5.6
Pelvic Inflamm. Dis.	19	14.8	25	8.9	9	11.5	14	11.3
HIV/AIDS/AIDS Rel.	–	–	–	–	–	–	–	–
Hepatitis B	10	14.8	22	7.9	6	7.7	10	8.1
Genital Herpes	13	10.2	35	12.5	11	14.1	12	9.7
Genital Warts	23	18.0	45	16.1	12	15.4	15	12.1
Thrush	82	64.1	172	61.4	48	61.5	77	62.1
Pubic Lice	45	35.2	55	19.6	20	25.6	21	16.9
Other STDs	5	3.9	4	1.4	1	1.3	1	0.8
Never had any STDs	21	16.4	47	16.8	21	26.9	22	17.7

Most of these infections were only contracted once: 62 percent of the *Sex Workers 1986* sample, 44 percent of the *Sex Workers 1990* sample, 50 percent of the *Private Workers* sample and 60 percent of the *Brothel Workers* sample caught STDs on only one occasion. Also, most of the diseases were not necessarily sexually transmitted, viz. thrush or minor infections like warts, herpes and lice. Moreover, less than half of the diseases of the *Sex Workers 1990*, *Private Workers* and *Brothel Workers* were contracted from clients. There is a good reason for this, because 70 percent of the *Sex Workers 1986*, 95 percent of the *Sex Workers 1990*, 83 percent of the *Private Workers* and 89 percent of the *Brothel Workers* used condoms on every occasion at work compared to only 43 percent of the *Sex Workers 1990* and one-third each of the *Private Workers* and the *Brothel Workers* who used them on every occasion in their *private* sexual relations. Interestingly, although two-thirds of the *Cleo Women* used condoms in their sexual relations, less than a quarter of these did so on every occasion.

There are many other health concerns of prostitutes. Two-thirds of the sample of *Private Workers* and over 60 percent of the *Brothel Workers* suffered from stress; a quarter of the *Private Workers* and over a third of the *Brothel Workers* suffered depression; and more than a third of the *Private Workers* and a fifth of the *Brothel Workers* suffered a sense of isolation. Also, more than a quarter of the *Private Workers* and nearly a third of the *Brothel Workers* had suffered the loss of sexual pleasure. But probably the greatest concern should be expressed over the extent of tobacco consumption amongst sex workers: just over half of the *Sex Workers 1986*, well over two-thirds of the *Sex Workers 1990*, nearly two-thirds of the *Private Workers* and 82 percent of the *Brothel Workers* smoked cigarettes. A third of the *Brothel Workers* smoked in excess of 30 cigarettes a day. As only about a quarter of Australian females over the age of 18 (and one-third of men) smoke (ABS 1992, p 82), female prostitutes must be considered among those with the highest risk of tobacco-related illnesses. Such heavy dependence on nicotine may be correlated with the stress mentioned above, or simply a response to the boredom many sex workers say occupies the greater part of their working day.

CLIENTS OF SEX WORKERS

Everyone knows that prostitutes see many men as clients. But just how many does the average female sex worker service? Table 8.14 indicates how many clients the women in four samples saw during their 'best' week. Private prostitutes see fewer clients because of the nature of their work and the clients are mostly regulars. Street workers, on the other hand, see the largest number of clients in a week and have the lowest proportion of regulars. Women clients are rare and are usually wives or lovers of men who hire prostitutes for 'doubles'.

Table 8.14
Number of Clients During Female Prostitutes, 'Best' Weeks

Number of Clients	Sex Workers 1986		Sex Workers 1991		Private Workers		Brothel Workers	
	(n=128)	%	(n=322)	%	(n=78)	%	(n=124)	%
0–20	22	17.1	159	49.5	55	70.5	57	45.9
21–30	41	32.0	88	27.4	10	12.8	34	27.4
31–40	34	26.6	37	11.5				
41–50	16	12.6	14	4.4	9	11.5	29	23.4
Over 50	14	10.9	18	5.5				

Most clients are married. According to the *Sex Workers 1991* sample the women saw clients in the following ethnic ratios: 1 in 4 clients were Anglo-Saxons; 1 in 9 were Italians; 1 in 9 Greeks; 1 in 9 Chinese; 1 in 13 Arabic; 1 in 13 Japanese; 1 in 19 Southeast Asians; 1 in 30 Northern Europeans; 1 in 36 Eastern Europeans; 1 in 63 Aboriginal Australians; 1 in 63 Pacific Islanders. In social class clients of the sex workers were more evenly spread, as Table 8.15 shows.

Clients request many services, as shown in Table 8.16, but a comparison with services offered by prostitutes (Table 8.10) indicates that sex workers do not necessarily do exactly what the client wants.

The major problem that prostitutes have with clients is convincing them to wear a condom. Incredibly, in this age of AIDS, some clients still try to see sex workers without wearing them.

Table 8.15

Social Class of Clientele of Female Prostitutes

Social Class	Sex Workers 1986 (n=128)	%	Sex Workers 1991 (n=322)	%	Private Workers (n=78)	%	Brothel Workers (n=124)	%
Working Class	16	12.8	19	5.9	3	3.8	18	14.5
Working/Middle Mix	37	28.6	80	24.9	20	25.6	43	34.7
Middle Class	15	11.3	37	11.5	14	17.9	15	12.1
Middle/Upper Mix	12	9.0	30	9.3	20	25.6	10	8.1
Mixture of All Classes	49	38.3	141	43.9	18	23.1	31	25.0

Table 8.16

Services Most Requested by Clients of Female Prostitutes

Service	Sex Workers 1986 (n=128)	%	Sex Workers 1991 (n=322)	%	Private Workers (n=78)	%	Brothel Workers (n=124)	%
Masturbation	9	7.2	68	21.2	13	16.7	14	11.3
Kissing/Cuddling	13	10.4			47	60.3	73	58.9
Full French (Fellatio)	22	17.3	77	24.0	25	32.1	43	34.7
Sex (Coitus) Only	21	16.1	72	22.4	21	26.9	40	32.3
Part French & Sex	42	33.1	283	88.2	60	76.9	100	80.6
Greek (Anal Sex)	6	4.5	71	22.1	5	6.4	46	37.1
Fantasy Jobs	7	5.1	34	10.6	22	28.2	29	23.4
Heavy Bondage	3	2.4	10	3.1	2	2.6	1	0.8
Lesbian Acts	4	3.0			22	28.2	22	17.7

According to the *Sex Workers 1991* sample, two-thirds of their clients claim that condoms reduce feeling, a third use the phrase 'it's like wearing a raincoat in a shower', over 60 percent say they are 'clean' (in an effort to persuade the prostitute not to insist on a condom), and more than 40 percent claim that it makes them impotent. Some desperate clients will offer considerably more money for condomless sex. Although most clients nowadays submit to wearing a condom without complaining, the fact that very few of them ever visit a brothel with one in their pocket is indicative of intent. Also, since the advent of AIDS and most brothels' insistence on condoms, business has fallen by at least 50 percent (though, as pointed out earlier, probably other factors are also at work here).

There are various degrees of bondage and discipline, and some light bondage such as a spanking is done by many ordinary sex workers. But services that require drawing blood or causing extreme pain are usually the province of the specialist: the bondage mistress, or 'dominatrix'. Only a very few of these specialists will offer themselves as submissives, in which *they* receive the pain and allow themselves to be bound. The reason why so few agree to be submissive is that bondage sessions are highly charged fantasies in which the client sometimes loses control.

> People go crazy in sessions sometimes, but because we're usually dominant in the arrangement we can control the situation... One [guy] tried to jump out of a top-storey window once, but his dick was tied to the ceiling. Had his dick not been tethered he would have killed himself. We had to jump on him and hold him down, and he cried for about 15 minutes. They get pretty close to breaking sometimes, but as a mistress you have to learn people's breaking point. (Martine, bondage mistress, Kings Cross)

Another problem, which fortunately is not very frequent, is that of clients turning violent. Table 8.17 indicates the extent of this sort of violence on the job.

Table 8.17
Client Violence Against Female Prostitutes

Type Of Assault	Private Workers		Brothel Workers	
	(n=78)	%	(n–124)	%
Rape	8	10.3	8	6.5
Non-Violent Robbery	8	10.3	5	4.0
Violent Robbery	1	1.3	5	4.0
Bashing	4	5.1	6	4.8
Stabbing	0	0	3	2.4

In the *Sex Workers 1986* sample a third of the women had experienced some kind of non-sexual violence, 11 percent experiencing it on more than seven occasions. A fifth of these women had been raped at work. These disturbing statistics mean that prostitution is the most dangerous occupation usually undertaken by women. It also indicates how little protection is provided sex workers, even from police, who often take the view that 'if they weren't there then it wouldn't happen to them'. Some of the acts of violence are particularly brutal and seem to be motivated by a deep-seated misogyny.

> I had broken all the rules of the working girl. I went to work late, walked into a house after everyone had left and broke the rule that you do not work alone — and I picked him up in a back lane. Therefore it was my own fault. He undressed and sat there holding his silly little thing and said: 'Suck it!' ... I glared at him and said: 'You filthy mongrel!'. Had I put my head down he would have slipped a noose of wire ... around my neck. When I refused he whipped out a cut-throat razor. I ended up with 27 stitches in my hand, four in my nose and five in my throat... I was able to fight my way out of it ... even with everything I owned practically hanging loose. And that gave me a great deal of satisfaction. (Jeanette, brothel worker, East Sydney)

Unfortunately prostitutes, like Jeanette, often blame themselves for their own victimisation, just as many other female victims of male violence do.

CONCLUSION

In this chapter I have investigated the lives of female sex workers as illustrated in findings from surveys made over a period of eight years and in comments offered by some of the women. What these sources demonstrate is that sex workers' lives outside prostitution are not fundamentally different from those of other women. Prostitutes are not the purveyors of disease that many people assume them to be, and neither are most of them drug addicts. Where differences do exist, as in their criminal record and in the extent to which they are victims of sexual assault, these are not outcomes of sex work itself but occur most often outside prostitution and are a response to others' perceptions of prostitutes.

Similarly with the findings on female prostitutes' initial coital experiences. These experiences are not so much predetermining factors for prostitution as they are events which, when coupled with other experiences, enable women to make a rational decision about entering prostitution. The fundings offer more substantial evidence for a realistic analysis of prostitution than do some theorists who seek the aetiology of female sex work in drug addiction, pimps and infantile psyches. These latter analyses have long underpinned popular misconceptions about prostitution, especially in the mainstream media such as the cinema (see, for instance, Perkins 1989). As we have seen throughout this chapter, though, the reality of prostitution is very different.

9

MALE AND TRANSSEXUAL PROSTITUTION

Garrett Prestage[1]

Male prostitution is not always included in studies of prostitution. There is a tendency to think of prostitutes only as women and their customers only as men. This is not surprising in a gender-biased society where sexuality has largely been defined in masculine terms and women's role in sexual relations has been thought of primarily with regard to (heterosexual) men's expectations and desires. Nor is this tendency surprising given the overwhelmingly widespread heterosexual presumption: whenever issues of a sexual nature are considered they are usually thought of in heterosexual terms and any deviation from exclusive heterosexuality is considered merely an unusual aberration; sometimes mentioned as an afterthought but more often ignored altogether. Even the most recent publications on sex work fail to properly take male prostitution into consideration. This is difficult to achieve as male and female prostitution are, in many ways, quite different. As an example, analyses of feminism and female prostitution generally ignore male prostitution and how it might impact on a feminist analysis of prostitution. This is not surprising given that the feminist debate about prostitution which most authors address has also completely ignored male prostitution, thereby making problematic any analysis of the debate that also takes account of male prostitution.

The information presented here is based primarily on research conducted by the author in association with others. It draws partly on research which was conducted in 1983: a survey investigating drug and alcohol use among gay and lesbian youth (Bennett 1983); and a series of indepth interviews with male prostitutes (Perkins and Bennett 1985). It also draws on more recent research: an evaluation of HIV/AIDS education within the sex industry (Lovejoy et al. 1992); a study of men who have sex with other men but who are not socially attached to, and do not identify with, the organised gay community — the Bisexually Active Non Gay Attached Research Project or BANGAR (Hood et al. 1994); and a longitudinal study of clinical and behavioural aspects of HIV/AIDS in the lives of a cohort of gay and bisexual men — the Sydney Men and Sexual Health Project or SMASH (Kippax et al. 1994). Observations made about male and transsexual prostitution throughout this chapter relate to sex work in Sydney.

MEN AND WOMEN IN PROSTITUTION

Prostitution is, to a large extent, a very different experience for men and women. This reflects the differing economic circumstances of men and women, as well as what appears to be a basic difference (at least socially) in male and female sexuality, probably as a consequence of the relative power of men and women. Male-to-female transsexuals[2] engaged in prostitution seem at most times to be in a position which corresponds more to that of the other women, but in some situations they are more akin to the men. Occasionally, transsexual prostitutes appear to be in a relatively unique position which is unlike that of the other women or that of the men.

Women are far more likely to enter prostitution for economic reasons: a lack of alternative employment options and the prospect of a relatively high income compared to other employment options available to many, especially unskilled, women. As a result they tend to make prostitution a full-time occupation from which they derive all or most of their income for a period of several years, sometimes decades: it is their 'job' and so they call themselves 'sex workers'.

For men this is not the common pattern. Although some — a relatively small minority — make prostitution a full-time occupation, most men who engage in prostitution do so casually and tend to derive only a small proportion of their income, irregularly, from such activity. In fact, even among those who make prostitution a full-time occupation it is only a minority who do so for more than a few months. Few men engaging in prostitution would see it as their 'job'.

These differences are reflected in the distribution of prostitution in the population. Very few women — between 0.03 percent and 0.16 percent — enter prostitution (Perkins 1991, p 17) and the proportion of women who use the services of a prostitute is probably lower still. It is very likely that the proportion of men who enter prostitution is even lower than that of women, but a large proportion of men use prostitutes' services. On the other hand around 20–25 percent of gay men enter prostitution, and a similar proportion use prostitutes' services, during their lives (Bennett 1983; Kippax et al. 1994; Hood et al. 1994). Obviously not all these gay men make a career in prostitution. Rather, this high percentage among gay men indicates the casual nature of male prostitution. The SMASH data from a cohort study of gay and bisexual men in Sydney (Kippax et al. 1994) showed that, while about 7 percent of the respondents were currently accepting money for sex from time to time if it were offered, only 3 percent actually saw themselves as male prostitutes. Also, the similarity between levels of sex work and the use of prostitute services suggests that the use of prostitution and performing prostitution are not too dissimilar for men (especially gay men) and seem to present fewer challenges to them than to women.

Women rarely mention sexual gratification or pleasure as a motivating factor or even as a consequence of prostitution. If it occurs it is usually viewed as incidental: women work in the sex industry because that is how they obtain their income. On the other hand, although most men in prostitution would mention the economic benefit of sex work, they are also far more likely than the women are to mention sexual gratification as being an additional motivating factor (see the personal account of working as a male prostitute in Chapter 6). In the SMASH study only 1 percent of the respondents said that they were engaged in prostitution because they had no other choice (Kippax et al. 1994), indicating that most of those men who were in prostitution were doing so at least partly out of choice. In contrast, male-to-female transsexual prostitutes are much more dependent on sex work even than other female prostitutes, thanks to their lack of viable alternatives free from prejudice and discrimination (Perkins et al. 1994).

There is another very basic difference between male and female prostitution. Although prostitution encompasses the full range of sexual preferences and desires, the vast majority of female prostitutes perform their services on a heterosexual basis, while the vast majority of male prostitutes do so on a homosexual basis. The common factor is that there are few female clients. However, the organisation of work around heterosexuality is very different from the organisation of work around homosexuality because of the nature of sexual stigma. For men to purchase sexual services from women is far more acceptable — and, in some ways, is viewed as a fairly ordinary aspect of male sexuality — than for them to purchase those same services from another man. It is with regard to the sexuality involved in prostitution that the situation of male-to-female transsexual prostitutes appears to be quite distinct from either that of the men or that of the other women. Even though most transsexuals would claim that what they do is heterosexual prostitution, they would also agree that their male clients often choose them on a different basis. The reality is that, although some male clients do not question that the transsexual prostitute is, in fact, a woman, there are many others — very possibly most — who choose transsexual prostitutes specifically. And they do so for a variety of reasons: some simply like the sensibility and particular appeal of the 'trannies'; some are attracted by the 'kinkiness' of sex with a transsexual; some are attracted by the idea of (experimenting with) sex with another man but are reluctant to choose a partner who actually is a man; and some enjoy particular sexual activities which require that their partner has a penis even though they prefer female partners. In this regard it is interesting that among transsexual prostitutes those who are pre-operative male-to-female transsexuals (ie they still retain a penis though they live and appear as women) have been increasingly in demand in recent years.

Men and women in prostitution often have very different perspectives in relation to their clients as well. Women tend to regard their clients somewhat warily and it is not uncommon for a woman to be abused by her (male) client or to be forced to engage in activities she would not otherwise choose — 34 percent report being assaulted and 20 percent being raped (Perkins 1991). Men, on the other hand, appear to have little to fear from their clients — male prostitutes very rarely report assaults and those which do occur are more likely to be from clients. Indeed, the male clients of men are more likely to be fearful of exposure regarding their homosexual behaviour and so tend to be more wary of the male prostitute than the reverse. It has been argued elsewhere (Perkins and Bennett 1985) that this relationship between prostitute and client is related to social stigma. For women sexuality in general is often stigmatised and the abusive term 'whore' reflects the degree of stigma attached to prostitution for women. On the other hand, there is no corresponding form of abuse for men because prostitution, whether as client or as 'hustler', can be viewed as actually promoting their masculinity in the form of the 'stud'. Yet men engaging in male-to-male prostitution, both clients and workers, face the heavy stigma attached to homosexuality. Women working in prostitution have little in common, sexually or socially, with their male clients, while the men face similar problems to their male clients resulting not from the prostitution so much as from their homosexual behaviour.

Male-to-female transsexuals seem to be in a particularly difficult situation in this regard: they tend to suffer the stigma of both, depending on the circumstances and the perspective of their clients and others — and they are also stigmatised as transsexuals. In general their clients have little in common with them: the BANGAR study (Hood et al. 1994) suggests that the partners of male-to-female transsexuals tend to view themselves as heterosexual and do not often see themselves as behaving in a homosexual manner, yet neither do they usually regard their transsexual partners in the same way as other female partners. In a sense these men often seem to view their transsexual partners merely as a sexual tool, a means to explore their sexuality. It is not surprising, then, that transsexual prostitutes should report relatively high levels of abuse from their clients — 45 percent report being assaulted and 34 percent report being raped (Perkins et al. 1994).

In general, then, male sex workers tend to be less economically dependent on prostitution and are less likely to make a commitment to a career in prostitution. They are also more likely to report some degree of sexual satisfaction through, and sexual fascination with, prostitution. Men in prostitution are far more likely to perform homosexual activities than heterosexual and, if they suffer any stigma, it is more likely on the basis of that homosexual behaviour than the prostitution. In this particular regard they often share a common history with their male clients and so are much less likely to suffer abuse from their clients. Within such a framework the issue of 'exploitation' tends to be much less relevant to the situation of men in prostitution.

Male-to-female transsexuals in prostitution are in a relatively unique position, although in some ways they are like the male workers and in others they are like the other women. However, in the end their situation is no different from that of the other women or the men because, even though it is possible to describe general tendencies, the fact is that the particular circumstances and perspectives involved must be considered in every case before a true account of a particular sex worker can be given — and this must be done with regard to the specific issues of 'work' and 'sex'.

MALE HOMOSEXUALITY IN PROSTITUTION

Of fundamental importance in understanding the situation of an individual male sex worker is the issue of sexuality: how the sex worker views himself sexually and whether the sex work he does involves heterosexuality, homosexuality or both.

In 1985 it was argued that most men engaging in prostitution were homosexual both in their practice and in their self-identification (Perkins and Bennett 1985). This was based on the perceptibly larger presence of young gay men within the growing gay community; their observably greater frequency on the street 'hustling' scene; the growth of male parlours; and the greater ability of young gay men to compete for male clients than their heterosexually identified counterparts. This trend has continued over subsequent years with young heterosexually identified men increasingly restricted to the Kings Cross area unless they are willing to compete on the same terms as young gay men (which means they must be prepared to engage in a broad range of sexual activities, including receptive oral and anal intercourse as well as affectionate practices). Young heterosexually identified men have even begun to work in male parlours where their ability to set limits on the range of sexual practices they engage in is often much more restricted.

However, some more recent studies (Prestage and Hood 1993) suggest that this simple distinction between heterosexual and gay male workers may be inappropriate. It would appear from these studies that the concept of a heterosexual self-identity, at least among men, is both complex and uncertain. 'Heterosexually identified men' can include those who have sex with women only, men only and both men and women; and can include those who live a fully heterosexual social life — regardless of their sexual practices with men — and those whose heterosexual social life is only superficial and may conceal a gradual, though often uneasy, transition to a homosexual social life. A heterosexual self-identity usually is based on the importance of personal and social attachments and relationships and is not a good indication of actual sexual behaviour.

This is also true of a gay self-identity although the particular issues are somewhat less complex due to the fact that a gay identity is a positive assertion of association with a highly stigmatised group, the very basis of which is their sexual behaviour. This is a clear linkage and few would make such a self-identification without it having a strong resonance with their own personal situation both socially and sexually. This is reflected in the relatively low proportion of homosexually identified men who are not exclusively homosexual in their current sexual behaviour (Hood et al. 1994; Kippax et al. 1994). Unfortunately, given the subtleties of the association between sexual identity and sexual behaviour found in the BANGAR study (Prestage and Hood 1993), there are no reliable studies of heterosexual men from which it is possible to ascertain the actual level of homosexual behaviour within that population.

Within such a perspective heterosexual self-identification among men engaging in prostitution is particularly problematic. It is simply not possible without a study such as BANGAR, which was particularly sensitive to these issues, to determine whether those (young) men who have been labelled as heterosexual and who engage in male prostitution are, in fact, heterosexual or are merely asserting their self-assessment of their personal and social attachments and relationships rather than describing their sexual desires and behaviour.

Clearly, those men working in male homosexual prostitution who view themselves as heterosexual tend to have a very different relationship to their work compared to those who view themselves as homosexual or even bisexual. They are unlikely to enjoy the work as much or to view it as anything other than a purely economic proposition, often claiming that they do it only because they lack any alternative means of income. Also, the range of activities in which they are willing to engage as part of their work is often much more restricted. However, there are certainly some heterosexually identified male workers who engage in a full range of sexual practices with their male partners and who enjoy their work, for a variety of reasons. Some even claim to gain some measure of sexual pleasure from the work and to engage in male homosexual prostitution partly because it fulfils certain erotic fantasies. Such men demonstrate the complexity of heterosexual classification.

There are very few female clients — although they have become far more common in recent years than they once were. This being the case, it is virtually unheard of for a male worker to work solely with female clients. Male workers with female clients usually have a predominantly male clientele — even those workers who identify as heterosexual. Moreover, given the predominance of young gay men in male prostitution, it is likely that most male workers with female clients actually view themselves as homosexual or gay. But, the important issue here is that male workers are very unlikely to work with a woman unless they are able to receive some sexual pleasure from such behaviour. In simple terms, they need to be able to 'perform'. Even those who work in parlours and escort agencies are unlikely to be assigned to work with a woman unless they have agreed beforehand to do so. This appears to be a more common occurrence than its counterpart among female workers (ie working with another woman). The common factor is that working with a woman very often occurs in the form of a three-way: it is not uncommon for heterosexual couples to seek the services of a prostitute, either male or female; or for a male client to seek the services of either two women together or a male worker and female worker together. It is rarer that a female client alone will seek the services of a prostitute, much less the services of two prostitutes together — whether they be male, female or one of each.

This being the situation, it is simply not possible for a heterosexually identified male prostitute to entirely avoid engaging in homosexual behaviour. If he sees this purely in economic terms (ie as 'work') and derives no erotically based pleasure from it (ie it is not 'sex'), then this fact has little meaning in terms of his sexual identity. Those who do derive such pleasure present further difficulties in understanding both male sexuality and the nature of male prostitution.

How should we understand the situation of the male clients of male workers? Male sex workers universally state that most of their male clients are married men or men living in a de facto relationship with a woman. Not all of these men are 'closeted' gay men or even bisexual men trying to negotiate their particular sexual desires within the context of an ongoing heterosexual relationship. Many of them, like those found in the BANGAR study (Hood et al. 1994), are simply heterosexual men who have sex with men for a variety of reasons: some do so to fulfil a specific sexual fantasy which cannot be fulfilled with a woman; some because they are curious and want to experiment; some because their female partner wants to watch or to enjoy two men together; some because they have concerns about their sexuality and want to try sex with men to test themselves. This behaviour need have absolutely no impact on their heterosexual self-perception, nor on any aspect of their lives other than the particular occasions (sexual moments) when they engage in such practices. In the BANGAR study it was evident that for many men the sexual moments were compartmentalised and were given no importance beyond those moments — and a large proportion used male prostitutes during those sexual moments, and those who did use male prostitutes were, in fact, less in contact with gay men and the gay community than those who did not. Although most did, in fact, define these interactions with other men as 'sex', they did not often label it as 'homosexual'. It was simply 'sex'. This being the case, there is no reason to presume that male workers who are heterosexually identified, regardless of whether they receive any sexual pleasure from male homosexual prostitution or not, need question their heterosexuality as a consequence of that behaviour.

Some may claim that issues of sexuality do not necessarily relate to the issue of prostitution, which may be true if prostitution is simply 'work' and is never 'sex'. However, the reality is that prostitution does always involve sexual activities, at least for the client. Even though these might sometimes be mixed up with fantasies of dominance and submission, they are always erotically based fantasies. Very often the male prostitute also uses prostitution to fulfil certain erotic fantasies, or derives sexual pleasure from the activities involved. If he does not, then, at least with regard to his situation, it may be possible to argue that sexuality is not an issue. An interaction can be sexual only if each of the participants themselves perceive of it in that way.

As to the question of homosexuality, this is a much more difficult and complex issue. As the BANGAR study (Hood et al. 1994) demonstrated, men often interact with each other in a clearly sexual manner, and even recognise such interactions as sexual, without any suggestion on their part either that that behaviour is homosexual or that they themselves are anything but heterosexual. This being the case, it is not possible to easily categorise all sexual interaction between a male prostitute and a male client as homosexual other than in clinically descriptive terms which can easily mislead. The meanings of such interaction for the individuals concerned are the only true indicators of its nature.

HIV AND MALE PROSTITUTION

There is little data concerning the impact of HIV on male prostitution. What little there is suggests that the situation of the male workers is similar to that of the women: male workers are relatively well informed about HIV and AIDS and rarely engage in high-risk behaviours while working. In fact a recent evaluation of HIV services within the sex industry found that the male workers were even better informed about HIV transmission and AIDS than were the women and were less likely to engage in unprotected intercourse (Lovejoy et al. 1992). This finding is largely related to the men's much more consistent exposure to HIV education through the gay community.

The impact of this high level of awareness of HIV among male prostitutes is even reflected in the findings of the BANGAR study (Hood et al. 1994), which was concerned only with men who were not associated with the gay community and who rarely even identified with other men who have sex with men. Those men in this sample who had paid for sex with a male prostitute during the previous six months were far more likely to have used a condom during anal sex than were those who had not paid for sex, even though the former were actually more likely to have engaged in anal intercourse. This greater tendency to use a condom also applied in the case of those who had been paid for sex during the previous six months. The men who had been paid for sex were also much better informed about HIV transmission.

STREET PROSTITUTION

There are two broad forms of male street prostitution in Sydney: that which occurs coincidentally with casual ('amateur') male-to-male sexual contact at 'beats' (cf Prestage 1992; Bennett et al. 1989 for descriptions of beats); and that which occurs in locations specifically known as places where male prostitution occurs.

Suburban Beats: There are a very large number of public locations (parks, streets, public conveniences) throughout the metropolitan area where men meet for casual and anonymous sexual contact. Most suburban areas would have at least one such location. The men who frequent beats range from relatively openly gay-identified men to heterosexually identified men who are curiously seeking their first — and very possibly last — homosexual contact. Occasionally a (usually young) man will be offered money for such sexual contacts and these offers are often accepted. The men who make such offers, according to the young men who receive them, are usually married or living in a de facto relationship with a woman or in some form of ongoing heterosexual relationship. This very casual form of prostitution is not easily described as 'work', particularly given that the young man involved very often might otherwise have engaged in the sexual behaviour anyway, even had he not been offered money. Rarely, a young man will regularly cruise a local suburban beat specifically to trade sex for money. Even in these cases it is usually only as a casual source of extra income and rarely precludes sexual contacts which do not involve material reward.

Rural Beats: Like suburban beats, most rural towns have at least one beat. Unlike suburban beats, though, rural beats tend to be the only location in the area where men wishing to make sexual contact with each other can do so. Often this means that such beats tend to be much more social than are suburban beats: they are the physical centre for an otherwise hidden local social network and therefore tend to include a broader range of men, especially those who are more firmly gay-identified. In metropolitan areas these gay men have numerous other options for socialising with, and meeting, other gay men. Nonetheless, these differences between suburban and rural beats do not lead to large differences in the incidence, or nature, of male prostitution in such places. It is generally true that male prostitution is even less common in rural beats because proportionately there are more gay-identified men and because many of those using rural beats are attached to a social network — which makes anonymity more difficult for anyone using these beats for prostitution, either as client or worker. This view is generally supported by the observations of the Rural Outreach Workers of the AIDS Council.

Regional City Beats: Beats in larger regional centres tend to be similar to rural beats in that there is very little in the way of an organised gay 'scene' to draw away the more gay-identified men. However, regional centres are more populous and the larger number of men using beats allows greater anonymity and, therefore, there is a greater incidence of prostitution. Certainly the AIDS Council Beats Projects in Wollongong and Newcastle have both identified a few young men using local city beats for prostitution purposes on a semi-regular basis.

Darlinghurst Streets: Unlike other beats, one particular beat operates on a section of street in Darlinghurst beside the main gay commercial area. It exists specifically for the purposes of male prostitution and this has become a generally accepted location. The prostitution which occurs from here is neither circumstantial nor accidental; young men come to this location solely for the purpose of prostitution; their clients choose this location knowingly to purchase their sexual services. The young men working here are usually gay or bisexually identified, although some heterosexually identified men can be found among them. They may be regular workers who see themselves as such or occasional casual workers or even young men who decide to go there once for any number of reasons, economic or otherwise. The clients are usually married men or in ongoing heterosexual relationships, although they can include gay men and heterosexual couples. The negotiation process is no different from that which occurs in any other form of street prostitution.

Kings Cross Streets: There is another location for male street prostitution in Kings Cross which is very similar in most respects to that in Darlinghurst except that there are fewer gay-identified workers and even fewer gay-identified clients in that area. It is not at all uncommon for a heterosexually identified male client to be serviced by a heterosexually identified male worker from this location.

'Trannie' Street Scene: There is one location in East Sydney where the workers are all male-to-female transsexuals ('trannies'). Although superficially it may appear like any other form of female street prostitution, the difference can be found in the attitude of the clients. They are like clients elsewhere: usually married men or men in ongoing heterosexual relationships. But, there is a much more evident mood of hostility in the area — the trannies are often subjected to abuse and sometimes this comes from the men who are their clients. These clients do not usually appear to regard trannies like other female workers, nor is there the fairly 'civilised' and mutually accepting interaction found in male prostitution; sometimes trannies are even treated as 'freaks'. Clearly, some men choose to find a prostitute in this area specifically because they are seeking a transsexual prostitute, for any of many different reasons.

PARLOURS AND AGENCIES

There are several male parlours operating in Sydney. These mainly function as a mixture of brothel and escort agency, though their day-to-day operations are not very different from those of similar female establishments. There is usually a manager with a number of young men working each shift. When a client arrives or telephones he is given a description of each of the men available. If he comes to the premises in person he is shown each of the young men in whom he expresses an interest. The client then makes his selection. If the client wants the young man to come to his home or hotel he is obliged to provide a telephone contact for security. Management takes half the takings and the worker retains the other half from each of his clients.

Male parlours seek male clients through advertisements in the gay press, in sex magazines and in local suburban newspapers. Although some of this advertising does not explicitly state that the service is primarily for male clients, the style of advertising definitely has a male focus. Toward the end of 1993 at least one male parlour began experimenting with advertising to attract female clients as well. This has met with only limited success so far but, although it is still not possible for a male prostitute to work solely with women and earn enough to survive, women are a growing proportion of the clientele.

The male clients of male parlours are little different from those of male street workers (or, indeed, of female prostitutes). Most of them are married or in an ongoing heterosexual relationship though the range is just as broad as that found on the streets or in beats. As might be expected, most of the workers in male parlours are young gay men. Some may identify themselves as bisexual but very few would view themselves as heterosexual. Working in a parlour involves a greater commitment to prostitution and usually means less ability to limit the range of sexual activities required. These factors make working in a male parlour difficult for a heterosexually identified man.

Several of the male parlours also operate as trannie parlours with a number of male-to-female transsexuals working on each shift. These trannie parlours advertise in the various sex magazines and in local suburban newspapers. They are promoted as parlours offering transsexual prostitutes and so they naturally attract a clientele who specifically seek this sort of service. Even so, those who work in these parlours describe their clients in the same way as do other prostitutes: their clients are almost all men and most are in ongoing heterosexual relationships, but they cover the full range of sexual behaviours and orientations.

PRIVATE WORKERS

Many male prostitutes work privately. They usually receive their clients at home though they will sometimes do out-calls. The men who work privately tend to charge about the same as the parlours — but of course they keep all the proceeds themselves — and they advertise themselves similarly. Private male prostitutes are almost always gay identified, though a few are bisexual. It is very rare for a heterosexually identified man to make the commitment to a career in male prostitution which working privately entails. The clientele of private male prostitutes is no different from that of the parlours or the street workers. Certainly some male prostitutes working privately advertise themselves in ways which may appeal to women as well as men, but it is simply not possible for a male prostitute to build a career in the sex industry primarily on the basis of a female clientele. Survival as a male prostitute requires a largely male clientele and working privately necessitates having a broad sexual repertoire — including receptive sex and affectionate and sensual sex practices — as well as, of course, a ready acceptance of, and comfort with, engaging oneself in homosexual activities. Any unwillingness or discomfort can often be recognised by clients and, particularly for private workers, a regular clientele is essential to a successful career.

BAR WORK

Although it is not a widespread practice it is true that male prostitution does occur in bars. Male prostitutes do not generally frequent bars specifically to find clients but occasionally, as is the case at beats, a young man frequenting a gay bar will be offered money for sex. Of course, not all those who are offered money in a gay bar are male prostitutes or would even consider seeking such offers, but that does not necessarily stop them from accepting.

There are a few bars which, while not clearly attached to the organised gay community, tend to attract 'curious' heterosexually identified men and some 'closeted' homosexual men who would be fearful of discovery in a gay bar. These less gay-attached bars may also attract male-to-female transsexuals and young male street hustlers who do not view themselves as gay. In such a mix, offers of money for sex are not as uncommon as in the gay bars; and it is not unusual, after some conversation, for a young man or a trannie to offer sex for money.

A few gay bars employ young men to perform striptease in the bar but, although there are sometimes quite erotic performances, no physical contact occurs. Of course, the opportunity is there for offers of money to be made and followed up but this is neither organised nor encouraged by the managements. Gigolos sometimes work in certain bars, picking up female clients in a manner not dissimilar to that of other male and female prostitutes. But these men depend largely on male clients for most of their income (Perkins and Bennett 1985, pp 204–10).

SEX WORK IN SEX VENUES

As is the case in bars, male prostitution does not commonly occur and is not organised in male-only sex venues such as gay bookshops and video arcades or gay saunas and sex clubs. In fact, in most such places the management expressly forbids any form of prostitution. However, it certainly does occur informally, if infrequently. Offers of money are occasionally made to young men and, particularly in the adult video arcades, young men will sometimes ask for money in exchange for sex. Those making such offers are not usually gay-identified men and those requesting money are usually young street hustlers who normally identify as bisexual, although sometimes they may be heterosexually identified.

A recent phenomenon is the development of male peep shows at which customers pay to watch a young man strip and perform an erotic dance. Although no actual physical contact occurs at the time it is certainly possible, as with strippers in the bars, for offers of money to be made and followed up later in private.

In the early 1980s young men were occasionally employed by gay sex clubs as 'sex slaves', often chained to a wall or locked in a cage, naked, and required to perform sexual activities with the clientele. This no longer occurs — largely because of concerns about the *Disorderly Houses Act*. Occasionally sex performances are staged at some gay dance parties (including performances by young lesbians) but these are usually unpaid activities staged by the performers themselves.

'PERSONAL SERVICES'

An unusual aspect of male prostitution occurs within the gay community: the provision of 'personal services'. This can include strippergrams, nude waitering for private parties, nude house-cleaning or similar activities. This sort of service is advertised, usually by private workers (though occasionally an agency will offer such a service), within the gay press. Sexual activity may not always be required by the client though it is often expected, and not all those offering personal services extend them to actual sexual activity though they usually will if the offer is acceptable. This is an almost wholly gay aspect of male prostitution. Most men offering these services are gay-identified and most of their clients are gay-identified men.

Of course, strippergrams and similar services are offered by specialised agencies outside the gay community. These services are explicitly non-sexual and often use models and dancers needing a supplementary source of income. The clients of these services are predominantly heterosexual (in both identity and behaviour) and the services could hardly be included in any analysis of prostitution. But the opportunity is there for offers of money for sex to be followed up later in private.

CONCLUSION

This chapter has explored the world of male and transsexual prostitution, in all its enormous diversity. It encompasses sex between men as well as sex between men and women, although the activities need not be viewed either as 'sex' or as 'homosexual vs. heterosexual'. It all depends on the meanings ascribed to the behaviours by the participants. Transsexual prostitution can be viewed as a particular variation on sex work, with methods more like those of female prostitutes but with clients who respond to them in a variety of ways: as women; as 'sexotic' women; or as men in 'drag'. Most interesting about these sorts of prostitution are the insights into identity and sexual meaning that they offer social scientists. Indeed, armed with such insights, it is possible to re-examine many aspects of sexuality, including female prostitution, from a quite different perspective.

10

THAI SEX WORKERS IN SYDNEY
Linda Brockett and Alison Murray

Thai sex workers[1] in Sydney have been called 'sex slaves' working in 'a haven for the spread of AIDS'.[2] But little formal research has been done with these women, who have entered the industry in significant numbers since the mid-1980s. Over half of Sydney's commercial sex establishments employ Asian workers (usually Thais) to fill a client-created demand for the 'exotic'. Twenty percent of these 'specialise' in Asian workers and cater to Asian clients in areas such as Haymarket, Burwood and Cabramatta.[3] The development of this 'Asian sex industry' reflects the increasing mobility of female labour within the region and the establishment of a sophisticated underground recruitment and immigration system and, of most concern, features workers who are marginalised by communication barriers, poor bargaining power and 'invisibility'.

In 1993, 80 percent of all female migrant sex workers in Sydney were from Thailand. Over 90 percent of these women arrived in Sydney bonded to a verbal contract agreement that outlines both terms and conditions of employment and the scheduled repayment of debt for recruitment, passage and placement within an establishment. This system undoubtedly exploits the Thai women, but they are far from a homogeneous group. We will examine how the system operates, the migration of Thai women and reasons for working in Sydney, their relative status in the industry, whether their working life changes over time and whether their expectations are met.

THAI WORKERS ARRIVE IN SYDNEY

> I came here on contract three years ago with four other Thai girls. We had to pay back $12,000. It took me nearly two months. A Thai girl I met at the parlour (brothel) then told me she'd come out here two years earlier, and the fee was $8000. Some girls who came ten years ago didn't have a contract at all — they just arranged it with their boyfriends. Now girls are paying up to $25–30,000. I'm just glad I came when I did! (Jane, Marrickville, 1992)

Sexual Health Centres (SHCs) started seeing Thai workers for checkups and certificates[4] in the mid-1980s. SHCs provide free, anonymous medical services without a Medicare card (which are restricted to Australian residents), so Thai workers often visit with a range of health and welfare problems not strictly related to sexual health.[5] In a six month period 247 visits were made to Sydney SHCs by Thai working women,[6] while outreach to parlours shows that Thai workers also visit other SHCs or general practitioners (GPs); but many have no contact with existing health services.

There is a rapid turnover of Thai women in the industry, so it is difficult to estimate the total number. Parlour visits indicate that 200–300 Thai workers are employed in Sydney at any one time. The length of stay varies from as little as one week to permanently. The average is six to 18 months: about the time it takes to work off a contract debt and send money home. Visits may be terminated by immigration raids, when women who have overstayed their visas are detained and have to leave the country. Their return air tickets are usually forwarded anonymously to the immigration department.

Thai women are the largest group of migrant sex workers in Sydney, and can be compared with other workers from non-English-speaking backgrounds. After Thai women, workers from mainland China are most numerous, followed by those from Malaysia, Singapore, the Philippines and Hong Kong. Occasionally we have met women from Laos, Burma, Vietnam, India, Indonesia, Korea, Japan, Lebanon and South America. Most of the Chinese women have legitimate visas so, while working in the sex industry may be isolating and confusing for those who speak little English, for these women there is less fear of authorities or pressure from parlour managements. In the few cases where Chinese and other migrant women are involved in debt-contracts, they are generally made independently and open to negotiation. Rumours that Indonesian and Vietnamese women are being contracted like Thai women have not been substantiated to date.

BACKGROUND OF THAI WORKERS AND FACTORS IN MIGRATION

Most Thai workers in Sydney are from rural areas in the north/north-east of Thailand, and moved first from the village to the capital and second from Bangkok to Australia — although some travel instead to Japan, Germany or Singapore. Despite the move to the city, the family and the traditional rural culture retain their importance.

> I hated Bangkok. Too fast. Pollution everywhere ... like the air had died. Every time I returned home [to Nan province] I felt myself become alive again. (Julie, Cabramatta)

Rural-urban migration is a response to rapid industrialisation in Thai cities which have expanded at the expense of the rural sector. The capitalist land-owner system has worsened rural poverty (Phongpaichit 1982; Hirsch 1990) so that landless villagers are increasingly seeking work in the cities. Work-based migration was previously male-dominated, but increasing urban-rural disparities and the loss of productive male labour to urban centres has led women to transcend traditional family roles and become key income earners. Women left with a choice between staying to look after the family and property or going to look for work in the city are frequently choosing the latter.

> I came to Bangkok two years ago when my family had to sell our land to pay off debts. In our village now, only half the people own the land they work... (Nui, worker in a Patpong bar)

With few formal jobs available, prostitution is one way for women to support themselves and their families. The prospect of working for big dollars in a rich country may be even more appealing: the international flow of prostitution reflects not only client demand and entrepreneurial initiative but also economic inequality between countries. Thai women in Sydney argue that the economic advantages are considerable.

> In Bangkok there is not much work for women with no skills… My friend told me I could work in Japan and make a lot of money, so I worked in the sex industry there for a few years … now I've come to Australia to see if things are better. (Tina, Sydney inner city)

> It costs a lot to get an education, and it's been hard since my father died. Why not make the most of your rich country? It makes more sense than being a waitress in Bangkok. There is no money to be made there. (Lina, Kings Cross)

> It comes down to how much money you have in your hand at the end of the night. A good night in Sydney, I make $400. A good night in Bangkok, I make $20. It's simple. (Mary, Haymarket)

Entering sex work is thus an economic decision, and a brave one given that Buddhism and Thai society teach women 'don't let more than one man gain access to your body' (Hantrakal 1983, p 7). Thailand has 'a culture of polygyny and concubinage which apparently legitimates the commoditisation of women' (Phongpaichit 1982, p 6; see also Murray 1991, p 105) so prevailing morals both despise and create prostitution. While the media focus on foreign sex tourists in Thailand, Thai men form the majority of sex industry clients.

> All Thai boys get drunk and go to the brothel. It is culture. (Mary, Haymarket)

A changing moral order has accompanied the capitalist economy. In rural areas new material values can affect attitudes to prostitution, particularly when women are able to remit large sums of money from Bangkok or Sydney.

I think my parents must know that I work as a prostitute, but they don't talk about this to me because I make a lot of money. They can have a better life. They have a nicer house. But even so, when I told my mother I was coming here [to Sydney] she cried. (Ann, Parramatta)

In the literature on the global sex trade, Asian women are often objectified as victims of a ruthless slave market. This view is too simplistic and ignores the rational choices women have made. We have heard many different perspectives from Thai women; from those who prefer sex work because they earn lots of money, favour Australian men or find life easier; to those who feel embittered, angry and oppressed. Though a few are forced into prostitution or sold to agents by parents — one woman believed she was to work in a restaurant in Bondi but found herself in a Chinatown parlour — most Thai sex workers have chosen the work as the best option available at the time.

Economic burdens prevail among reasons for migrating, while some women are often also fleeing an unhappy or violent domestic situation. About 50 percent are supporting children, as well as siblings, parents and extended family. Meanwhile, others want to learn about the 'rich world', find a husband and learn English.

I'm here to learn about life. What is wrong with that? I want to take the opportunities that come my way. (Sunny, Sydney inner city)

THAI WORKERS AND THE POLITICS OF SYDNEY'S SEX INDUSTRY

Like other migrant women from a non-English-speaking background, Thai women face a lack of economic opportunities in Sydney.

I'm a hairdresser by trade, but no one would give me a job doing that here. And one of the Chinese girls I work with is a teacher — she can't get a job because of language. (Jill, Ashfield)

Immigrants 'tend to be concentrated in unskilled or semiskilled manual occupations typically offering low pay, poor working conditions, little security and inferior status' (Lin and Pearse 1990, p 208; see also Martin 1984, pp 110–21, and Game and Pringle 1983, pp 120–40). But sex work is unique as 'immigrant employment' because it offers a very high income (ranging from $700 to $2000 per week).

> I haven't been to university and I don't need to go. I earn more money as a prostitute than I would as an accountant in Thailand. (Helen, Parramatta)

The organisation of the sex industry in Sydney is very different from that in Thailand, where women work in bars, massage parlours, teahouses, restaurants, coffee shops, nightclubs, escort agencies, big hotels and alleyside brothels. In Sydney, most Thai women work from parlours or occasionally as escorts. In Thailand's tourist areas clients pay a bar fine to spend the night with a dancer while in Sydney clients pay an agreed fee for a specific time and service, usually half-French and sex.[7] Thai workers in Sydney might have a relationship with an ex-client but on the whole liaisons remain short and strictly professional, unlike the 'mia chaaw' (rented wife) situations found in Thailand.

Most Thai women entering Sydney's sex industry have little sex work experience; they may have dabbled in sex work in an independent or informal way, such as picking up 'paying boyfriends' in restaurants. Those women with prior experience have often gained this overseas: the Japan-Singapore-Australia sex work circuit is quite common. In one Haymarket parlour three newly arrived Thai workers had come directly from Singapore and said the work was 'busy', the money 'okay' and the clients 'awful'. Once in Sydney, the women might not make as much money as they expected, and may become entangled in further debts and extortion so that they have to keep working.

> If I break my contract then the agent has threatened to tell my parents what I am doing. I can't let that happen. (Anna, Bondi)

This woman, affected by a serious STD infection and constant pelvic pain, also found it difficult to take time off work, reduce the number of clients she saw or insist on safe sex. She was refused time off to undergo an important surgical procedure. Occasionally women are physically forced to keep working and have little freedom to move beyond the parlour setting on their own; or they are moved from parlour to parlour to maximise profitability. When passports, tickets and visas are taken away they have no bargaining power. Groups of Thai women are escorted by a parlour minder or 'boyfriend' to sexual health checkups, and occasionally women have talked about 'escaping' a particular situation. Working illegally leads to stress and fear, increased by a lack of knowledge of Australian laws on prostitution. Thai workers often believe that selling sex itself is illegal, when in fact offering sex in a massage establishment or working without an appropriate visa are the usual grounds for police apprehension.

Parlours in the metropolitan area are close to arterial roads and shopping centres. Many parlours with Thai workers are in areas with an established local Asian population, such as Haymarket, Kings Cross, Cabramatta and inner western suburbs. Thai workers who have completed contracts have begun to seek work in other parts of Sydney where there is less competition from other Thai workers, and more autonomy.

At least 75 parlours in Sydney employ Thai workers. Visits to these establishments with safe sex information and supplies are coordinated by Sydney SHC and SWOP (Sex Workers Outreach Project), and only a handful refuse entry and the condoms.

> Condoms? What for? We don't use those things here! (Bouncer, parlour in the inner west)[8]

'Asian parlours' typically have Asian decor like Buddhist shrines and incense, and mostly Indo-Chinese and Chinese clients. Thai workers play cards between customers, listen to popular tapes and nibble on Thai takeaway food. In some parlours workers can cook rice, and guests are offered green tea. Accommodation and transport to and from work are often available for new arrivals (Borthwick 1992). When contracts are completed, workers leave this arrangement for an independent life with a partner, family or friends.

'Asian parlours' do not necessarily have Asian owners. Many 'invisible' owners employ a manager to be the front person, usually a middle-aged women (the madam or mamasan) who is responsible for the day-to-day business, hiring staff and keeping the books. Sex workers themselves only rarely have a management role or a financial stake in the establishment.

THE HEALTH OF THAI WORKERS

The parlour management has a great deal of influence on the working health of Thai workers through rules laid down by the house: 'management seemed unlikely to intervene in favour of condom use. Mostly their concern was to work as smoothly as possible around the few workers who insisted on condoms to accommodate the client with another less fussy worker' (Borthwick 1992, p 4). The decision to practise safe sex is usually left up to the worker; however, the situation can make it virtually impossible to consistently practise safe sex.

> If a client won't wear a condom, I usually see him anyway. I haven't finished my contract and the boss hates trouble. Almost every customer that walks in here wants sex without a condom. If I won't see him, someone else will. It'll take me years to earn any money if I make them all wear condoms! I try every time, but I don't want to lose the customer. (Tina, Cabramatta)

Most Australian workers insist on safe sex, but because of client attitudes there is still a demand for unsafe commercial sex. This lucrative market is now largely supplied by Thai workers who, even when aware of the risks, do not have the same bargaining power as Australian workers. Economic necessity, poor English, inadequate health and welfare support, illegal work status, discrimination and cultural barriers perpetuate the isolation and disempowerment of Thai sex workers. They are often stereotyped as 'passive', an image which contributes to client perceptions and demands.

> He wants me soft, he gets me soft. I say, 'Come on, darling, I make you feel good'. He likes Thai girls, they don't argue. We play the game he wants, we make him happy, he comes back, we make more money. And that is why we're here. (Mary, Haymarket)

For some Thai women, lack of a common language with clients

often means that arguing is awkward, and the importance of sending remittances to dependants may mean they are prepared to sacrifice their health. English-speaking workers rely on dirty talk, tease, massage and general conversation to keep penetrative sex to a minimum, while Thai workers may be unaware that they are being paid less and doing 'extras' such as anal sex or full-French (oral sex to orgasm) for nothing. Conversations with Thai workers show that their level of understanding about HIV transmission is low, although most are aware of the dangers of AIDS and fear infection; they often ask questions about HIV/AIDS such as, 'if he licks me, will I get it?'. However, the lack of condom use is not simply caused by ignorance or personal choice of the women, but also by the force of circumstances created by parlour management, agents and clients.

Besides the increased risk of HIV infection, low condom use also creates a range of other sexual health problems. In 1988–90, 89 percent of gonorrhoea cases seen at Sydney Sexual Health Centre were Asian sex workers (Donovan et al. 1991). STD infections can be extremely serious and can lead to pelvic inflammatory disease, cervical cancer and infertility. There have been only three reported cases of HIV infection among Thai workers in Sydney (to mid-1993), and the women concerned are believed to have contracted the virus before arriving in Sydney. Many women on contract claim they are HIV-tested before departure. However, the high rate of STD infection shows the potential for HIV infection through unsafe sex, and Donovan et al. (1991, p 521) conclude: 'Attempts to keep Asian prostitutes out of Australia will not prevent Asian prostitutes from perhaps playing a role in the future in the spread of HIV-1 infection in Australia. On the contrary, persecution of these women could undermine the education and other valuable interventions already being developed'.

The Sydney SHC set up a Multicultural Health Promotion Project in 1990 to address the specific issues faced by Asian workers (Sydney Sexual Health Centre 1991; Brockett 1992). In conjunction with SWOP, information, support and counselling have been provided both through outreach and at sexual health centres and specific language materials have been produced including a Streetwize comic and a video. The objectives are not only to increase knowledge levels about STDs and HIV/AIDS and about access to safe sex supplies, but also to empower workers to uphold their rights to personal safety at work. Therefore strategies targeting parlour management and clients are also essential.

CLIENTS AND THE SEX INDUSTRY HIERARCHY

> A lot of customers don't want to use condoms, don't care about us. They think they are not getting their money's worth if we use condoms. (Ann, Marrickville)

Thai sex workers in many parts of Sydney cater largely to an Asian clientele, and frequently encounter problems over condoms. Australian workers who see Asian clients insist on condoms even though Australian-standard condoms are too big. But when groups of Indochinese youths arrive at Asian parlours late at night, drunk and sometimes aggressive, Thai women often find it difficult to negotiate with them. These men may also demand more than one orgasm after one payment. Thai workers see Australian clients too, who expect massage and conversation as well as sex and may have spent time in Southeast Asia as servicemen, businessmen or tourists/sex-tourists. Workers say they prefer older clients who see themselves as a 'father figure'. In several cases Thai women have later developed personal relationships with clients. On the other hand, there has been a disproportionate level of violence against Asian workers, such as the murder of a Thai sex worker in an inner west parlour and the murder of a Filipina street worker in the Royal National Park in 1991.

What status do Thai women have in Sydney's sex industry? Thai women under contract seem to be at the 'bottom of the heap', particularly in terms of working conditions, health and the exercise of personal rights. Australian prostitutes have greater solidarity thanks to sex worker groups, lobbying and extensive AIDS education. Almost all Australian sex workers now consistently use condoms, and this includes street workers, older workers and heroin users formerly at the bottom of the worker hierarchy. Sex workers who do not practise safe sex are often considered to be undermining the health rights of all workers; for this reason Thai workers who see clients without condoms are resented and ostracised by others. This is despite the fact that given more power and autonomy, most Thai workers would insist on 100 percent condom use.

> Don't you think we want to use condoms? Don't you think we worry about AIDS? It is so much harder than you think... (Ann, Marrickville)

Thus these workers have the lowest status in an already maligned industry and experience high levels of discrimination, exploitation and client violence. They slip through the structures of welfare support provided for Australian residents although their health and safety are constantly at risk. However, although they are exploited and excluded from the mainstream, Asian workers have developed some limited peer support. Older or more experienced workers take new workers to sexual health clinics, and workers who speak some English pass information to those who don't.

> The older [more experienced] women in the parlour tell us where to go and what to do. We trust them because they have had to cope already. (Mae, Cabramatta)

Despite the difficulties of working under contract, women see it as a necessary step towards achieving financial independence. The development of parlour subcultures and spending time off together helps them cope with a new culture and language and an arduous working life.

Being at the 'bottom of the heap' is not always the case for Thai women. Life invariably becomes easier and more fruitful with the completion of the contract. By that time the women have a better grasp of English and are more familiar with Sydney, and they can take control not only of work but of health and lifestyle as well. Workers attending sexual health clinics generally have fewer STD infections once they have been in Sydney for some time.[9] They can seek work in establishments that encourage safe sex, or even work privately, and take time off when necessary.

> There is no point trying to change anything for Thai girls under contract. They need the money and have to do anything expected of them. Save your energies for helping Thai girls after the contract

— that's when they have the power to determine their future. (Kate, Parramatta)

Over time many Thai women become increasingly empowered. We have spoken to women who over several years have developed important relationships, established a home life and made sufficient money to improve the quality of their life as well as that of their families in Thailand. Others have worked in Sydney until they made enough money to return to Thailand and settle down. For them it has 'all been worth it'. But success is increasingly difficult to obtain. Increased contract debts, the tightening up by the immigration authorities, the impact of HIV/AIDS and tough economic times have increased competition and reduced the numbers of clients. Thai women continue to arrive in Sydney with dreams that are not now so easily realised.

CONCLUSION

Thai sex workers in Sydney are alienated by the authorities, by the broader Thai community and by a society which does not readily tolerate women providing sexual services to make a living. Despite the difficulties, we are seeing more women taking control in the workplace and benefiting from increasing condom use. One Thai worker estimates that her condom use with clients has increased from 10 percent to 90 percent over the past twelve months — and while it is harder for contract workers to insist on condoms there is increasing awareness of STDs and HIV/AIDS.

In summary, the work space and practice of Thai sex workers in Sydney is in many ways unique. They are working in a semi-formal and largely underground industry (as far as tax, health and immigration departments are concerned). Their income is far higher than in comparable migrant women's occupations, set against which there may be enormous debt repayments, obligations to support dependants in Australia and overseas, and compromised health. Working in Sydney is often seen as 'taking a gamble' by Thai women who face cultural conflicts and dilemmas in choosingbetween family security and their own health and well-being.

11

PROSTITUTION AND PUBLIC HEALTH IN THE ERA OF AIDS

Christine Harcourt

The most common social response to the presence of sexually transmissible diseases (STDs) and other stigmatised conditions is to assume that they are harboured and spread predominantly by a small minority of aberrant individuals who do not conform to 'normal' patterns of behaviour. Such a belief serves the double purpose of removing the threat of disease from 'decent' people while reinforcing the norms by which decency is defined. In the case of STDs commercial sex workers have commonly been identified as both the source and the vectors of disease. A highly coloured statement on these lines was made by the Vice Commission of Chicago in 1911: 'Prostitution is pregnant with disease, a disease infecting not only the guilty but contaminating the innocent wife and child in the home with sickening certainty' (cited in Brandt 1987, p 32).

The analogy between the procreative functions of the female body and its role as an incubator and dispenser of disease is an ancient one and is clearly linked with other beliefs about the destructive power of unrestrained female sexuality. It was given new meaning with the development of the germ theory of disease and the increasing 'medicalisation' of social interventions in the nineteenth and twentieth centuries.

The concept of a 'pool' or 'reservoir' of infection within the female prostitute population was behind the administrative rationalisation of the English Contagious Diseases Acts of 1864–69 which were largely replicated in legislation in Queensland, Tasmania and Victoria. In 1909 the editor of a Western Australian newspaper called for his state to introduce a local Contagious Diseases Act, 'because syphilis is becoming dangerously prevalent and because the only effective means of checking it is to put the women of the town under some restraint' (cited in Davidson 1984, p 174).

There is no doubt that prostitutes have a much greater than average chance of being exposed to a variety of sexually transmissible conditions. Also it is characteristic of a number of STDs to remain symptomless or 'silent' for long periods in women, permitting many contacts to take place before the condition resolves spontaneously or is treated. Economic and social restrictions often prevent the taking of adequate protective health measures by prostitutes, as their stigmatised and unregulated workplaces do not permit paid sick leave or easy access to conventional medical resources. Nevertheless, the link between prostitution and the epidemiology of STDs has probably never been as simple as much of the earlier literature suggests.

In this chapter, unless otherwise stated, I refer to female prostitution. Very little epidemiological material has been published about male or transgender (transsexual) prostitution and it is very rarely discussed in relation to sex industries in developing countries.

I look first at some of the issues which determine the public health impact of a sex industry on the community in which it is located. The structure and impact of prostitution varies enormously with cultural conditions and is not simply related to the size of the industry. The problem of identifying cause and effect is compounded by the inadequacy of global data on STDs and the fact that much of the data which is available is collated from 'captive' and unrepresentative populations.

Next, I survey the literature over the last decade which has linked prostitution with the spread of STDs. Rather more has been written about the role of prostitution in the epidemiology of the human immunodeficiency virus (HIV) than in the spread of the traditional STDs. Some studies have identified prostitutes as the probable source of infection in index cases, but many more deal with the prevalence of STDs and HIV in prostitutes themselves. Major differences appear between the developed world and the developing world in the epidemiology of prostitution-related STDs, including HIV and the acquired immune deficiency syndrome (AIDS).

Finally, I describe the public health impact of prostitution in Australia and specifically in New South Wales, since the beginning of the AIDS epidemic. I draw some conclusions about the positive effects on the industry of the presence of active sex workers' support groups, the proliferation of services aimed at sex workers and other target groups in the community, and some changes to law enforcement practices. The outcomes compare very favourably with situations described elsewhere.

COMMERCIAL SEX WORKERS AND STDs

The role of prostitution in the maintenance and spread of significant levels of STDs within the community is a complex one and very variable. However it is not simply the number of prostitutes, or even the number of commercial sexual transactions that take place, which determines how much of a given society's STD burden will be prostitution-related. It depends to some extent on the STD in question and even more 'on the relative role of prostitutes in providing sex in a community' (Plummer and Ngugi 1990, p 71). The role of prostitutes as source contacts is clearly higher in societies where the sexes are segregated and there is an expectation that women will refrain from sexual activity outside of marriage.

Factors which affect the working conditions and general health of prostitutes and their sexual partners are also important. These may include legal restraints which force workers 'underground'; cultural inhibitions preventing the practice of safer sex; and economic and political factors which largely determine whether or not they have access to rapid and effective treatment.

One other aspect which critically affects the wider impact of some STDs is the 'socio-geographic space' of the core group. That is, the degree to which sexually active people choose sexual partners within their own community or status groups, thereby imposing a 'natural boundary' on infections (Potterat 1992, pp 16–17). Commercial sex workers by definition have few restrictions on their choice of sexual partners. However, some provide services to clients from a much wider range of backgrounds than others. The variation may come about either because the prostitutes or their clients move from one location to another or because clients are drawn from a range of different status groups within one community. In Britain street workers move between cities to avoid police attention and in Australia some women travel in a circuit between rural towns and the metropolis. In many places prostitutes work on truck routes with clients who travel long distances between sexual encounters. Higher status prostitutes in large cities may work predominantly with clients who are professional and business travellers and over-seas visitors. By contrast, low status brothel workers in industrial or suburban centres may draw most of their clients from the near locality, even perhaps from a single industrial labour force. Similarly, 'private' sex workers in New South Wales often have a limited clientele of whom a relatively large number are 'regulars'. Where prostitutes and/or their clients are very (geographically and/or socially) mobile the impact of prostitution-related STDs on the community as a whole is potentially much greater.

In general the epidemiological role of prostitution in STDs is higher in developing countries. It may become even greater in periods of war, rapid social change, economic crisis or colonisation, where the usual cultural barriers which define acceptable sexual relationships are disrupted and traditional social units are destroyed. In these circumstances large numbers of women may be driven into prostitution under conditions where their health is likely to be at the greatest risk. Many African, Latin American, Asian and recently some southern and eastern European countries, currently fall into this category.

PROBLEMS IN ESTIMATING PROSTITUTION-RELATED STDS

Globally, STDs are greatly underreported and permit only the iden-tification of trends rather than precise numbers. The information which is available comes largely from reports from public STD clin-ics and from laboratories under government regulation. Very little

information is gathered from private medical practice and consequently countries like the United States with a large private sector
seriously underreport STD rates. Other information is obtained by
a process of extrapolation from studies of specific groups such as
STD clinic attenders, prostitutes, mothers and babies, military
recruits and detained populations. The data that are available suggest that worldwide the problem of STD control is as big as ever but
that in the developed world the level of some acute bacterial STDs
may have improved since the mid-1980s. However, even among
the more economically advanced countries there exist enormous
differences in STD rates. See, for example Table 11.1.

Table 11.1
Gonorrhoea Rates per 100,000 Total Population

Country	Year	Rate
USA*	1987	324
Canada*	1986	138
Sweden*	1987	31
Australia†	1987	31
Japan‡	1989	4.4

* Holmes et al. 1990: 20.
† Hart, 1992: 117.
‡ Kawana, 1992: 3.

By 1990 the rate of gonorrhoea in Australia had declined to
14/100,000 and in the United States to 277/100,000 (Hart 1992,
p 117; US Dept of Health 1991, p 13). In the absence of reliable
national STD statistics the level of prostitution-related morbidity is
generally assessed through contact reports from patients undergoing
treatment and/or by extrapolation from the prevalence and incidence of infection in the sex workers themselves. However, both
methods have limitations. Estimates based on contact reports rely
on a retrospective assessment of the contact person as a 'prostitute'.
In this situation many factors, including feelings of guilt, prejudice,
confusion and justification, may play a part. Further, the concept
'prostitute' varies across cultures. In many regions, while it may
often be possible to purchase sex for money or goods, there is little

evidence of a distinguishable 'professional prostitute' population.

More frequently estimates are based on the clinical assessment of sex workers themselves. Here we need to be aware that often the subjects are recruited because they attend public clinics; have identified themselves because they have symptoms; have been detained; or are undergoing treatment for drug-related or other conditions. They may in fact be representative only of a portion of more seriously disadvantaged commercial sex workers in the community, with a higher than average morbidity.

Nevertheless, the general picture is clear enough when a consistently high prevalence of STDs is found in both clients and sex workers selected against different criteria. This has been the case in several recent studies conducted in developing countries in response to the AIDS epidemic.

SEX WORKERS AS SOURCE CONTACTS FOR STDS

In Nairobi, Kenya, 'Prostitutes are implicated as source contacts for >90% of men with gonococcal urethritis ... and for two thirds of men with genital ulcers ...' (D'Costa et al. 1985, p 64). In Somalia, positive syphilis testing in men has been linked with sexual contact with prostitutes. Also in this study 80 percent of men with gonorrhoea reported recent sex with a prostitute (Ismail et al. 1991). An uncontrolled study of 51 HIV positive men in Vellore, India, found that 92 percent 'had probably acquired HIV infection from prostitutes' (John et al. 1993, p 421). A somewhat lower but still very significant proportion (40%) of gonorrhoea and syphilis infections in Singapore is attributable to contact with prostitutes (Wong et al. 1992). And 'In Malaysia, prostitutes have been most often cited as primary contacts for men seeking treatment in sexually transmitted disease (STD) clinics' (Ramachandran and Ngeow 1990, p 334).

The figure may also be high in some parts of the United States. Researchers in Colorado estimated that prostitution accounted for 33 percent of gonorrhoea in males and for 27 percent of overall morbidity, assuming '0.3 infected contacts per infected man' (Potterat et al. 1979, p 60).

However, a different picture emerges in other developed countries where we find the proportion of prostitution-related STDs in the male population is much lower. In a British study the proportion over a five-year period was estimated to be approximately 1 percent per year in Sheffield and 16 percent per year in London (Woolley et al. 1988, p 392). Australia, which I discuss in a later section, has a similar very low prostitution-related infection rate.

PREVALENCE AND INCIDENCE OF STDs IN SEX WORKERS

Clinical assessments of sex workers often reveal very high levels of infection. Many such studies have been conducted in Africa in the last decade in response to the AIDS epidemic and almost all have shown a disturbingly high prevalence of STDs and a tendency for multiple infections to coexist.

A study conducted in Nairobi in 1984 found that up to 70 percent of sex workers had at least one STD at first visit, with a prevalence of 58 percent for gonococcal infection, and a projected yearly incidence of 572 percent. Among the lower socio-economic group one-third had two or more infections simultaneously (D'Costa et al. 1985). Table 11.2 summarises the findings from a number of studies conducted in African countries over the last decade.

Table 11.2
Prevalence of STDs in Commercial Sex Workers in Africa (reported from 1986 to 1993)

Author	Year	Country	n	Gonorrhoea %	TPHA+ %	Ulcers %	Chlamydia %
Kreiss	1986	Kenya high-low status	90	11–55	11–52	0–50	
Mabey	1988	Gambia	31	32	74		
Ahmed	1991	Somalia	155		69		
Cameron	1991	Kenya	123			32–34	
Nkya	1991	N. Tanzania 2 areas	106	47–56	71–75	14	25(a)
Kaptue	1991	Cameroon	168				38
Zekung	1993	Cameroon	273	3	36	30(b)	
Traore-Ettiegne	1993	Côte d'Ivoire	278	31	20	21	3

TPHA	Treponema pallidum haemaglutination assay (test for syphilis)
(a)	Workers from only one area (n=47) were tested for chlamydia
(b)	Reported as genital 'lesions'

Other STDs commonly found in African prostitutes include herpes simplex (Oldfield et al. 1993), genital warts (Kreiss et al. 1992) and trichomoniasis (D'Costa et al. 1985). In general, the level of infection in African prostitutes is alarmingly high and has serious implications not only for their immediate sexual health but also because many of these conditions are linked in a synergistic relationship with HIV and AIDS (Wasserheit 1992).

Similar levels of infection have been described in prostitutes from other developing countries. A study of Malaysian prostitutes revealed high rates of gonorrhoea (14.3%); chlamydia (26.5%); positive syphilis serology (13.6%); herpes (39.7%); and genital warts (8.5%) (Ramachandran and Ngeow 1990).

Results from four published abstracts from the IXth International Conference on AIDS/IVth STD World Congress in Berlin in 1993, describing STDs in prostitutes from India, Sri Lanka, Northern Thailand and Bolivia are presented in Table 11.3.

Table 11.3

Prevalence of STDs in Commercial Sex Workers in Developing Countries (reported in 1993)

Country	Author	n	Gonorrhoea	Chlamydia	TPHA+	Ulcers
India	Jana	450	11.0		63.0	6.0
Sri Lanka	Samarakoon	253	12.0	13.0	45.0	
N. Thailand	Limpakarn-janarat	159 brothel	24.0	30.0	37.0	9.0
		103 other	10.0	11.0	30.0	2.0
Bolivia	Vega	91 brothel	24.2	16.7	26.4	9.9
		161 club	3.1	6.8	3.1	3.1

TPHA   Treponema pallidum haemaglutination assay (test for syphilis)

In developed countries rates of syphilis, gonorrhoea and other acute bacterial diseases among sex workers have generally fallen to lower levels since the mid-1980s. This has been attributed to an increase in condom use, better and more comprehensive health surveillance of sex workers and increased awareness and knowledge of STD prevention among sex workers, and subsequently their clients, as a result of intensive anti-AIDS education campaigns. Figures for six countries are given in Table 11.4.

Table 11.4
Prevalence of STDs in Commercial Sex Workers in Developed
Countries

Country	Author	Year	n	Gonorrhoea	TPHA+ %	Chlamydia %
USA	Nayyar	1986	300	9.3		25.3
Netherlands	Nayyar	1986	60	8.3		16.6
Netherlands	Ruijs	1988	24	8.0	4.9	16.0
Belgium	Mak	1990	154			
Israel	Samra	1991	64(a)	0	1.5	25.0
UK	Ward	1992	304	2.5	2.4	7.5
Spain	Palacio	1993	758	10.9	25.1(b)	14.9

TPHA   Treponema pallidum haemaglutination assay (test for syphilis)
(a)   64 methadone clinic attenders including 38 declared prostitutes
(b)   FTA+ Fluorescent treponemal antibody test (specific test for syphilis)

Whereas gonorrhoea prevalence rates in prostitute populations in many developing countries are above 10 percent and range to over 50 percent in some African studies (see Tables 11.2 and 11.3), the range in a number of recent studies of sex workers in developed countries is from 0 to 10.9 percent (see Table 11.4).

More importantly, there is evidence of declining rates over the last decade in studies from Europe and the United Kingdom. There has been a marked decline in both gonorrhoea and chlamydia rates in registered and unregistered Viennese prostitutes between 1980 and 1989 (Stary et al. 1991). A study carried out in Sheffield in Britain concluded that there was a 'pronounced reduction in the number of cases of gonococcal urethritis acquired from local prostitutes' (Woolley et al. 1988).

MARGINALISED PROSTITUTES IN DEVELOPED COUNTRIES

Even in countries where levels of some STDs are falling there remain pockets of high prevalence which are generally associated with the more marginalised sections of the sex industry. These include groups such as adolescent prostitutes, people who are drug-dependent and unregistered and/or illegal immigrant prostitutes.

An editorial review of the literature on adolescent prostitutes found that most studies detected significant levels of gonorrhoea and other STDs in these groups (Markos et al. 1992). Teenage prostitutes are often caught in a complex network of lifestyle problems involving homelessness, lack of economic and social support, drug use, exploitation and alienation. Their involvement in prostitution may be casual and transitory, divorcing them from the mainstream industry and most of the resources available to adult prostitutes. The impact of crack cocaine and the exchange of sex for drugs has been a major factor in the spread of STDs among black youth in the United States (Schwarcz et al. 1992).

As a general rule, in developed nations a high level of illicit drug use by prostitutes is closely associated with raised levels of STDs. It is also the single biggest factor associated with the spread of HIV infection among prostitutes in the developed world (Potterat 1993). The need to fund their own drug dependence forces prostitutes to work in conditions over which they have less control and diminishes their ability to regulate their lifestyle and to seek health care. The tendency (often encouraged by dealers) for users to provide sex for drugs, further reduces access to disposable income and aggravates their alienation from society at large.

The ill effects of injecting drug use (IDU) have often been described but there is also a good deal of evidence that other drug dependencies have similar effects on the epidemiology of STDs. In the United States in particular, cocaine (and especially crack cocaine) use has not only been linked with the spread of gonorrhoea in young people but has also been related to a syphilis epidemic among prostitutes and their sexual partners (Farley et al. 1990).

In European countries where prostitution is legalised, it has been noted that unregistered prostitutes and those from minority or immigrant backgrounds often have a higher level of STDs than do registered or native-born prostitutes. A study in The Netherlands found that immigrant status was an independent risk factor for STDs among female STD clinic attenders (74 percent of whom were prostitutes) (Hooykaas et al. 1991, p 381). In Vienna, gonorrhoea was diagnosed 20 times more often in unregistered prostitutes who were screened following a summons by police than it was in registered prostitutes who were screened regularly (Stary et al. 1991). Unregistered prostitutes largely comprise the groups already mentioned as being at greater risk: adolescents, those with serious drug dependence and immigrants. High levels of syphilis were also found in unregistered (immigrant) prostitutes in Turkey (Agacfidan et al. 1993). In the United States a prostitution-related outbreak of chancroid (a disease rarely reported in North America) was largely confined to a community of illegal immigrants who had had sex with a small number of 'door-to-door' prostitutes (Blackmore et al. 1985).

HIV/AIDS IN DEVELOPING COUNTRIES

More has been written about prostitution in the past ten years than in the entire period of recorded history prior to the global epidemic of HIV infection. This unprecedented interest is prompted by the knowledge that HIV is predominantly heterosexually spread and that in many countries female prostitutes have the highest exposure to the infection in the population. The distribution of HIV infection in commercial sex workers is as varied as is the distribution of STDs. Figure 11.1, reproduced from a recent review, shows infection rates in prostitutes from a large number of sub-Saharan African countries (Mann et al. 1992, p 54).

In most parts of Asia and in South America, HIV infection rates in sex workers remain quite low (below 1 percent in several recent samples), but there are some dramatic exceptions where prevalence has risen very rapidly over the past three or four years. Prostitutes from Haiti and Martinique were found to have prevalence rates over 40 percent (Mann et al. 1992, p 53). In Dominica, 49 percent of 'international' prostitutes were HIV positive (Koenig 1989).

Thailand and India are the Asian countries where the epidemic currently has greatest impact. In a study published in 1987 there were no HIV positive results detected in 2880 female prostitutes in Bangkok (Traisupa et al. 1987). By 1991 there were reports of rates over 20 percent in many parts of the country (Mann et al. 1992, pp 53–4), ranging as high as '72% of low income prostitutes in Chiang Mai province' (Ryan 1991). Similarly, in South India HIV prevalence in female prostitutes 'increased from 1.8% in 1986 to 28.6% in 1990, with a doubling time of 0.95 years' (Simoes et al. 1993). In Bombay a nearly tenfold increase (up to 20 percent) was recorded over three years (Mann et al. 1992, p 53).

Factors commonly associated with a high risk of HIV seroconversion for sex workers in developing countries are: a history of

Figure 11.1: HIV Seroprevalence for Commercial Sex Workers in sub-Saharan Africa, circa 1990

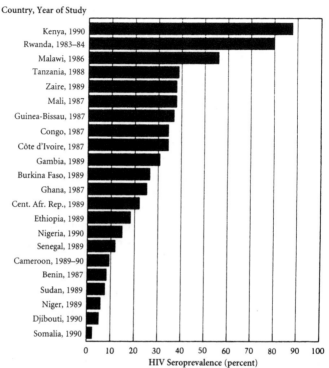

Source: Figures compiled by the Centre for International Research, U.S. Bureau of the Census
Note: Includes infection from HIV-1 and/or HIV-2

ulcers and other STDs (Plourde et al. 1992; Pepin et al. 1991) and having a low socio-economic status (Kreiss 1986; Ryan 1991). In reality these two risk factors are interdependent. Low-status prostitutes have least control over their work conditions, see more clients but earn less money, often have more dependents, and have poorer general health than other sex workers. It is also probable that their clients are similarly disadvantaged and therefore more likely to have untreated infections at the time of contact.

There has been an explosive increase in HIV infection among prostitutes in many parts of the developing world and there appears to be little chance of stemming the epidemic in these locations in the short to medium term. In addition there are many areas which are potentially at high risk but for which we have very little current information. These include South China, Eastern Europe and many Muslim countries.

HIV/AIDS IN DEVELOPED COUNTRIES

The progression of the HIV epidemic among female sex workers in the developed world has been slower than in the developing world and largely confined to marginalised groups, particularly those who are drug dependent (European Working Group 1993; Potterat 1993). Injecting drug use is one of the major risk factors for HIV seropositivity in the United States and Europe; and prostitutes in these countries generally show a similar pattern of infection to the rest of the population. A large study in the United States indicated that 'risk factors for AIDS in female prostitutes may be similar to those in other women living in the same geographical areas'. Black and Hispanic prostitutes were more likely to be HIV positive than other prostitutes, but IDU was significantly associated with HIV seropositivity in female sex workers irrespective of race or ethnic background. Seventy-six percent of HIV positive prostitutes had injected drugs (MMWR 1987). A similar large, multicentered study in Europe found HIV seroprevalence of 31.8 percent in IDUs compared with 1.5 percent in non-IDUs (European Working Group 1993). Both the European and American studies found high levels of condom use (78–80%) among prostitutes' clients and attributed the lack of heterosexual HIV spread within the sex industry, even among IDUs, to this factor. European data are given in Table 11.5.

There are clearly major differences in the impact of HIV/AIDS on the sex industries of developing and developed countries which can be explained largely in terms of comparative sexual health. In the main, female prostitutes in developing countries have less control over their work conditions, less access to health care, and greater exposure to other STDs and HIV. For cultural and economic reasons they are less likely to use condoms.

In developed countries sexual health was monitored and better controlled even before the AIDS epidemic. Since the mid-1980s there has usually been a favourable behaviour change within

Table 11.5

Prevalence of HIV in European Sex Workers

Country	Author	Year	Number	HIV positive $n\%$	
				IDU	Non-IDU
Austria	Stary	1991	approx 842	0 (a)	0 (a)
Belgium	Mak	1990	154	0/1 (0)	1/153 (0.8) (b)
Denmark	Krogsgaard	1986	101	0/1 (0)	0/100 (0)
Germany	Smith	1986	399	0/1 (0)	0/398 (0)
Italy	Conte	1987	29	22/29 (75.9)	
Netherlands	Haastrecht	1993	199		3/199 (1.5) (b)
Spain	Pineda	1992	519		12/519 (2.31)
Spain	Echevarria	1993	121	8/25 (32)	1/96 (1)
Scotland	McKeganey	1992	159	4/115 (3.5)	0/44 (0)
Switzerland	Lüthy	1987	123	14/18 (78)	1/102 (1) (b)

(a) An unspecified number of IDUs were included in this study
(b) All HIV+ in these groups were immigrants from AIDS-endemic countries

sex industries, assisted by government and non-government health and education programs, and by the ready availability and acceptance of condoms. An accident of history and demographics ensured that the epidemic had its greatest impact on the gay community: a community unlikely to spread HIV infection to female prostitutes by their sexual behaviour. Consequently, in much of the sex industry in the developed world, the advent of AIDS has led, so far, to an overall improvement in sexual health in spite of some negative political and legal responses to the threat of heterosexual spread.

HEALTH ASPECTS OF PROSTITUTION IN AUSTRALIA

Australia is now among the developed countries with a very low level of prostitution-related morbidity. There has been a dramatic decline in gonococcal infections in resident prostitutes and evidence of a reduction in other acute bacterial STDs over the last decade (Philpot et al. 1991; Lovejoy et al. 1991; Harcourt et al. 1989). Since 1987 surveillance reports from South Australia (Hart 1992), Victoria (Department of Health and Community Services 1993), New South Wales (Donovan et al. 1991b) and Queensland

(Criminal Justice Commission 1991) have consistently indicated that a very low proportion of gonorrhoea in the community is related to the local prostitution industry. The Brisbane Special Clinic estimated in 1989 that the relative risk for female sex workers of developing an acute bacterial STD was about half that of other female clinic attenders (Criminal Justice Commission 1991, p 31). Few heterosexual men now report acquiring STD from local prostitutes (Hart 1992; Donovan et al. 1991a).

There is still no documented case of a female prostitute in Australia receiving or transmitting HIV infection during sexual intercourse with a client. A small number of Australian resident HIV positive female sex workers have been identified: all had injecting drug use as a probable source of infection (Donovan 1990). Injecting drug use is also a factor in the higher rates of HIV infection found in male and transsexual prostitutes in Sydney (Morlet et al. 1990).

One study has shown that female prostitutes were at greater risk of infection from their private partners than from clients because of their reluctance to use condoms with lovers (Philpot et al. 1988). There are also venues within the Australian sex industry where women work under duress and/or in conditions where health and safety issues are disregarded. These workplaces employ marginalised sex workers with poor English skills and are often contravening immigration laws. They have less access to health care, but frequently have much higher levels of infection than mainstream sex workers (Donovan et al. 1991b). There are also unconfirmed reports of other sex industry establishments employing underage and drug-dependent prostitutes.

Some Australian clients of prostitutes are problematic because they actively seek out workers who do not practise safer sex, or they visit prostitutes overseas in areas of high HIV and STD endemicity. There is evidence of Australian men being infected with HIV while on 'sex tours' in Asia (National Centre in HIV Epidemiology 1991). An early report described a case where HIV was apparently contracted from a sex worker in Germany (Cooper and Dodds 1986). Australian clients of overseas prostitutes are far more likely to report STDs than are the clients of local prostitutes (Hart 1992; Donovan et al. 1991a).

THE HEALTH OF SEX WORKERS
IN NEW SOUTH WALES

Among 70 prostitutes screened at their place of work in a Sydney brothel in 1980 and 1981 there was a weekly incidence of gonorrhoea of 10 percent and a prevalence at initial screening of 13 percent (Donovan 1984). A clinic-based survey made in 1983–84 found comparable rates of gonorrhoea among female sex workers attending the Sydney Sexual Health Centre (Jones 1984). Ten years later, an examination of laboratory records at the Centre revealed only one case of gonorrhoea in an Australian resident prostitute, over a two-year period (Donovan et al. 1991b). This represents 0.5 percent of the total number of cases in females investigated at the Centre during that time (1988–90) and corroborates another finding that there had been an overall decline of 90 percent in case numbers of heterosexually acquired gonorrhoea between 1981 and 1989, with an average yearly decline of 30 percent (Donovan et al. 1991a).

In a comparative study of English-speaking prostitutes working in a variety of locales in the Sydney metropolitan area, conducted between 1985 and 1988, significant decreases were reported in the five-year incidence of gonorrhoea, genital herpes and trichomoniasis (Philpot et al. 1991). Chlamydia infections, however, did not show a similar decline. This apparent stability may be partly explained by improved detection methods and a heightened awareness among health professionals of the prevalence and the risk of infertility and long-term morbidity associated with this infection. Early results from the study showed that, over five years, female prostitutes had a 40 percent chance of being infected at least once with chlamydia. Ten percent had been infected three or more times (Philpot et al. 1988).

Viral STDs such as herpes and papilloma virus infections are less easy to quantify because of the long latency periods of these infections and the vagaries of the clinical diagnosis. In 1991 Philpot et al. found a decrease, from 51 percent in 1985 to 25 percent in 1988, in the number of prostitutes diagnosed with herpes. Clinical evidence of genital or anal warts remained at about 25 percent but abnormal cervical cytology increased from 16 percent to 33 percent, of which 43 percent (33/76) were wart virus-related, four were herpetic in origin, and 17 (22%) showed precancerous changes of varying severity (Philpot et al. 1991).

Lovejoy et al. (1991) also described a reduction in self-reported acute STDs (gonorrhoea, trichomoniasis and pelvic inflammatory disease [PID]) in 1990 compared with 1985–86.

HIV INFECTION

In 1985 in Sydney there was great consternation over the perceived imminent threat of the heterosexual spread of HIV via prostitution, and public concern was expressed by several politicians including the then Premier, Neville Wran. As a consequence a contentious amendment to the *Public Health Act* 1902 was passed in December 1985 to allow some diseases (ie HIV/AIDS) to be declared 'proclaimed diseases'. The amendment Act requires medical practitioners to notify a proclaimed disease immediately upon discovery and imposes a $5000 fine on anyone who, knowing that he or she has a proclaimed disease, has sexual intercourse with another person without first informing that person of the risk and receiving voluntary consent.

There was no first-hand evidence of a spread of HIV from female prostitutes in Australia but a high level of concern persisted and rumours prevailed. The Report of the New South Wales Select Committee Upon Prostitution, brought down in 1986, anticipated that increasing numbers of female prostitutes would become infected with the virus and would contribute to its spread in the heterosexual community (Parliament of New South Wales 1986, p 170).

Three years later, media speculation rose exponentially when Sharlene, a self-confessed HIV positive sex worker, gave a sensational television interview. But by that time several large studies had been conducted or were under way and there was still no evidence of significant levels of infection within the sex industry (Harcourt 1989; Donovan 1990). The situation remains largely unchanged towards the end of 1993 with only a very small number of HIV positive workers identified, most of whom were probably infected through injecting drug use. As noted earlier, no confirmed case of transmission to a prostitute's client within Australia has been reported. In 1991 it was estimated by outreach workers that fewer than 20 sex workers, including males, transsexuals and females, were infected with HIV. Nearly all worked on the street and the infected females and transsexuals were all known to inject drugs (Criminal Justice Commission 1991, p 137).

CHANGING CONDITIONS AND SAFER SEX

The low HIV infection rate among female prostitutes may be attributed in part to the low level of infection in the heterosexual population as a whole (National Centre in HIV Epidemiology 1991). At the same time, changes have occurred in the industry which have had a beneficial effect on the incidence of all STDs.

The high level of STD observed by Donovan (1984) in his earlier study was mainly attributed to the extremely large number of clients (an average of 80 per week) seen by the women and the rarity of condom use. Since that time prices have risen in brothels, and the fear of AIDS and an economic decline have led to a reduction in demand for prostitution. Parlour prostitutes now see an average of approximately 20 to 25 clients per week with a great deal of fluctuation between 'good weeks' (38 clients on average) and 'bad weeks' (average 13 clients) (Lovejoy et al. 1991; Philpot et al. 1991; Philpot et al. 1988). Most importantly, however, there has also been a very considerable increase in condom use by parlour prostitutes (male and female) since 1986.

This change has been attributed to AIDS publicity and the educational work of both health professionals and the Australian Prostitutes' Collective (APC) (Harcourt and Philpot 1990, p 143). The APC was a community-based group which held its first informal meeting in Sydney in 1983, modelling its organisation on an English prostitutes' group. Within a year it had published its first official newsletter and volunteers (workers, ex-workers and supporters) were making contact with brothel workers and managers all over Sydney advocating self-determination and safer sex practices for prostitutes wherever they worked. The APC was funded by the State Government between 1986 and 1989, and built up considerable rapport and influence with most sectors of the industry, including many managers. The Collective met with internal conflicts and an incoming conservative government withdrew its funding after failing to resolve the organisational difficulties. After funding ceased much of the outreach work was taken over by the AIDS

Bureau-funded Sex Workers Outreach Project (SWOP) auspiced by the AIDS Council of New South Wales.

During the 1980s there were also changes in the pattern of law enforcement against prostitution in New South Wales which led to a less punitive and more laissez-faire approach to the regulation of the industry (Egger and Harcourt 1993). As a result much of the corruption and criminality associated with the industry was reduced and a climate more conducive to creating an effective health and welfare outreach program was created.

Prior to 1986 it was generally accepted that most independent sex workers (including street workers) were better able to negotiate with their clients for safer sex (using condoms) than were parlour workers who were subject to the wishes of their managers (Parliament of New South Wales 1986, pp 163–7). Between 1985 and 1988 condom use by the clients of female prostitutes in New South Wales had increased from as low as 5 percent to 88 percent (Harcourt and Philpot 1990, pp 144–5). More recently, in a study of 280 female sex workers, 98 percent reported constantly using condoms at work (Lovejoy et al. 1991, p 15). Over 70 percent of the subjects in these studies were parlour workers, but the samples also included escorts, privates and a small number of street workers. Condom use is also reported to be very high in the four or five male brothels which operate in the inner suburbs of Sydney (personal communication from SWOP outreach workers).

The increase in condom use, the greater awareness of health issues, and the impact of outreach work done by peer groups and health professionals has led to an observable decrease in acute STDs among female prostitutes (Harcourt et al. 1989). And many who use condoms all the time now find it unnecessary to attend weekly for STD checkups. Nearly half of Lovejoy's 1991 sample reported that they attend on a fortnightly or three-weekly basis. Venereologists in New South Wales have encouraged this trend as they have found much less evidence of disease, especially among more mature female prostitutes (CJC 1991, p 139).

Private Partners and Personal Relationships

Although they may use condoms consistently with paying clients, female prostitutes are less likely to use them in their private relationships or with 'regular clients' (Harcourt and Philpot 1990; Lovejoy et al. 1991). Lovejoy et al. also found that prostitutes reported that they more often contracted an STD from a private partner than from a client. This is of concern because it appears that up to one-third of female prostitutes may have had a recent partner who was himself at risk of HIV infection from IDU or bisexuality (Philpot et al. 1988). However, this finding may be partly offset by the fact that female sex workers seem to have fewer private sexual partners than do other women of similar age. A proportion (20%) were in a stable marriage or de facto relationship, approximately 5 percent were exclusively lesbian in private life, and others (14%) deliberately avoided private sexual encounters during periods when they were working (Lovejoy et al. 1991).

INTERNATIONAL PROSTITUTES

There is, however, one part of the industry in New South Wales where infection rates are still unacceptably high and that is the parlours which employ contracted overseas workers. In a previous section I noted the problems faced by marginalised international prostitutes who are driven by economic circumstances to work overseas. These women are quite distinct from the (usually young, comparatively well-educated) women who work as prostitutes overseas to fund a travelling holiday and who usually fit easily into the mainstream industry.

In Australia most low-status international prostitutes come from Asian countries. Currently most are from Thailand and Malaysia. They work in parlours which are often only identifiable through advertisements in the ethnic press and which are usually managed by men of non-English-speaking background (Brockett and Murray 1993; Sydney Sexual Health Centre 1991). Many of the employees are women who are working illegally in Australia on short-stay tourist visas or expired work visas. Often they are heavily indebted to their employers and agents and work under restrictive contracts until the debts are repaid. They appear to be subject to a good deal of coercion by management and clients, who are culturally disinclined to use condoms.

Eighty-nine per cent of cases of gonorrhoea in females, seen at the Sydney Sexual Health Centre between 1988 and 1990 were in prostitutes born overseas (71 percent from Thailand and 25 percent from Malaysia), although this group formed only 17 percent of total attendances by female patients (Donovan et al. 1991b). Similar but unpublished data has been collected at Parramatta Sexual Health Centre. Staff at Kirketon Road Centre also deal with many cases of gonorrhoea of similar origin (CJC 1991, p 140). These observations are particularly disturbing given the high levels of HIV infection in Thailand, the association between HIV infection and the presence of other STDs, and the secretive and inaccessible mode of operation of these parlours (Sydney Sexual Health Centre 1991).

Many of the Asian women who work in parlours attend public STD clinics weekly for checkups and treatment, and are assisted by interpreters and the use of health promotion literature printed in their own languages. But they can do little to protect themselves without the cooperation of managers and clients.

The clients are particularly difficult to access as they come mainly from non-English-speaking backgrounds and do not commonly present to public STD clinics. It is not clear whether health education and HIV prevention messages are reaching them, or if they relate the messages they do receive to their own situation. However, staff employed in the 'Multicultural Health Promotion Project' at Sydney Sexual Health Centre and SWOP outreach workers have recently managed to access all brothels known to have contract workers and some progress is being made in conveying health education messages.

HIV infection has not, so far, appeared to catch hold in these establishments but the risk cannot be overemphasised because of the enormous epidemics currently engulfing the workers' countries of origin.

CONCLUSION

The epidemiological impact of female prostitution is clearly much greater in developing countries than in the developed world. The reasons for this are complex and interrelated but nevertheless identifiable. Cultural factors play a large part in determining both the proportion of men in a community having sexual contact with prostitutes and the ability of prostitutes to negotiate condom use and safer sexual practices. Political and economic factors may limit access to adequate health care, information and education sources and improved working conditions. They may also lead to the exploitation and social neglect of vulnerable members of the sex industry in cases where there is a perceived dependence on income from sex tourism.

In developed countries, including Australia, prostitution has less impact on public health. Indeed, since the advent of AIDS the relative role of the sex industry in the epidemiology of some STDs in these countries seems to have declined further and there is as yet little evidence of a rapid rise in HIV infection from this source. However, this situation is largely the result of changes made by sex workers, health and welfare professionals, and administrations in response to the threat of AIDS. It is essential that these benefits are not lost either through a growing complacency or through policy changes which may inhibit access by sex workers and their clients to adequate health care, information and outreach together with safer working conditions.

Recent changes in the sex industry in New South Wales clearly show that better public health outcomes are achieved when sex work is largely decriminalised and sex workers have personal autonomy and a choice of work venue. Marginalised prostitutes and their clients continue to be exposed to serious health risks. It is therefore essential to develop strategies which reduce the numbers of marginalised sex workers and maintain and improve the conditions achieved by workers in the mainstream sex industry in this state.

12

Female Sex Work and Injecting Drug Use: what more do we need to know?

Rachel Sharp

This chapter concentrates on female sex workers in Australia who are injecting drug users (IDUs), in the light of what is known about their health and their use of health services. Much attention has been given in contemporary commentaries on prostitution to this subgroup of workers because of their being at least doubly at risk. This is a function of, on one hand, their sexual relations with both paying and non-paying sexual partners, and the risk of contracting sexually transmitted diseases, of which HIV/AIDS excites most public attention. On the other hand, the practice of intravenous ingestion of drugs may involve damage to their health, either directly via the drugs themselves through overdosing or through impurity or indirectly via the transmission of viruses such as hepatitis and HIV through needle sharing or other risk practices which involve exposure to contaminated substances (Bellis 1993; Plant 1991; McKegarney and Barnard 1992; Pineda 1992; Van de Hoek et al. 1988; Shedlin 1990).

Chris Harcourt (Chapter 11) provides an excellent overview of research on sex workers and their health, including the broad picture regarding injecting drug users (see also Harcourt and Philpot 1990). It is worthwhile summarising very briefly the main findings, before turning to the substance of this chapter which dwells on what we don't know.

Globally, we know that there are huge variations in the incidence of STDs among both commercial sex workers and IDUs. Since the HIV/AIDS pandemic much research has focused on the incidence of HIV infection among prostitutes and ways to prevent the virus spreading. That research reveals big variations among prostitutes in their pattern of drug use in general and intravenous drug use in particular, but shows a higher rate of intravenous drug use than in a comparable non-prostitute population and a higher rate of drug use generally. In Australia, large-scale surveys have estimated that less than 2 percent of the general population are IDUs. Several studies of prostitutes, using samples selected by different methods, have estimates ranging around the 10–15 percent level. In many countries in the developed world it seems that there is a positive correlation between IDU and HIV infection, and Australian studies of prostitutes reveal the same relationship. Those few workers known to be HIV positive are likely to have contracted the disease via intravenous drug use or via sexual contact with drug-using partners. Harcourt has estimated that about one-third of sex workers are at risk through their sexual contacts with bisexual and/or drug-using partners. Intravenous drug-using sex workers tend not to be distributed evenly in the industry or completely representative of the sex industry's demography.

Studies in developed countries have shown that the more marginalised workers — the adolescent, occasional and immigrant workers — are usually more prone to inject, as are those who work from a less secure workplace, such as street workers, and those in strip clubs and escort agencies. Studies of HIV risk practices have indicated that IDU sex workers are more likely to have intercourse without a condom and to have sexual partners who are also users. In a recent study (Lovejoy et al. 1992) less than 4 percent of New South Wales sex workers overall admitted to sharing needles, but 8 percent of street workers and 15 percent of club-hotel workers reported they had done so — and this in a context where there is a fairly extensive availability of free needle exchanges, where syringes can be purchased from pharmacies and where there has been quite extensive outreach work among sex workers more prone to use drugs intravenously. As the rate of HIV infection among Australian intravenous drug users is now more than 5 percent, at least in Sydney, and the 5 percent level has been thought to be a crucial barrier, there is obviously no room for complacency (Wodak 1991).

GAPS IN KNOWLEDGE AND RESEARCH

Let us turn to the question of what we don't know. With a few notable exceptions (Loxley and Davidson 1991; Mugford 1988; Sharp et al. 1991; Moore 1992), Australian drug researchers tend to operate with a medical model of illicit drug taking, regarding it as harmful and pathological and not treating it as a socially constructed and mediated activity. It will be suggested that we need to refocus some of our research attention to provide us with a much more detailed understanding of the social, cultural, economic and political context in which injecting drug use occurs and of the situations in which commercial sexual exchanges co-exist. Without such refocusing there is a danger that health promotion campaigns may fall on deaf ears. Those wishing to understand the inner workings of the sex industry require more of the insights which can be gained from qualitative studies. Such insights help us to avoid the danger of falling victim to the popular stereotype of sex workers as feckless, out-of-control people who work primarily to support a drug habit and who are relatively immune to warnings about the health risks of their work or to the broader public and social implications of their activity.

The gaps in the research on injecting drug use and sex work are partly a function of the priorities of funding agencies. They tend to be more impressed with reliable and replicable statistics than with the insights which can be yielded via carefully planned qualitative studies. In such studies, reliability and replicability take second place to the need to gain an understanding *from the inside* of the subtleties of context, social meanings and the texture of everyday life (Moore 1992). Only thus can we make sense of any particular known fact about a certain population. We may, for example, enquire whether the fact of injecting drug use per se is causally significant — whether any known differences between injecting and

non-injecting drug users are crucially related less to the drug taking itself than to the social context of drug taking, perhaps to be
accounted for by other variables such as homelessness, differences
in moral codes, attitudes to leisure and recreation. Injecting drug
use and sex work may both be dependent rather than independent
variables (Sharp 1992). The causal sequences involved in sex work
and injecting drug use require more than large-scale quantitative
studies if we are to avoid arriving at too hasty conclusions.

In social science it is commonplace to realise that the two segments of society about whom relatively little is known are those
right at the pinnacles of power, and those at its weakest margins.
People subject to extreme social stigma such as IDUs have a vested
interest in keeping their secrets and often rightly regard the attention of social researchers as an unwelcome intrusion into their personal space. Similarly, at the other end of the social scale, those
whose privileged social position depends on the withholding of
information resist any intrusion on their privacy. How often do we
read carefully constructed research reports of the day-to-day planning of the boards of multinational companies, their financial
strategies and manoeuvres and their directors' use of leisure and
recreational time?

What we know about drug-injecting prostitutes depends, at
least partially, on what they will allow us to know: on information
gleaned from them as they carry out their legitimate right to use
health services such as drug treatment centres or sexual health clinics. This knowledge has to be seen in the light of the self-selected
nature of the sample and interpreted accordingly. Research has
often demonstrated that, for example, those who inject drugs and
use drug treatment services form only a relatively small proportion
of the total number of drug takers, and are not necessarily typical
of the total population of those who take drugs (Holden 1989;
Hartnoll et al. 1985; Erickson 1987). We also know that there is a
wide variety of social and cultural milieux in which injecting drug
use occurs, and a broad spectrum of ways of relating to drugs
which may never produce the need to access health services about
drug related problems. The greater proneness of street prostitutes
to drug use in general and injecting drug use in particular that is
shown by surveys may have more to do with the way in which we

select our samples than with the actual incidence of drug use in the population. Similarly, the relatively low rate of injecting drug use among sex workers who work in brothels or parlours may be more a result of the penalties which could follow disclosure, given the anti-drug practices of many parlour managements, than an accurate description of the actual rate of injecting drug use (Lovejoy et al. 1992).

It has been said that sex workers are relatively likely to have partners who are themselves injectors, regardless of whether or not the sex worker is a user. As we have observed, it is widely believed that prostitution is resorted to because it provides a more lucrative means of supporting a drug habit than do more conventional occupations. We need to know far more about the economics of prostitution and its interrelations with the economics of the drug trade at its various levels such as supplying, dealing and consumption. Ethnographies of drug-taking communities have revealed that most consumers are also petty dealers, and the same is likely to be the case with sex workers either at the centre or at the margins of the illicit drug trade (Pearson 1987; Walters 1985). The extent to which financial considerations weigh upon the sex worker and are related to the specifics of the circumstances in which paid sex and/or injecting occurs is information that would be useful for targeted health promotion campaigns. It would also be advantageous to ascertain in precisely what ways the patterns of legal control and regulation of sex work and of drug taking impinge upon the everyday life of the sex worker and constrain what is done, or not done. We already know that there is a social structure to the sex industry with more stable and secure elements structurally differentiated from those less secure. The extent to which this structure itself is a function of legal control and regulation and is capable of being changed, were patterns of regulation altered, would be useful information. If those in the more marginal sections of the industry are there because these sections have patterns of policing, control and social and legal regulation which are different, then this is relevant information for more finely tuned health promotion strategies. We are ignorant as to precisely why some sex workers prefer, or end up, working from the street. We know little about questions of labour turnover, patterns of recruitment and formal and informal mechanisms for training new workers into the expected patterns of behaviour and established ways of doing things.

Let us focus now on street workers. Most of our knowledge about street workers comes from their self-report via structured questionnaires or interviews obtained in the field or from sexual health or drug clinics. As Chapter 17 on the methodology of conducting field work among sex workers makes clear, most of the instruments used in such surveys are short, to the point and specifically designed not to interfere with the demands of the work place. Such surveys, while yielding valuable data, will never be able to document the subtleties of behaviour as it occurs in the natural setting (Waldorf 1980). Just as in the case of non-commercial sexual transactions it is usually impossible to carry out an ethnographic observational study focusing, for example, on the details of negotiation regarding condom use, so it is with commercial sex. We can only go on what participants say happens, or want you to think happens, which gives rise to transformations between the raw data and the reported data.

While this problem is a common one in survey analysis, it is magnified when dealing with stigmatised activities or groups. It is fairly easy to see this with respect to condom use in an industry where business has been adversely affected by the HIV epidemic. To admit to not using condoms at least in the work place is to admit to helping to undermine the industry. The same goes for admitting one's drug use in an industry where clients are reported not too enthusiastic about having sex with drug-affected workers. But what about the inter-section of drugs and sex in the same setting? Drug research has often used the concept of disinhibition to refer to the effects of drugs upon individuals' resolve. We have already noted the relatively high amount of drug use generally among sex workers, the common explanation being that the work often requires drug use to soothe away the stress and lessen the tension springing from the very nature of the work. But this assumption may be the result more of the researchers' prejudices than of accurate observations about the role of drugs in sex work. We need to know, too, much more about the drug use of clients and about their expectations regarding drug use accompanying paid sex (Lovejoy et al. 1991). We do not know what proportion of clients are themselves injectors and under what circumstances injecting would take place with a sex worker. Nor do we know if such episodes are conducted safely in response to health promotion campaigns on condom use and needle sharing. Also, are any of these clients likely to form a prostitute's regular clientele. In such a case, caution might be thrown to the winds just as we know condoms in such cases are sometimes discarded. Most studies of sex workers' clients (to the extent to which they exist at all) have been studies of the sex workers' assessments and judgements of their clients rather than direct and first-hand studies of clients themselves (Lovejoy et al. 1991). We know relatively little about the typical clients of street workers as opposed to those who frequent parlours. Indeed, we know relatively little about what actually transpires between street workers and client, or, indeed, the physical and social circumstances in which paid sexual encounters occur.

This lack of knowledge is aggravated when we also consider the relative dearth of information generally about life on the street. Some of our knowledge comes via those charged with conducting outreach among street workers or whose brief is specifically concerned to address, say, the problems of homelessness among inner city youth or the needs of those known to be heavily addicted to drugs. Evidence presented to various select committees on prostitution and other perceived social problems is notoriously affected by prevailing social standards and does not necessarily capture the range of life on the streets or the subtle and informal social controls through which it is informally regulated (Australian Capital Territory 1991). How injecting drug use is integrated into this social structure and the complexities which surround it would require a range of expensive and carefully thought out ethnographic research studies that so far only a few funding agencies have had the foresight to finance (anywhere in the world). Without such studies it is difficult to mould effective health promotion strategies which can effectively target the health beliefs and harm minimisation strategies which already exist and could be strengthened. We are rarely dealing with individuals who are not located in some manner in a social context (Harding and Zinberg 1977) with its own internal pattern of norms and social sanctions. This is the case even when the foci of our attention are those whom opinion leaders in the wider society often regard as totally bereft of social conscience and social support.

Another issue on which our knowledge is deficient is the question of gender and drug treatment agencies and the complicating effect of the occupation of sex work for those seeking or desiring treatment for drug-related problems. Other studies have noted the complaints made by many women that drug treatment agencies tend to show a lack of attention to the specificities of women's lives and responsibilities, including their roles as mothers and child carers (Rosenbaum 1985; Sharp et al. 1991). This may mean that those most likely to be accessed by researchers via drug treatment centres are less than typical of female users as a whole. Similarly, some studies of sex workers have pointed to their reluctance to access health agencies specifically targeting sex workers and to concerns in some quarters that counsellors are sometimes too judgemental and insufficiently sympathetic to the social lives of workers and the culture of prostitution. If these concerns have any grounding, they are likely to be doubly relevant to those engaged both in injecting drugs and in prostitution.

THE IMPACT OF HIV/AIDS ON DRUG HABITS

Harcourt in Chapter 11 makes mention of the relatively small number of sex workers, including male, female and transsexual workers, who are HIV positive. She also claims that, as far as can be known, not one sexually transmitted case of HIV seropositivity has occurred in Australia as a result of paid sex; most sex workers who are HIV positive having become so as a result of injecting drug use. Again, here, we are limited in our knowledge about the sexual and drug-using activities of sex workers with their friends and partners in the non-commercial arena. Most such studies are not first-hand but rely on the reporting of sex workers (Lovejoy et al. 1992). From these studies we know that sex workers are only slightly more likely to use condoms in their private lives than are non-sex workers and that, where injecting drug use occurs, it may sometimes involve sharing among friends or with those one trusts.

We don't know other than approximately what proportion of sex workers' partners are users. Nor do we know the numbers of sex workers supporting, financially, a partner's use. Neither do we know the needle-sharing proclivities of such partners. But what we do know raises questions of the utmost importance for HIV prevention. Despite the availability of needle exchanges and much successful agitation about the dangers of sharing needles, sharing still occurs and indeed is responsible for an increasing proportion of new cases of HIV each year. It is too simplistic to argue that such 'sharing' is indicative of the general irresponsibility of those who take drugs intravenously or, indeed, by any mode if they are illegal. Sharing may be part of the cultural universe of those subject to double stigmatisation. It may be so deeply integrated within the subcultural underworld and tied in with its everyday array of communally articulated survival strategies, in conditions of marginality and exclusion, that the breaking of the habit of sharing may be extremely difficult to achieve. And efforts to bring this about may be far more difficult than, say, encouraging someone always to use their own toothbrush, or since some people attach symbolic significance to sharing a toothbrush shift from the use of a 300–sheet toilet roll to one containing 500 sheets (Sharp et al. 1991). Here we need to focus far more on detailed analysis of precisely what is being shared and what might be the possible functional substitutes for a ritual which holds deep significance. That significance may itself be related to the need to maintain solidarity and secrecy in the face of an external threat in the form of law enforcement officers. If so, the more worrying and more challenging the task in that it calls for change in the patterns of legal regulation, something very difficult to achieve.

We noted above the question of those sex workers who are also HIV positive, whom it is believed became so as a result of their drug use rather than their sexual practices. We are unaware of just how many drug-using prostitutes continue to work in the industry after diagnosis, or who are HIV positive and don't know it. We also can only guess at what might be the impediments to leaving the industry, especially if drug use is heavy and the need to sustain the habit uncontrollable. There is some evidence (somewhat anecdotal) that gay HIV positive people sometimes resort to injecting drug use as a response to their status and as a means of coping with it. One wonders what the incentives would be for someone trebly marginal, and open to stigmatisation with respect to three areas of their practice, to leave an industry which pays better and where others may be, perhaps, more tolerant towards their affliction. Services targeting sex workers have paid special attention to those who are HIV positive and their often unique needs. But we know there is a dearth of the full range of supportive systems dealing with such matters as child care, accommodation and income support. These matters affect all who are chronically sick in our community, not just those with HIV. One can confidently assume that more needs to be done in these areas.

Another issue which we know relatively little about concerns the fine line which often exists between the casual sex worker (who often would not even dream of thinking of herself as being engaged in sex work) and those more centrally involved. It is well known that some people, especially young people living on the margins of our society, may exchange sexual favours for accommodation, food, cigarettes, alcohol and other drugs (Australian Capital Territory 1991). We know that many young people have fallen victim to pathological family setups and poor education and to the collapse of the youth labour market which has been especially difficult for those without family support. It is widely believed that such groups can easily fall into a drug-taking subculture, where the interaction between sexual practice and drug-using could prove particularly risky. We do not know, though, very much about the underlife of our cities and the location of drug taking in such a context; nor about the role which casual sex work may play in both the consumption of pleasure and the provision of what are often necessities. We certainly know more about those marginal people likely to gain the attention of law enforcement agencies or of what has been termed the 'soft police force' of social workers, moral entrepreneurs and what have you. We know little, however, about those whose activities are such as to keep them out of the beady eye of the law.

Another area of shocking ignorance relates to the question of drug taking and injecting drug use outside the realm of English-speaking inhabitants. Not a great deal of work has been done on non-English-speaking sex workers other than Southeast Asian workers (Brockett and Murray 1992) and little is known about their drug use in general, let alone their injecting practices. We do know, however, that some migrant groups come from countries of origin where there is a more tolerant attitude to the use of drugs in various spheres of social life. There is a need for more multicultural analyses of both drug use and sex work.

Such studies also need to penetrate the border which exists around the issue of Aboriginal health. Should we assume that prostitution does not exist in either urban or rural Aboriginal communities or is it the case that our research has been too ethnocentric, too reluctant to cross cultural boundaries? The inadequacy of health promotion campaigns on HIV issues in Aboriginal communities, especially outside the main urban areas, is already a matter of some public concern. One of the costs of Aboriginal or other ethnic groups' self-determination vis-à-vis health may be the neglect of problems related to stigmatised social practices.

SOME LINES OF COMPARATIVE ANALYSIS

We know that patterns of drug use vary tremendously across regions and across class and other social boundaries. Included are particular patterns of drug intake and the way these are affected by fashion, subcultural milieu and style. An appropriate harm minimisation strategy which seeks to reduce the tendency to inject drugs in favour of ingesting by less harmful modes, would depend on some understanding of the particular social factors which present barriers to a shift away from injecting. Research undertaken among injecting drug users in some places where the HIV incidence is very high and where there have also been longstanding traditions of prostitution (Edinburgh, for example) shows that there have been remarkable successes in preventing the epidemic spreading — whereas a few years ago a catastrophic health crisis had been predicted. Other places where injecting drug use is common, and especially among sex workers, such as in the United States, have not been nearly so successful. We need some understanding of the reasons for the success of certain strategies rather than others (Thomas et al. 1989).

Edinburgh's experience prompted a thoroughgoing community response stretching into schools and colleges, local government, social service agencies and health and welfare organisations. It has had the aim of targeting the general population about the need for self-care and the altering of social customs and practices with respect to condom use and needle sharing. Sex worker organisations in this concerted campaign, as in Australia, have played a vital role in sharing responsibility for community health (Plant 1990). It is interesting to ask why sex worker organisations have been much more successful than drug user organisations in promoting health in their respective and overlapping communities. Both prostitution and injecting drug use are morally stigmatised, so this difference is intriguing. If we knew the answer to the question we would have made a great advance in safeguarding not only sex workers and their clients and partners but the larger population as well.

13

AIDS EDUCATION AND PREVENTION STRATEGIES IN THE SEX INDUSTRY

Carol Stevens

Australia's response to AIDS has been proactive and effective, as evidenced in HIV infection rates declining from 2786 in 1985 to 352 in 1993 (National Centre in HIV Epidemiology, 1993). The success is underpinned by the National HIV/AIDS Strategy, which has provided a framework for an integrated response to the HIV crisis and a plan for action spanning a range of policy and program activities. One of the Strategy's objectives is to promote the development of community norms which support the establishment and maintenance of safe behaviours within populations whose activities place them at greatest risk of infection.

Funding of education and prevention programs recognises that the design and delivery of these programs are most effectively taken at the community level and by members of the targeted groups, in consultation and in conjunction with government funding bodies. The goals are achieved primarily through the provision of free condoms, free lubrication, free needles and syringes for intravenous drug users (IDUs), free HIV/AIDS testing, AIDS-related counselling and the provision of primary health care.

The primary public health measure implemented to combat the spread of AIDS infection was the setting up of Sexual Health Clinics (SHCs), Kirketon Road Centre, the Sex Workers Outreach Program (SWOP), drug centres and other specialised services. Badlands provides short-term accommodation for sex workers who are also drug users. Together these organisations provide a comprehensive service to sex workers. Their overall aim is the well-being of sex workers and IDUs and they are based on a one-stop model of primary health care. Outreach delivers education and prevention services, counselling and support to sex workers. Outreach aims at establishing peer norms and peer group support for sustained behavioural change leading to a decrease in HIV/AIDS infection rates. For many workers in the sex industry, contact with an outreach worker will be their first point of contact with service providers other than medical ones.

SAFE SEX PRACTICES IN THE SEX INDUSTRY

While the general public's image of sex workers has been tinged by cases such as that of Sharlene, the HIV positive sex worker who was portrayed as infecting the 'innocent' populace (Donovan 1990), it is generally recognised that the sex industry in New South Wales has been exemplary in its adoption of HIV/STD prevention measures (Perkins 1991). This view is supported by the dramatic decline in gonococcal infections among resident sex workers as well as reductions in other acute bacterial STDs over the last decade (Lovejoy et al. 1991; Philpot et al. 1991; Harcourt et al. 1989). Significantly, no resident female sex worker is known to have been involved in the transmission of HIV during commercial sex activities, and only a small number of Australian resident HIV positive female sex workers have been identified, the probable source being the use of unclean needles (Donovan 1990). However, with contracted overseas workers there have been three cases reported of HIV to mid-1993 and, between 1988 and 1990, 89 percent of gonorrhoea cases seen at a Sydney health clinic were Asian workers (Brockett and Murray 1992). The overall success of the education and prevention policies had its foundations laid by the early efforts of prostitutes' organisations. These organisations advocated self-determination and safer sex practices for sex workers. In New South Wales, largely thanks to the efforts of the Australian Prostitutes' Collective, there was a massive increase in condom use by female sex workers, as recorded at a Sydney STD clinic, from a low five percentage in 1985 to 87 percent in 1988 (Harcourt and Philpot 1990).

While the education and preventive programs implemented in New South Wales to date have been successful in reducing HIV/AIDS and STD infection rates, it is not clear which components of the programs are most effective. To find out what leads to the adoption of 'safe sex' practices by both sex workers and their clients, a survey funded by the NSW AIDS Bureau was conducted among sex workers and brothel managements in 1992 (Lovejoy et al. 1992). This study and the collection of data were carried out by Garrett Prestage and Roberta Perkins. The more important findings of this survey are given below.

THE SURVEY SAMPLE

In all, 388 sex workers filled in the questionnaire; 291 (75%) identified as female, 66 (17%) as male, and 21 (5.5%) as male-to-female transsexuals, transvestites or cross-dressers (hereafter referred to as 'transsexuals'). As some survey questions were not answered by some respondents and as most of the questions were multiple-response items, the numbers and percentages reported throughout this chapter relate to the number of responses to each item or variable.

SUPPORT AGENCY SERVICES

The practical items most frequently received by sex workers at agency sites are listed in Table 13.1.

CHANGES IN BEHAVIOUR

The most frequently cited change in behaviour in response to education and prevention programs was the increased use of condoms with clients. Just less than 10 percent of the sample reported that they had commercial sex without a condom within three months prior to participating in this study. One area of concern to AIDS educators, in relation to sex workers, has been their sexual activities off the job. Understandably, people have a psychological desire to have 'unprotected' sex with their lover or private sex partner. As well as this psychological need, for sex workers not using a condom is symbolic of the 'specialness' to themselves and their partners of the

Table 13.1

Services or Items Received

Item	Female	Male	Transsexual	Total Cases
Free condoms	245 78%	49 15%	18 5%	312 100%
Free clean needles	55 64%	22 25%	8 9%	85 100%
Information about safer sex	179 80%	36 16%	9 4%	224 100%
Information about my sexuality	35 68%	12 23%	4 7%	51 100%
Information about drugs	50 72%	14 20%	5 7%	69 100%
Drug or alcohol counselling	21 77%	5 18%	1 3%	27 100%
Bashing/domestic violence counselling	11 73%	2 13%	2 13%	15 100%
Other counselling	34 79%	5 11%	4 9%	43 100%
General health advice	91 78%	17 14%	8 6%	116 100%
Free lube	190 76%	46 18%	14 5%	250 100%
Free rubber gloves	32 71%	8 17%	5 11%	45 100%
Free dental dams	20 74%	2 7%	5 18%	27 100%
Career advice	8 61%	3 23%	2 15%	13 100%
Family reunion advice	2 50%	1 25%	1 25%	4 100%
Family planning advice	20 87%	2 8%	1 4%	23 100%
HIV/AIDS testing	167 82%	28 13%	7 3%	202 100%
Accommodation advice	8 42%	7 36%	4 21%	19 100%
Other counselling or information	21 63%	5 15%	4 12%	30 100%

relationship (Perkins 1991). The increased use of condoms outside of work (222–57%) and the decrease in the number of sex partners off the job (25%) were the next most frequently cited changes in behaviour. The high percentages of workers across the gender groups who use condoms off the job compares very favourably with condom use in the general population (Perkins 1991). Of significance is the fact that 83 (21.5%) reported changes in sexual behaviour via the 'way I use illegal drugs'; this number is almost all the IDUs in the sample. In relation to types of sex work, most encouraging is the change in behaviour in illegal drug use reported by 50 percent of club/hotel workers and 46 percent of street workers.

ADOPTION OF SAFE SEX PRACTICES

The reasons reported for the adoption of safe sex practices are listed in Table 13.2.

The continuing promotion of general AIDS awareness will serve to remind people that the threat is there and, hopefully, should counter the emerging general perception in the community that the AIDS scare is over, or has been overblown. This perception has led some sex workers and clients to be less vigilant in relation to safe sex practices. That a growing number of individuals have become less vigilant is understandable, given that the infection rates of HIV/AIDS in Australia are so low. The frequency of the need for ready availability of condoms (191–49%) and clean needles (56–14.5%) highlights the importance of maintaining these AIDS services. Positive results indicate that 'self-efficacy' related to AIDS preventative actions is high, with 204 (53%) reporting the reason for adopting safe sex practices as being 'a decision to protect myself'.

CLIENTS AND UNSAFE SEX

Overall, 228 respondents (59%) reported having had trouble with clients' reluctance to use condoms. Almost all the clients creating trouble were males attending female sex workers (193–85%), compared with similar reports from 25 male sex workers. Given the general level of awareness of AIDS in the community these figures are disappointing although research highlights the fact that most males are reluctant to use condoms and, further, that this is a cross-cultural phenomenon (Lule and Gruer 1992; Hong, Lee, Kok et al. 1993).

Table 13.2

Reasons for Adopting Safe Sex Practices.

Reason	Female	Male	Transsexual	Total Cases
Clients more AIDS-aware	121	17	10	148
	81%	11%	6%	100%
Condoms more readily available	151	28	12	191
	79%	14%	6%	100%
Resources provided by AIDS agencies	55	11	5	71
	77%	15%	7%	100%
General AIDS awareness	156	33	14	203
	76%	16%	6%	100%
No change	30	7	3	40
	75%	17%	7%	100%
Change in workplace policies	49	1	3	53
	92%	1%	5%	100%
Information provided by AIDS agencies	58	12	5	75
	77%	16%	6%	100%
Knew someone with AIDS	51	21	5	77
	66%	27%	6%	100%
Clean needles more available	38	11	7	56
	67%	19%	12%	100%
Decided to protect myself	156	36	12	204
	76%	17%	5%	100%

When confronted with condom avoidance, 226 (58%) of sex workers refused service, 185 (48%) talked about AIDS/STDs, and 143 (37%) told clients about the house rule. These results indicate that the sex worker education programs have been successful in implementing three of their guiding principles: firstly, in creating a supportive environment for personal change; secondly, by empowering the sex community to achieve a fuller ownership of its endeavours and destinies; and thirdly, by increasing options to allow people to exercise control over their own health and to make choices conducive to health. The National HIV/AIDS Strategy proposes to develop community norms that further encourage and maintain safe behaviour.

UNSAFE SEX PRACTICES

In this discussion, 'unsafe sex' means unprotected vaginal intercourse and receptive and insertive anal intercourse with a person whose HIV serostatus is unknown. Overall, 34 instances of unsafe sex were reported in the survey. Of the 30 sex workers reporting these instances, 17 were female, eight male and five transsexual. Two respondents reported instances of two of the three types of unsafe sex activity and one 16-year-old male reported instances of all three types. Ten instances of unsafe sex were reported by individuals under the age of 18 years, eight instances by respondents aged between 18 and 25 years, 13 by those between 26 and 40 years, and two by those over 40 years. (See Table 13.3 for details.)

Did unsafe sexual behaviour occur through ignorance of the risks involved? Fifteen (of 30) who reported unsafe sex practices had not received any workplace training and 18 (of 30) no AIDS-related counselling. Only six respondents had received neither workplace training nor counselling. The length of time that respondents who had had unsafe sex had been working indicates that lack of awareness of the dangers should not have been the problem. Ten of the workers who had had unsafe sex had been working between one and two years, and eight between five and ten years; while of the 'new' workers (ie individuals working for between two and six months), only two had had unsafe sex. One person who had 'unsafe sex' had been working between six and eleven months. These figures suggest that it is the more experienced workers who are most likely to have unsafe sex, which raises the issue of risk assessment and 'negotiated safety' which is discussed in the next section.

Six IDUs reported 'unprotected' vaginal intercourse, three 'unprotected' receptive and four 'unprotected' insertive anal intercourse. One 16-year-old and one 17-year-old male street worker engaged in 'unprotected' receptive and insertive anal intercourse.

REASONS REPORTED FOR HAVING 'UNSAFE SEX'

Two male sex workers reported not using a condom because they did not have one at a time of working. Two females, one male and one transsexual had 'unsafe sex' because they 'just felt like it'. Of the females engaging in unsafe sex because they 'just felt like it', one was 35 years old, had worked in the industry five to ten years, had not received any workplace training, but had discussed AIDS-related issues with a counsellor. Another female was 37 years of age, had also worked five to ten years, had not received workplace

Table 13.3

Age and Workplace of Respondents and Instances of 'Unsafe Sex' Practices

	Vaginal i/c without a condom			Receptive anal i/c without a condom			Insertive anal i/c without a condom			
	F	M	T[a]	F	M	T	F	M	T	Total
Age										cases
<18 years	1	1	2	0	2	1	0	2	1[b]	10
18–25 years	2	0	0	2	0	1	0	3	0	8
26–40 years	12	0	0	1	0	0	0	0	0	13
Over 40 yrs	2	0	0	0	0	0	0	0	0	2
Not stated	0	0	0	1	0	0	0	0	0	1
Totals	**17**	**1**	**2**	**4**	**2**	**2**	**0**	**5**	**1**	**34**
Workplace										
Brothel	13	0	0	1	0	0	0	1	0	15
Own place	1	0	0	0	0	0	0	0	0	1
Bars	0	0	0	0	0	1	0	0	0	1
Priv. resid.	3	0	0	1	0	0	0	0	0	4
Escort agency	1	0	0	1	0	0	0	0	0	3
Beats	0	0	0	0	1	1	0	1	0	2
Streets	3	1	2	0	1	1	0	2	1	9
Totals	**21**	**1**	**2**	**3**	**2**	**3**	**0**	**5**	**1**	**37[c]**

(a) Transsexuals
(b) Some transsexuals can achieve erections.
(c) Multiple response item

training, and had not discussed AIDS-related issues with a counsellor. The male was 16 years old, had worked between one and two years, and had not received either training or counselling. The transsexual was 19 years old, had worked for two to four months, and also had not received any workplace training or counselling.

Of the respondents who reported the reason for sex without a condom as 'the client made me do it', three were females aged 28, 31 and 32, all of whom had discussed AIDS-related issues with a counsellor. Two had worked for between two and four months and had received workplace training. One had worked for between one and two years, but had not undergone workplace training. When the data on these workers' strategies for dealing with a client who is reluctant to use a condom were examined, it was found that, while not reporting that they 'refuse service' they did report positive strategies of charming, negotiating or persuading, and one reported 'fooling them', perhaps by using 'trick sex' (using a hand instead of the vagina without the client's awareness). One could infer that those situations where the client 'made them' practise unsafe sex involved some form of physical coercion.

Ten females reported that the reason for unsafe sex was that it was with a 'regular client'. Of the respondents who reported having 'unsafe sex' because they were 'offered more money', two were males aged 19 and 23, and one a transsexual aged 19. All three had received workplace training, and two had had discussions with counsellors on AIDS-related issues. Four female respondents had penetrative sex without a condom but 'did not believe it was dangerous'. Only one of these had received workplace training, but all four had had AIDS-related counselling indicating that they may have been sure that there was no element of risk involved.

The above findings raise the issue of risk assessment procedures that some workers use. Of the individuals who did not believe that non-use of condoms is dangerous, two females reported checking up on the client and two that the work was with a regular client. The two female respondents who had had 'unsafe sex' because they 'just felt like it' had worked for between five and ten years. The findings of the present survey indicate that, although older sex workers might engage in 'unsafe sex' practices, it is usually in the context of 'negotiated safety'. In contrast, juveniles and young adolescents consistently have unprotected sex even though they have some level of awareness and knowledge of the dangers (Caron, Davis, Wynn et al. 1987; Mickler 1993). It appears that more behaviourally oriented interventions aimed at increasing personal skills and overcoming youth's 'egocentrism' are necessary to encourage wider safe sex practices. As well, more social support is required so that using a condom becomes a peer 'norm'.

'UNSAFE SEX' PRACTICES AND FEAR OF CATCHING HIV/AIDS

Eleven females engaging in vaginal or receptive anal intercourse were not 'very much' afraid of catching AIDS. Bearing in mind that a proportion of the female respondents had engaged in some risk assessment this result is not surprising. Their attitude could be considered a reasoned response, given that they court danger every time they have commercial sex. They appear to be confident that their expertise will protect them. But for some workers denial could be a factor, a defence mechanism which allows them to get on with the job.

Of concern is the fact that there were three instances of males having 'unprotected' insertive anal intercourse who were not 'very much' afraid of catching HIV/AIDS. (Table 13.4 summarises the survey data.)

Table 13.4
Unsafe Sex Practices and Level of Fear of Catching AIDS

	Vaginal i/c without a condom			Receptive anal i/c without a condom			Insertive anal i/c without a condom		
	F	M	T[a]	F	M	T	F	M	T
Not at all	0	0	0	1	0	0	0	1	0
Very slightly	5	0	0	1	0	0	0	1	0
Moderately	2	0	1	1	0	0	0	1	0
Very much	10	1	1	1	2	2	0	2	1[b]
Total	**17**	**1**	**2**	**4**	**2**	**2**	**0**	**5**	**1**

(a) Transsexuals
(b) Some transsexuals can achieve erections

INTRAVENOUS DRUG USERS

Overseas experience indicates clearly that the likelihood of a future spread of HIV infection and AIDS in Australia will tend to centre on IDUs, their sexual partners and their children. In the present survey, 85 sex workers (22%) reported getting clean needles from agencies when they visit them. Of this group, 55 were female, 22 male and eight transsexual. Thirteen of the 85 reported sharing an unclean needle in the three months prior to our interview with them. Ten of these people were female and three male. Four worked in brothels, one for an escort agency, four on the street, three in clubs/hotels, and one on the beats. Two were under 18 years of age, eight between 18 and 25 years, two between 26 and

40 years; for one, age was not stated. Of the 13 respondents who had shared an unclean needle, nine had received AIDS-related counselling compared to four who had not, and five had had some workplace training compared to eight who had not. Only three respondents had received neither training nor counselling.

Seven of the 13 sex workers who shared an unclean needle reported being 'very much' afraid of catching AIDS, while three were 'very slightly' and one 'moderately' afraid. Two were 'not at all' afraid. It is interesting that nine of the 13 had received counselling. Of the seven who were 'very much' afraid, two reported as a reason for sharing an unclean needle that they 'knew the others well'. Four respondents reported that it 'was with their regular partner' and four that they 'went first'. (Multiple responses were permitted in the survey.) Again, there is evidence of some form of risk assessment occurring which indicates that the education and preventive messages are being heeded.

On the positive side, no IDUs reported that they used an unclean needle because they were too stoned or drunk to be careful or because the needles got mixed up or they didn't think about it. Given the widespread availability of free needles it is disappointing that seven workers reported no needles being available, including one 16-year-old respondent who asked: 'Why aren't clinics open for needles at the weekend?'. While it is reassuring that only 13 respondents reported using unclean needles, it is important to remember that many individuals working in the sex industry, particularly in clubs/hotels and on the streets, are IDUs. The importance of maintaining services, such as providing clean needles and counselling to these individuals, is underscored by the finding that 83 (21%) cited as the reason for the adoption of safe sex practices 'the way I use illegal drugs', and 56 IDUs cited the 'availability of clean needles'.

For HIV/AIDS testing, significant numbers of IDUs were found to use their own doctor (40–47%) or sexual health clinics (32–38%), with only three people using any of the mobile outreach buses. None of the IDUs used a brothel management's doctor or were tested at work. Multi-purpose health clinics were also popular for AIDS/STD testing, with more than 50 percent of the 85 IDUs reporting having used these centres.

KNOWLEDGE OF HIV/AIDS MODES OF TRANSMISSION

The primary aim of HIV/AIDS education programs is to get across the message that any form of penetrative sex without a condom is a high risk activity. However, medical research shows that pre-ejaculatory fluid and saliva may be considered low risk transmission fluids. When the survey responses are judged 'correct' or 'incorrect' on the basis of the educational message, the majority of sex workers appear correctly informed with regard to penetrative sex with ejaculation but appear not to heed the educators' advice with regard to forms of penetrative sex without ejaculation. Table 13.5 indicates these and other responses given by our sample.

Forty-six (16%) of the females, 16 percent of the males and three transsexuals were not aware that 'unprotected' vaginal intercourse is a high risk activity. Evidence that the message most emphasised in AIDS education, that the highest risk activity is 'unprotected' receptive anal intercourse is getting through, is the fact that the lowest percentage of incorrect answers were given for this activity. All the same, six males and six transsexuals were unaware that receptive intercourse is a high risk activity for infection. Fifty-two (18%) of the females, 12 (19%) of the males and six transsexuals were not aware that insertive anal intercourse without a condom is a high risk activity. These figures indicate, although it is difficult to believe, that some sex workers were still not aware that engaging in any of these three activities places them at high risk for HIV infection.

Fortunately, as can be seen from Table 13.6, this lack of knowledge did not translate substantially into unsafe sex practices for the majority of respondents who answered incorrectly, suggesting that the AIDS education policy of 'a condom from start to finish' is being heeded.

Of the respondents who were not aware that 'unprotected' vaginal sex was a high risk activity, six had engaged in it; while 16 who were aware had had this form of unsafe sex. Most of these individuals had presumably 'negotiated the safety' of their encounters. Of particular interest are the 47 respondents who answered incorrectly yet did not have unsafe sex. Responses to the other two high risk activities show a similar pattern.

Table 13.5
Sex Workers' Knowledge of Modes of Transmission of HIV/AIDS

Activity		Correct Response	Incorrect Response
Vaginal intercourse without a condom			
	Female	241 (84%)	46 (16%)
	Male	51 (82%)	11 (18%)
	Transsexual	17 (85%)	3 (15%)
Insertive anal intercourse without a condom			
	Female	235 (82%)	52 (18%)
	Male	51 (81%)	12 (19%)
	Transsexuals	15 (71%)	6 (29%)
Receptive anal intercourse without a condom			
	Female	254 (89%)	32 (11%)
	Male	56 (90%)	6 (10%)
	Transsexual	15 (71%)	6 (29%)
Withdrawal before ejaculation			
	Female	143 (50%)	142 (50%)
	Male	33 (53%)	29 (47%)
	Transsexual	13 (65%)	7 (35%)
Going down on someone (ie French) without a condom			
	Female	99 (35%)	187 (65%)
	Male	13 (22%)	47 (78%)
	Transsexual	9 (43%)	12 (57%)
Taking semen in the mouth			
	Female	163 (58%)	119 (42%)
	Male	29 (48%)	31 (52%)
	Transsexual	11 (52%)	10 (48%)
Injecting drugs without sharing needles			
	Female	171 (60%)	113 (40%)
	Male	47 (76%)	15 (24%)
	Transsexual	10 (50%)	10 (50%)
Working with HIV positive workers			
	Female	128 (46%)	151 (54%)
	Male	38 (63%)	22 (37%)
	Transsexual	9 (45%)	11 (55%)

Table 13.6
Knowledge of High Risk Activities and its Relationship with Behaviour

Knowledge		Engaged in vaginal i/c without a condom	
	Yes	No	N/A
Correct	16	236	62
Incorrect	6	47	9
		Engaged in receptive anal i/c without a condom	
	Yes	No	N/A
Correct	4	234	68
Incorrect	4	47	20
		Engaged in insertive anal i/c without a condom	
	Yes	No	N/A
Correct	6	220	102
Incorrect	1	29	14

It is worrying that four individuals not aware that 'unprotected' receptive anal intercourse is dangerous had engaged in this activity. Of these four, one 16-year-old male IDU who had worked for nine months answered incorrectly to every question assessing knowledge of HIV transmission, and had engaged in all three high risk activities. One 17-year-old male IDU who had worked for two years without any AIDS-related counselling, and who had engaged in all three high risk activities also had very poor knowledge of HIV/AIDS mode of transmission. One 16-year-old male non-IDU who had worked for two years and *had* received AIDS-related counselling, and who had engaged in 'unprotected' receptive anal intercourse, answered, in response to being asked the likelihood of HIV/AIDS infection, 'a bit likely' to giving insertive anal intercourse and 'very likely' to receptive anal intercourse. While it appears that for these young men the problem is lack of knowledge of HIV transmission, we should reiterate the point that information alone, without some form of behavioural intervention, is not enough to bring about safe sex practices.

As only the three highest risk activities in Table 13.6 were surveyed in the questionnaire, we cannot assess the degree to which lack of knowledge translated into risk behaviour in the other activities. But there were unacceptably high percentages of females (42%), males (52%) and transsexuaals (48%) who believed that 'taking semen in the mouth' is not a high risk activity. The number of respondents who incorrectly believed that 'working with HIV positive workers' is a high risk activity (Table 13.5) is disappointing and indicates that the level of knowledge about HIV/AIDS is not high enough to overcome unnecessary fears, prejudices or discrimination. As one of the objectives of the National HIV/AIDS Strategy has been to elevate awareness to a level at which these problems would not occur, it appears that a more focused effort is required to achieve the goal. The confusion evident in the response data on 'injecting drugs without sharing needles' (Table 13.5) is odd. However respondents who answered incorrectly on this item did not show abnormal responses on any other items. Indeed, of the 83 IDUs 68 (82%) answered correctly; while of the non-IDUs 165 (54%) answered corrrectly and 125 (41%) answered incorrectly, indicating that a large proportion of sex workers who are not IDUs are ill-informed about the risk of transmission of AIDS through drug or needle use.

CONCLUSION

A major concern of health workers has been to help people to modify sexual behaviour in order to reduce the rate of new HIV infection to an annual rate of two persons per 100,000 (National HIV/AIDS Strategy 1993–94 to 1995–96). A variety of educational campaigms, using different mediums and instituted by different segments of the community, provide information and educate sexual partners to avoid activities that lead to the transfer of semen, blood and other body fluids. Another measure of the success of education programs is a reduction in STD infection. In New South Wales there have been marked reductions both in HIV infections (from 2796 in 1985 to 352 at June 1993; National Centre in HIV Epidemiology 1993) and in gonorrhoea and syphilis infections over the same period (males and females seen at STD clinics). The belief underpinning the educational programs is that knowledge of HIV/AIDS translates into changes in sexual practices, changes that result in a reduction in HIV/AIDS infection rates. The reductions have been attributed to heightened awareness of the risk of HIV infection. But recent overseas evidence indicating a reversal in the reduction of HIV/AIDS and STDs is a matter for concern. 'Rebound' effects in HIV/AIDS have been reported in Seattle and other US cities and in Amsterdam (McConaghy 1993). While HIV rebound effects have not been evident in Australia, a more carefree attitude towards the threat of HIV/AIDS is being reported by Sydney-based sex workers who since 1992 have seen both sex workers and clients becoming less vigilant with safe sex practices.

14

FEMINISM AND FEMALE PROSTITUTION

Barbara Sullivan

Over the last hundred years feminism has been the only political movement to regard prostitution as a central political issue. This is because, for most feminists, female prostitution has broad implications for the negotiation of power between men and women, and is related both to other forms of work that women do and to other relationships involving sexual-economic exchange, including marriage. This means that women — whether they are prostitutes or not — share a number of common problems. As the anarchist feminist Emma Goldman (1969, p 179) asserted in 1917: 'Nowhere is woman treated according to the merit of her work, but rather as a sex ... it is merely a question of degree whether she sells herself to one man, in or out of marriage, or to many men'.

This sort of approach creates both problems and possibilities for the formation of political alliances between sex workers and feminists. In emphasising the commonalities between women, between prostitutes and non-prostitutes, new avenues of political cooperation are possible and these have the potential to improve the position of all women, including sex workers. It is also important, however, that the significant differences between groups of women are not underestimated. Sex workers have some specific problems — for example, in relation to police and legal harassment — which other women will not share (at least not to the same extent) and may not even understand.

While some sex workers and sex worker organisations have explicitly adopted feminist approaches over the last two decades (see, for example, Margo St James in Pheterson 1989), many are highly critical of feminism. They argue that feminist approaches to prostitution are wrong and offensive to sex workers and they accuse feminists of being both anti-men and anti-sex (Bell 1987; Pheterson 1989). Sax, however, argues that the prejudices on both sides are fuelled by 'fables' about prostitution and feminism and by negative media images of the women's movement. In her view, 'the misunderstanding is especially caused by the stigmatisation of whores' and this allows feminists and sex workers to be 'played off against one another' (Sax in Delacoste and Alexander 1988).

While this is clearly an important issue, it does not go far enough in explaining many of the present tensions between feminists and sex workers or in explaining the ambivalence which many Australian feminists exhibit in extending political support to prostitutes. As Perkins (1991, p 387) has argued, the women's movement has never mobilised mass political support for prostitutes despite the significant problems facing women in the prostitution industry and the larger issues at stake regarding sexuality and men's power. At least partly, this is because prostitution raises uncomfortable questions for non-prostitute women, including many feminists, about their own relationships with men. However, I would argue that there are also substantial theoretical problems within feminism which inhibit the development of feminist political alliances with sex workers. In this chapter I explore recent feminist approaches to prostitution drawing out strengths and weaknesses, problems and inconsistencies. I argue that there is an urgent need for a feminist re-evaluation of sex work, one which both values the work that prostitutes do and maintains a focus on broader patterns of sex-based power.

PROSTITUTION AND FEMINIST POLITICS

Since the 1860s feminists have waged numerous campaigns around the issue of prostitution and these have often had contradictory effects on prostitute women themselves. On the one hand, feminists have acted directly in support of prostitutes. In the late nineteenth century and early twentieth century 'first wave' feminists in Britain and Australia fought against laws which provided for State registration of prostitute women, compulsory medical examinations, and detainment in a lock hospital — or jail beyond the terms of an original sentence — for those prostitute women found to have a sexually transmitted disease (Walkowitz 1980; Allen 1988). Feminist leaders, like Josephine Butler in Britain and Rose Scott in New South Wales, argued that such laws were degrading and unjust; they penalised women prostitutes but not their male clients for engaging in commercial sex and thus offered State support for the sexual prerogatives which men already enjoyed in relation to the sex industry. On the other hand, many first wave feminists also lobbied for the introduction of new criminal penalties on prostitution. These feminists were concerned to protect women and girls from sexual exploitation in the prostitution industry and to limit men's sexual power. However, as we now know, laws like these were disastrous for prostitute women. Despite an intended focus on bludgers (pimps) and the owners and operators of brothels, it was prostitute women who were most likely to be arrested and imprisoned under anti-prostitution laws (Allen 1990).

There are many similarities between present day feminist campaigns around prostitution and those waged between 80 and 100 years ago. Feminists in Australia are still concerned with prostitution both as part of a general involvement with sexual politics (the way that sex and power are related) and of a specific concern about the unjust treatment handed out to prostitutes. Although most prostitution laws in Australia are now couched in gender-neutral language, the buyers (men) and sellers (predominantly women) of sexual services are treated differently within the legal and judicial system. While male clients constitute the single largest numerical group within the prostitution industry, it is still prostitutes who are most likely to be arrested, fined and jailed (Sullivan 1992). Consequently, many Australian feminists support the decriminalisation of prostitution as a way of defending the civil and legal rights of prostitutes. Since the early 1970s feminists and feminist organisations such as the Women's Electoral Lobby have lobbied governments about the decriminalisation of prostitution. Such feminist support was instrumental in the decriminalisation of street soliciting initiated in New South Wales in 1979 and in the decriminalisation of brothel prostitution in Victoria during the 1980s.

However, the overall achievements in prostitution law reform over the last two decades have been quite limited. It is notable that many Australian feminists who support such law reform are also ambivalent about the extent and form of a 'good' decriminalisation process; very few advocate a complete decriminalisation and most look to the maintenance of some restrictions. For example, the feminist law academic Marcia Neave — who conducted the Victorian Government's Inquiry into Prostitution (Victorian Government 1985) — argued in favour of restrictions on prostitution advertising (in order to reduce the demand for prostitution) and a limited decriminalisation of street and brothel prostitution. There are also feminists in Australia who oppose decriminalisation; like their 'first wave' counterparts they want to use the law to protect women and girls from exploitation within the sex industry and to limit the sexual prerogatives of men. Consequently they lobby against measures — such as the licensing of brothels — which are seen to offer 'legalisation' or State endorsement of the sex industry. In Queensland, for example, feminists recently lobbied both for and against proposals by the Queensland Criminal Justice Commission that sex workers and brothel owners should be licensed and legalised.

It is clear, then, that there has been no single feminist politics in Australia in relation to prostitution. Feminists, like sex workers themselves, have adopted a range of different approaches to prostitution. However, the vast majority of feminists argue that there is something 'wrong' with prostitution. There are a few, like Gayle Rubin (1984) in the United States, who regard prostitution as 'harmless' or who embrace sexual politics which endorses all sexual activity, including prostitution. Feminists who oppose prostitution might, in the short term, be prepared to seek pragmatic solutions to some of the particular problems facing sex workers (for example by supporting decriminalisation) but they also usually have an overt or covert desire to abolish prostitution. This desire is based on specific judgements about prostitution as an activity harmful for women — both women who are sex workers and those who are not — and on more general arguments about the nature of 'good' sexual and work relationships. It is of course necessary to make judgements, moral and otherwise, particularly if broader feminist aims — to improve the situation of all women (including sex workers) — are to be met. In the remainder of this chapter I critically examine key feminist judgements about prostitution.

AUSTRALIAN FEMINIST THEORY AND PROSTITUTION

In the 1970s feminists in Australia, Britain and the United States began to draw out the connections between marriage, prostitution and other forms of 'women's work' (see, for example, Millett 1971; Aitkin 1978; Scutt 1979). By the mid-1980s, it was clear that two quite separate views were emerging within feminism. Some argued that prostitution was 'work' but that it also had a lot in common with other gendered relationships, including marriage. But other feminists argued that there were vital distinctions between prostitution and other forms of work as well as between prostitution and other sexual relationships; these distinctions were then used to support a feminist condemnation of prostitution.

The view that prostitution is 'work' which has a lot in common with other 'women's work' is premised on feminist arguments about the servicing of men which women undertake in both their public and their private lives. From this perspective all women — whether they are secretaries, prostitutes or academics — are forced into servicing, sexualised roles as part of their employment. It is then simply the degree of overtness which separates the prostitute from other women workers (Scutt 1979). This sort of argument has been explored in a variety of different ways by recent Australian feminists. Anne Summers (1975), for example, argued that prostitution had played a central role in Australian history. This was both because many of the convict women transported to the Australian colonies between 1788 and 1867 were casual prostitutes in Britain and because the organisation of convict settlements meant that all women (particularly convict women but, at a later point, also free immigrant and Aboriginal women) were subjected to an 'enforced whoredom': in order to survive they were forced to trade sexual services for food, clothing and shelter.

According to Summers this situation shifted in the colonial period in Australia when women were increasingly divided into 'good' and 'bad', either 'God's Police' or 'Damned Whores'. It became the assigned role of 'good' women (a category that included married women, celibate spinsters and early feminists) to discipline and divert 'bad' women from their evil ways. But the overall effect of this process was to divide and classify women as either 'maternal figures who are not ... sexual or as whores who are exclusively sexual'. Summers argued that these stereotypes functioned to discipline all women for they ignored or actively repressed 'good' women's sexual needs (for 'good' women were represented as asexual) while all sexually active women were 'bad' and to be treated like prostitutes. Thus it was in the interests of all women for these stereotypes of appropriate sexual behaviour to be broken down. Summers thought that one way this could be achieved was for 'good' women' to refuse their traditional policing functions and for feminists to publicly identify themselves with those who were designated as 'bad' — that is, prostitutes, lesbians and prisoners.

Summers' arguments were taken up by many Australian feminists in the 1970s and early 1980s. Like Jackson and Otto (1984) they argued that the dichotomy between female prostitutes and non-prostitute women was 'a form of social control of female sexuality' which 'makes the support of prostitutes by other women a matter of self-interest rather than moral imperative'. However, this approach was also seen to involve a significant 'dilemma' for feminists: how to provide effective support for prostitutes in the short term without compromising a feminist opposition to prostitution in the long term (Jackson and Otto 1984). While prostitution was regarded as the most blatant form of sexual exploitation, such exploitation was also seen to take place in other areas and relationships, such as marriage. Moreover, like all women, prostitutes had a right to bodily self-determination. If the laws controlling prostitution were indeed 'laws on property, forbidding women to sell something (their bodies) that can only belong to men' (Bacon 1976–77), then feminists could not adopt a stance which advocated the legal suppression of prostitution despite what was regarded as its inherent sexual exploitation.

Several Australian feminists argued that the resolution of this 'dilemma' could be achieved by a focus on prostitution as work (Aitkin 1978; Jackson and Otto 1984). In this way feminist support could be confined to areas of immediate concern to prostitute women such as wages and working conditions. Consequently feminists could lobby for the decriminalisation of prostitution as a necessary precondition for improvements in the working conditions of sex workers. The analysis of prostitution as work was widely adopted by feminist activists in Australia during the late 1970s. As suggested above, this did not mean that feminist arguments about the need to abolish prostitution disappeared; this issue was temporarily 'set aside' as immediate industrial issues came to be regarded as the most appropriate focus of a feminist response to prostitution. The feminist conceptualisation of female prostitution as women's work did provide an important initial impetus in some states for the formation of new political alliances between feminists and sex workers. Consequently, arguments about the need to decriminalise prostitution began to emerge on mainstream political agendas.

THE FEMINIST CRITIQUE OF PROSTITUTION AS WORK

Despite the political possibilities which would appear to be attached to the conceptualisation of prostitution as work, some feminists from the 1980s onwards began to argue against this formulation; they argued that there were strategic disadvantages (for feminists and sex workers) in adopting a political/theoretical focus on prostitution as work or, quite separately, that prostitution was not like other paid work. Socialist feminists like Biles (1980), for example, argued that it was wrong to call everyone who worked in the sex industry a sex worker; in class terms prostitutes did not form a homogeneous group and could vary from 'the most extreme case of exploited and disadvantaged workers to ... women who own and manage the brothel or parlour in which they work'. The term sex worker, then, tended to obscure both important class differences and the struggle within the industry between sex workers and sex capitalists.

From a different perspective Cheryl Overs (1989) argued that there were disadvantages in addressing prostitution as sex work because the primary object of analysis remained the prostitute and — as in traditional analyses of prostitution — the client was rendered invisible. Thus the desires and aspirations of male clients — and the ways that these represent broader cultural practices and patterns of masculinity — remain both unprioritised and assigned to the realm of 'natural' male sexual needs. The visibility of prostitutes and the invisibility of clients has been an important problem in traditional accounts of prostitution. It is only since the AIDS crisis that research on the sex industry in Australia has begun to look at client behaviour.

In the 1980s and 1990s some feminists also began to argue that there were clear differences between prostitution and other paid work. Recently, for example, Christine Overall (1992, pp 705–24) has concluded that 'sex work differs in a crucial way from other forms of women's labour'. However, she found that many of the arguments which were used to condemn prostitution were without foundation. First, Overall examined the view that female prostitution was problematic because it involved particular dangers for women, such as disease, indignity, physical and psychological abuse and emotional pain. She concluded that danger and injury could not be considered essential elements of sex work. These factors, as Roberta Perkins (1991) has recently demonstrated in the Australian context, may be absent altogether in sex work. They may also, however, be a specific consequence of the illegality of many prostitution-related activities. Clearly, danger and injury are not unique to sex work because women are frequently subjected to disease, injury and psychological abuse in other workplaces such as offices and factories (as well as in their own homes). The fact that sex work occurs under a wide range of conditions and circumstances — some better, some worse — needs to be acknowledged.

Second, Overall examined the view that female sex work was wrong because women were coerced into it. She concluded that all workers face an absence of choice in relation to their work and that the presence of coercion and the absence of consent were features of many women's activities under capitalism and male dominance. Thus, there is a need to acknowledge both the presence of (economic) coercion in paid work generally and the agency which some women exercise in relation to sex work. Overall (1992, p 713) argued that: 'Some sex workers (perhaps most) appear to have little or no choice about their work; but some do have some alternatives, are explicitly conscious of them, and deliberately choose prostitution'.

Third, Overall examines the claim that sex work should be condemned because of its lack of reciprocity. Feminists and others often argue that intimate personal acts should not be sold on the market but should be exchanged between equals in a respectful relationship. As Overall points out (p 715), however, the retailing of intimacy is a common feature of modern life and of other paid work like therapy and massage. I would also want to add that, in the case of both therapy and massage, equality and reciprocity are not usually features of the professional relationship. Indeed, it is only in the last few decades that these values have been associated with 'normal' heterosexual relations. The enormous differences between men and women, particularly in terms of economic, social and political resources, mean that equality and reciprocity are rarely features of real relationships between adult men and women. If fairness, kindness and respect were also acknowledged as important values — both in the marketplace and in intimate relations — then there would be no reason why prostitution should continue to suffer a definitional exclusion from the realm of morally acceptable work.

Having established several grounds on which prostitution could *not* be distinguished from other types of women's work under capitalism, Overall goes on to conclude that there are other feminist grounds for opposing sex work. She argues that most of the servicing work which women presently do for men is 'reversible', that there is nothing in the nature of nurturing and domestic work which would prevent it being done by men for women, by men for men or by women for women in a postcapitalist, postpatriarchal world. Moreover:

> The value of office workers, sales clerks, cooks, cleaners and child care workers has a value independent of the (present) conditions of sexual and economic inequality under which it is done, and much of it would still be socially necessary in a postcapitalist, postpatriarchal world. (Overall 1992, p 718)

In Overall's view sex work is not 'reversible' because it involves an inherent 'commoditisation' of sex (which could not exist in a postcapitalist world) and because prostitution is essentially premised on conditions of sexual and economic inequality (which would disappear in a postpatriarchal society).

In my view this sort of feminist approach demonstrates a fundamental disrespect for the work that prostitutes presently do. There is no inherent reason why sex work should not also be 'reversible' (unless one adopts essentialist notions about male *and* female sexuality) or that in a postcapitalist, postpatriarchal world sex work would not be regarded as valuable. Even at present there are clear grounds on which to argue for a revaluation of the work which prostitutes do. Obviously, clients value the work of sex workers because they often pay a significant amount of money for these services. But sex workers also have specific skills and knowledge — for example, about the practicality of recommended regimes for safe sex — which are of value to the wider community. This knowledge has already been utilised by researchers and by state health departments in Australia in the planning of general AIDS prevention programs. Sex workers also have specific skills in the production of fantasy and sexual pleasure although, at present, this is a skill wholly focused on men. In a postpatriarchal world, where sex and power were connected (or not connected) in quite different ways from our own, sex work could well be performed by men or women and for male or female clients. In this case a desire to know more about (men's and women's) sexual pleasure might be the main reason for employing a sex worker.

Of course, this sort of approach is premised on an acceptance of a wide range of different sorts of sexual relationships. Sex is not inherently 'sacred'; it might be a part of lifelong partnership and parenthood but it might also be a part of non-monogamous, non-romantic relationships focused on play, companionship, learning about the world — and earning a living. I am not suggesting here that there are no problems within the prostitution industry as it is presently constituted; clearly, prostitute women often face substantial problems and the industry itself is quite blatantly a bastion of men's power. However, the sex industry is not unique in this regard because gendered power is a problem right across the board in

Australian society. My main point here is that problems and power in the sex industry are *contestable* and are not essential attributes of sex work and sex workers.

Carol Pateman (1988) has recently argued that prostitution is not like other work because the prostitution contract is not like other employment contracts. It is important to keep in mind that the main focus of Pateman's work is not prostitution per se but a critique within traditional political theory of liberal contractarianism. She is mainly concerned about the way that concepts of 'freedom' and 'consent' are used in the modern day to oppress women and workers. Pateman emphasises the coercive nature of all paid employment under capitalism but argues that the position of prostitutes is different from other workers both because of the dangers involved in sex work (for example, the fact that prostitutes are sought out by serial killers such as Jack the Ripper) and because of the work itself. In her view, it is the 'embodied' nature of female prostitution which means that it is not like other paid work. This is because, economically or otherwise, vulnerable women are coerced into 'selling sexual access to their bodies'. In our culture and time such 'sale of sexual access' is regarded as 'sale of self' (which is not the case with other embodied forms of labour such as professional sport, massage or therapy). According to Pateman, this means that prostitution looks less like an employment contract for sexual services and more like sexual slavery which, of course, is to be condemned.

It is important to note that Pateman does not argue that prostitution *is* sexual slavery; only that, in our culture and time, it *appears* like this (and consequently is usually experienced as such). Pateman raises an important issue here although it is as much about cultural meanings and their effects on individuals as about prostitution contracts. Those who reject the argument that prostitution is the 'sale of bodies' (and, therefore, sexual slavery) often contend that prostitutes sell only sexual services or the illusion of sexual intimacy. Clearly, however, it is difficult (if not impossible) to 'step outside' cultural meanings. For the community at large — and consequently often for both sex workers and clients — sex work is regarded as a profound sale of self. This is one of the main reasons why sex workers are disparaged and abused (by the community, clients, the legal and judicial system etc.) and why it is difficult to command respect for the work that sex workers do.

It is necessary, however, to acknowledge that different cultural understandings of prostitution can and do exist in the Australian community. In popular culture as well as in feminist history and fiction, prostitute women are often represented not as sexual slaves but as rebels and resistors of male power and as women who are cleverly seeking to maximise their conditions and opportunities in a problematic environment (see for example Daniels 1984; Horn and Pringle 1984). Pateman quite correctly draws attention to dominant cultural meanings of prostitution and to the effects of these on women. However, she then proceeds to reinforce these meanings by treating them as a suitable basis for a feminist condemnation of prostitution. Even from the perspective of Pateman's own argument, feminist efforts to intervene on behalf of prostitutes and to oppose the present practice of prostitution could be focused on shifting cultural meanings and on bringing marginalised discourses about prostitutes as rebels and empowered women into the mainstream. If prostitution is problematic because of contingent, culturally based assumptions about the bodily submission involved in sex work, then a feminist condemnation of sex work based on its perception as 'sexual slavery' will only reinforce those cultural assumptions. Such an approach will not advance the position of sex workers (who already bear the burden of a broad cultural condemnation) and it will not advance a feminist challenge to gendered practices within the sex industry.

To be fair to Pateman, though, her principal argument against female prostitution is about the relationship which she sees at present between the sex industry and male dominance generally. In her view the fact that men can purchase sexual access to women is intimately connected to the maintenance of their public and private power. She argues that masculinity and femininity are sexual identities which are confirmed in sexual activity and, in particular, via heterosexual intercourse; it is then in heterosexual intercourse that men create and maintain their sense of themselves as men and as women's masters. While Pateman does not emphasise this point, sexual intercourse is clearly the crux of the problem. But this sort of activity occurs in a wide range of heterosexual relationships, including both marriage and prostitution. While Pateman is not a supporter of marriage, she argues that it is the public nature of the sex industry which makes it particularly worthy of feminist condemnation because:

> When women's bodies are on sale as commodities in the capitalist market, the terms of the original contract (which is about men's civil power) cannot be forgotten; the law of male sex-right is publicly affirmed, and men gain public acknowledgment as women's sexual masters. (Pateman 1988, p 208)

Although Pateman's general point (about the connection between heterosexual activity and public power) is a convincing one, she does tend to understate the role of other public institutions like marriage. If men confirm themselves as women's civil masters in heterosexual activity within public institutions then both prostitution and marriage are problematic.

FEMINISM, PROSTITUTION AND MARRIAGE

Since the 1970s most feminists have emphasised the connections between marriage and female prostitution. Jocelynne Scutt (1979), for example, argued that marriage was a form of prostitution in which women received poor recompense for their work, were more vulnerable to violence (from their husbands) and had less control over their daily lives than sex workers. More recently, Tabet (1991) has argued that there is 'a continuum of forms of sexual service, not a dichotomy between marriage and the other relations implying sexual-economic exchange'.

I note, however, a disturbing tendency in some recent feminist work to draw new distinctions between female prostitution and marriage and to use these distinctions as a basis for condemning prostitution. I have already suggested, above, that Pateman makes an unfounded distinction between marriage and prostitution. Shrage (1989), for example, has argued that commercial sex, unlike marriage, is not 'reformable'. She contends that the actions of female sex workers and their clients are in complicity with the patriarchal domination of all women. In her view we should not blame sex workers but we should condemn prostitution. Christine

Overall (1992) would appear to agree with Shrage because she suggests that female sex workers perpetuate rather than challenge patriarchy. On this basis it 'therefore makes sense to defend prostitutes' entitlement to do their work but not to defend prostitution itself as a practice under patriarchy'.

In my view this position does *not* make sense. If the sex industry is particularly responsible for the subordination of women then it is not logical for feminists to defend prostitutes' rights to do sex work. But the argument that sex workers are particularly complicit in the patriarchal domination of women also does not make sense. As Elizabeth Grosz (forthcoming) has argued, there are no pure positions outside patriarchy and phallocentrism. None of us can escape complicity because our 'struggles are inherently *impure*, inherently bound up with what one struggles against'. We need then to refuse 'the fantasy of a position safe or insulated from what it criticises'. This makes it impossible to engage in work, political or sexual activity and not to some degree also be complicit in the perpetuation of existing structures of power; of course, non-engagement is equally impossible. This does not mean that all activities and relationships are equal; some may 'stretch' and challenge (rather than totally subvert) dominant paradigms while others will not take issue with the status quo. But it is not clear to me that many female prostitutes (as well as many married women) do not already challenge and stretch dominant paradigms in their personal and working lives.

This sort of position means that I disagree with Perkins (1991) who has argued that sex work is inherently empowering for women. She contends that a feminist re-evaluation of prostitution is needed because 'female prostitution is a social situation in which women have more power over sexual interactions than in any other circumstance involving both sexes interacting' (p 389); consequently, female prostitution should be regarded as a 'female control base' (p 391). Theoretically, and in the patriarchal imagination, prostitution and 'normal' sexual relations have been equated; in reality 'prostitutes are ... rebels of the patriarchy rather than totally subservient to it' (p 390). According to Perkins, because female prostitutes can set limits on the work they do, acquire economic power and 'knowledge of true male sexuality' they are 'a far cry from the common feminist assumption of prostitutes as the most explicit example of female oppression' (p 349).

Perkins' empirical investigation of a group of female sex workers in Sydney *does* provide a valuable corrective to feminist accounts of prostitution which represent prostitutes as special victims of patriarchy. As she suggests, there is a need for a feminist re-evaluation of prostitution. Her research indicates that female prostitutes are like other, 'normal', women and their clients are like other, 'normal', men. Also, many female sex workers would appear to assert a significant amount of control over their working lives and, like other employees (even under capitalism), can often feel empowered by their work. Perkins found that most of the women in her sample had not been arrested, raped or subjected to other assaults at work and the vast majority did not take drugs or, alternatively, did not increase their drug usage as a result of engaging in sex work. Moreover, they were more likely than other women to be orgasmic in their private lives.

O'Leary (unpublished) has recently criticised Perkins' study on several grounds that are convincing. She says that Perkins' sample is concentrated on the upper echelons of the prostitute workforce — brothel workers and call girls — and has not included ex-workers. Consequently, her results tend to be more favourable and to 'gloss over' the dangers which sex workers face. Certainly, while most women face significant dangers in their domestic relationships, they do not face the range of issues which female prostitutes do in the course of their *working* lives. Prostitution should still be regarded as a dangerous trade for women. O'Leary is also critical of Perkins' view that prostitution inherently empowers women. She says that female prostitutes can be empowered and empowering only within pre-existing patriarchal confines and that what is needed is an overall challenge to patriarchy. On the first part of this point I would obviously agree with O'Leary; as suggested above, none of us can step outside existing structures of power and dominance. However, in the end this means that I disagree with both O'Leary *and* Perkins. Prostitution is not inherently empowering for women but also it is not reasonable for feminists to condemn female prostitutes or even the sex industry for failing to deliver a killing blow to patriarchy.

CONCLUSION

Prostitution lies at an important intersection of feminist debates about theory and politics. As Roberta Perkins has argued, this means that movements for prostitutes' rights are well situated within feminist movements. But feminists also have a lot to gain from an engagement with sex workers and prostitution. For example, I had 'not noticed' the theoretical problems in many feminist accounts of prostitution — although I had been reading them for several years — until forced to deal with the angry responses of sex workers. At first I thought this anger could be explained largely in terms of a failure of communication between sex workers and feminists and by differences of opinion about the meaning of sexuality and sex work. Now, however, I would also want to acknowledge significant problems within many feminist accounts of prostitution which mean that they disparage both sex work and sex workers. Feminists need to develop accounts of prostitution which are respectful of what prostitutes do and yet maintain a focus on gendered structures of power in all work and personal relations. This means that we should question feminist accounts of prostitution which emphasise the distinctions between sex work and other 'women's work' or between female prostitution and marriage *and* which use these distinctions as a ground for a specific condemnation of prostitution. Feminist approaches which attempt to support sex workers but not the sex industry do not make logical or practical sense.

This is not to suggest that the differences between female sex workers and other women, between prostitution and other paid work or between prostitution and other sexual relationships should not be addressed. There are many specific issues and problems which demand attention. But differences as well as commonalities need to be acknowledged if effective political alliances between feminists and sex workers are to be forged in Australia; this would be to the benefit of both feminists and sex workers.

PART IV

WORKING WITH WORKERS

15

SOCIAL WORKERS AND SEX WORKERS
Louise Webb and Janice Elms

A lot of clients come in and see us and they want some help, some support, some counselling and some answers, and they know that there's a difference between them and us, and that's kind of like a barrier we need to cross in some way. Because they come in with a preconceived idea about the social worker, and I think that they have a perception and an expectation of us. And what we do in our work is to equalise the relationship as much as possible — it sounds like a lovely, good theory, but I think in practice we do it as much as possible, because we're respectful of our clients.

This statement was made by a social worker working with sex workers in Sydney. But, it might very easily have been made by a sex worker with reference to *her* clients. This chapter aims to bridge the boundary between the two types of workers by exploring the similarities and differences and the educational and counselling aspects of the work. Our task centres on the fact that community attitudes towards sex work are influenced by the way sex is portrayed in our society and that it is the role of the social worker and the sex worker in partnership to change those attitudes.

There is an attitude about women and sex and being a commodity and being at men's disposal and a lot of the laws reflect this. It's the community attitude towards prostitution. It's not so much any one of us as individuals. It's really, if you see prostitutes in a certain way, and then as a community pass a law, that puts all these people behind windows like reptiles then that commodity tone gets completely reinforced. I mean, it's like you're walking down the street and you're thinking what's available — in a real sense you're window shopping. (Tracey, social worker)

I think we're all prostitutes. Remember that! We all prostitute ourselves in some way. Selling yourself in general, presenting yourself. Not really sexually, but you know. It is one of the oldest professions in the world. There is nothing wrong with it. (Sylvie, sex worker)

In social work there are two types of services which sex workers are likely to access regularly. Social welfare agencies and advocacy organisations are sometimes linked but can often be at different poles. They both feel a certain affinity for sex workers but often on different levels. Social welfare agencies are concerned with primary health care, child rearing, emotional and social well-being of the individual client. Advocacy agencies strive to advance the rights of sex workers as a social group and to see their individual needs recognised. Social welfare agencies often initially educate sex workers on matters such as safer sex practices; advocacy organisations work together with sex workers to extend that education to the general public in order to change community attitudes. It is now accepted that sex workers participate in community education campaigns, give evidence before parliamentary committees and are interviewed in the media as authorities on the sex industry.

There are links between social workers and sex workers both in their professional arenas and their personal qualities. Both sex workers and social workers struggle to work for a living wage. Interestingly, neither profession has accomplished great improvements in its perceived status, perhaps because each is dominated by women. Or perhaps it is due to the fact that caring is required in both fields.

A lot of the girls have regulars. They even have guys who pay them $100 just to sit around and talk to them for an hour. Which is one of the better jobs. You just sit down with the guy for an hour and a half or an hour and just listen to his problems. He just wants a bit of female company. They don't want the sex, or anything like that. Sometimes they just want a bit of a kiss and a cuddle and a fondle or something like that, but that's it. (Sara, sex worker)

Individual personality is a key to both professions and the results, or how much they get out of their work, are dependent on how much they put into it. A social worker is extremely ineffective if she has no interest in her client. A sex worker builds up a stable of regular clients by giving more to her work, and hence has a greater financial return.

I see a completely different clientele because mostly women I see are in parlours and they're working for a number of reasons, most of them because their husband's out of work, their partner's out of work or in jail, they need to finish school. It's so different and because there is such a high turnover you get the sense that no one's really in the industry for very long. Some women want to open up, want to tell you all about their experience, because they have no one else to tell and that to me is always a real boost because they feel comfortable with me. A large number of women I see no one knows. Family and friends think they are doing office work or receptionist. It's completely hidden and no one can know. To be able to have access to talk to someone about it — even just to help them integrate with their partner at home because sometimes one of the most difficult things is to leave work and go home and be sexual with the person that they're really intimate with. I suppose for me that's a real boost and I think its a boost for them too — to know that they do have someone to talk to. (Michelle, social worker)

As a result of the individual service that both provide, confidentiality is a strict requirement of both professions. Confidentiality is an important matter for clients in each group, and in many cases sex workers also aim to keep their private identity unknown. It provides them with protection for themselves and for their families. It also helps to separate their working lives from their private, personal lives.

> I tell stories, lie to personal questions. You get good after a while. I have a different name, do my hair differently, speak differently, hold myself differently. I have a different life, and I am providing a service. (Sandy, sex worker)

The distinct separation between public and private lives is something that may differentiate types of social workers. Social workers who work directly on the street with sex workers probably also share a social life with them. Other social workers may specialise in areas such as housing or welfare and see sex workers purely as clients, not as friends or allies. They both provide a service to the sex worker and must both remember that her needs come first.

> The difficulty is that there seems to be a need to have some long-standing affiliation with those venues and if you stop going there you lose contact very quickly and it takes a long time to build back up. The best contact I ever had with a group was when I myself was out partying on the same four nights a week, so in some ways it was becoming not only my professional work but part of my social life ... I've withdrawn from that scene to some extent, I've lost contact with the group. It's very difficult unless you are out there at least two nights a week on a consistent basis to do that work. It is often very personality-based to be able to hang around the Taxi club [an all-night club] and blend in — I like it, but there are people at work that have big issues about going to those venues. (Lisa, social worker)

Sex workers and social workers must tailor their language to suit their respective clients. Clients' experience and educational levels vary widely, and both workers must be able to converse on many different levels. A social worker's client might be a sex worker who has been on the streets since her early teenage years and has had only primary education, or might be a graduate student who is involved in sex work to put herself through university. A sex worker's clients might range from a leading politician or educator to someone from another country who can barely speak English. Both workers have to be able to understand the needs of the wide range of clients whom they see and also to put them at ease. They must be able to communicate and gain the trust of their clients.

Education and counselling are a service that both workers must provide to their clients. AIDS awareness, infectious disease information and safer sex practices are matters that clients must be informed of if social workers and sex workers are to provide a competent service. The exchange of this information often involves highly charged emotional issues, such as women's sexuality and gender power relations. As well, social workers aim to empower sex workers and to teach them techniques of empowering themselves. Feminist attitudes and ideas are very effective methods to use. Rape, assault and the rights of sex workers are key issues that social workers and sex workers discuss. Most social workers endeavour to aid their sex industry clients in recognising their rights in this regard; to help them understand that, just because they provide sex as a service, no one has the *right* to take it from them or to rape them. Not the police, the clients or anyone.

Through the help of her social workers Sara has recognised her rights:

> The workers make the rules. If a guy makes them do it — that's rape. Stop, you have had your time, your time is up, and if they don't stop — that's rape. If I say 'no' and you don't do what I say — that's rape. I'm not afraid to put you up. Whether you're a worker or not, whether it is an older worker or a new one, you have the right to go to the police, just like any male or female in this world, whether you are a prostitute or not. It's not fair the way a lot of girls get treated like dirt. They get pushed over. They are not there to be used and abused. They are there to do a job. A lot of the girls just let themselves get used and abused — half the time because they have no control over it any more.

As Lucy, a social worker points out, when you listen to a lot of sex workers' life stories you find they get assaulted one way or another in the course of their day. And a lot wouldn't even dream of going anywhere near a support service because they know, as social workers know, that the chances of getting rape cases up and running are next to nothing. Sex workers are not getting proper sexual assault support services, let alone any hope of redress, because there is no real social justice for them in the courts. They are a category of people whom the community does not understand or approve of. They are robbed of social justice because of social attitudes. The only way to address the social injustice is to start providing real support services that are prepared to fight on their behalf. To do this there needs to be a buildup of group pressure to get the whole question of the assault of sex workers into the awareness of the general public. Services need to be able to support sex workers and to gain their trust, so that workers may feel comfortable in telling someone about an assault and have confidence that they will be believed and helped. Services need to care for the sex workers from the initial disclosure through to the court case, and often afterwards.

The violence that sex workers experience does not differ from the violence that is inflicted upon other women in society. Women in general have struggled very hard to have society recognise that violence against women is wrong and will not be accepted; this fight is still underway for the sex worker. It may be compared with the struggle women have had to get domestic violence recognised as a criminal offence. While it is a criminal offence to rape a sex worker, the courts, which may be reflecting societal attitudes, have not anywhere near adequately acknowledged this. Rape of sex workers is still rape. Society needs to recognise that sex work is a job like any other. And that sex workers are human beings trying to do a job and trying to do it properly.

> It's a job like any other. When I think about going to work, I don't think about going to work and having sex for money, I think about going to work, making money and socialising because I feel that social thing. Everyone there is about 25 years old, we all talk, we go out together occasionally. I can't see myself giving up the money and the lifestyle. It's a good life really. (Sandy, sex worker)

> Some of the advantages of working in the sex industry are that they can work from home, they can determine their hours, they can study, pursue other interests, and attend to family needs. (Leanne, social worker)

Street sex workers work independently of any formally structured group of colleagues or other workers, which differs from the situation of workers in a brothel. In this sense they can be very

isolated, though there is a sense of rivalry because they are competing for the same customers. But at times the isolation can be
overcome. For example, when a sex worker is in need they all help.

> One good thing about it is that they all stick together and they all
> watch each other's backs. They can rip each other off, but they all
> watch out for each other. (Sara, sex worker)

Social workers also can find difficulty vis-à-vis the isolation of
some sex workers. Liaising with clients at nightclubs and bars does
raise certain ethical issues. These are professional issues that have
been around for 20 years or more. As another social worker puts it:

> Do you sit there in a bar and have an orange juice and do you
> announce to every single person that comes up to talk to you, 'Hi,
> I'm a social worker'? It doesn't tend to go down too well. Then
> there's that confusion about who you are and why you're there and
> whether you're socialising or whether you're there for them. And
> too bad if you really are socialising because they'll assume you're
> there for them. And the boundary gets muddier and muddier till
> half the time you don't know whether you're socialising or on the
> job. (Tracey, social worker)

Social workers and social work agencies have difficulty in inte-
grating their work with individual clients and working for social and
political change. Social work agencies can create barriers between
sex workers and social workers which are difficult to deal with. The
boundary between a street social worker's work life and her private
life is very difficult to qualify. She must be a professional, but must
still attend to the needs of her clients. Where and how to access
clients is often a very real ethical dilemma. One street sex worker
pointed out that she could not imagine going out and having
dinner with her clients as escort workers do. This would be a
boundary for the street worker. Brothel workers also place certain
boundaries around the services that they provide in order to separate their private life from their work; no kissing is a common rule.
But for the social worker who wants and needs to moderate the
distance between herself and her client the rules are not so simple.

As we have indicated, part of the social worker's job is to help sex workers know their rights and how to utilise them. Sex workers are often vulnerable to abuse by the system because of the often transient nature of their occupation. Social workers can also help empower their sex-working clients to balance the power relationship with their customers. Teaching protective behaviours is a necessary part of caring for sex workers.

There are significant commonalities between sex workers and social workers. They share many common career burdens and roles. Given the role model of a competent social worker many sex workers have gone on to become social workers themselves and to work for their colleagues. The two groups need more generally to break down the barriers and realise that they can be friends and allies, working towards social and political change.

16

A HEALTH SERVICE FOR SEX WORKERS

Ingrid van Beek

The Kirketon Road Centre was established in April 1987, as a result of a recommendation of the New South Wales Select Committee of the Legislative Assembly Upon Prostitution. The Select Committee had been appointed in March 1983 with Patrick Rogan MP as Chairman, to investigate and report upon the criminal, social, public health and community welfare aspects of prostitution in New South Wales. The Committee met on 76 occasions and in April 1986 published its findings in what became known as the Rogan Report. One of the recommendations was that:

> The Government fund, and the Department of Health administer, a multi-purpose health centre in the Kings Cross area. The centre might be built upon existing facilities, perhaps in cooperation with St Vincent's Hospital. It should provide complete STD screening, diagnosis, and treatment; plus contact-tracing, counselling, contraceptive advice and treatment, Pap smears, and general health services. The aim of the department should be to make the centre as fully accessible and acceptable to prostitutes and other persons

who live and work in the inner city as possible. (Parliament of NSW 1986) (see Appendix in the present book for the findings pertaining to this recommendation.)

The recommendation was considered by the NSW Government and endorsed by the State Minister for Health, Barrie Unsworth. Specific, identifiable AIDS Program funding was then made available by the Federal Government and granted through the NSW Department of Health (AIDS Bureau) to the Sydney Area Health Service and Sydney Hospital, which would administer the centre.

In May 1986 a management committee was appointed to oversee the development and implementation of what was referred to as the Kings Cross Multi-Purpose Health Centre. The management committee included representatives from the Australian Prostitutes' Collective (APC) and other community-based services, to provide insight into the health and welfare needs of the target population. It was intended that when this phase was complete the management committee would also oversee the management of the Albion Street (AIDS) Centre and the Sydney STD Centre, which were also administered by Sydney Hospital at the time, thus ensuring complementarity of service provision. However, the management committee was disbanded at the end of its two-year term, in September 1988, and management responsibility returned to the Sydney Hospital Executive.

A shopfront site on the corner of William Street and Kirketon Road in Kings Cross was rented from a private owner and extensively refurbished during late 1986. On 6 April 1987 the Kings Cross Multi-Purpose Health Care Centre, renamed Kirketon Road Centre (KRC), was officially opened by the State Minister for Health, Peter Anderson.

SERVICE ROLE

In 1987 there was already an appreciation of the overlap between 'street youth' sex workers and injecting drug users (IDUs) in the area and of the relationship between their primary health care needs and the risk of HIV/AIDS and other transmissible infections. For this reason the originally recommended service role of KRC, which had been specific to sex workers, was broadened to include the area's drug users and street youth as well.

The following service aims were adopted:

- To prevent and minimise HIV/AIDS and other transmissible infections in 'at risk' youth, sex workers and injecting drug users in the Kings Cross and Darlinghurst area.

- To optimise the quality of life of clients with HIV infection and other transmissible infections.

A range of objectives were developed, aimed at providing an accessible and acceptable 'one-stop-shopping' service, which would meet the health and social welfare needs of the target populations. This setting would provide an understanding of clients' lifestyle, health status and level of HIV risk-taking behaviour necessary to effect the specific service aims at both individual and population level. KRC adopted a 'primary health care philosophy' (Stott 1983), encompassing the concepts of acceptability, accessibility, affordability and equity of health care provision, under the banner of 'Health for All' (WHO Alma Ata 1988).

The service was to be client-focused and to promote client empowerment and self-determination. While clients' lifestyle choices were respected, emphasis was placed upon informing them of how to reduce the potential harms associated with these choices. This later became more formalised as the 'harm reduction' approach (Buning 1990). Although KRC's role was to provide services to the three target populations referred to above, a number of services were developed specifically in response to the needs of sex workers.

DEVELOPMENT OF SERVICES AIMED AT SEX WORKERS

At first hours of operation were from 12 midday to 8 p.m., Monday to Friday. Medical, nursing, social work and clerical support staff were recruited to work as a multidisciplinary team with flexibility of duties and responsibilities. It was considered essential that staff be non-judgemental, non-doctrinaire and eclectic in their approach, and willing to work in a non-traditional health setting. Titles such as 'doctor' were dropped and all staff were known to the clients on a first-name basis. White coats draped with stethoscopes were banned and informal attire was encouraged.

KRC was never advertised publicly. The service became known to clients by word of mouth and by referral from other community-based agencies working with the target population. From the beginning KRC worked closely with the APC, outreaching to the sex workers and management of brothels in the area. The adoption of safer sexual practices and condom policies at brothels were promoted, and referral of sex workers to KRC for their sexual health needs, was encouraged. The centre had a relaxed, 'user-friendly' atmosphere and extended hours and was conveniently located. Clients could drop in at any time without having an appointment. All services were free and confidential. KRC being hospital-based, clients were not even required to produce a Medicare card, hence there was no need to verify personal identification, allowing anonymity and further assuring confidentiality. These were considered to be the reasons that KRC was soon used by many of the area's street and brothel sex workers for their primary health care needs.

In January 1988 KRC commenced a Needle Syringe Exchange Program (NSEP) after legislation was passed through the NSW Parliament allowing needle syringes to be dispensed to IDUs in order to reduce the sharing of injecting equipment and the inherent risk of infectious disease transmission among IDUs, their partners and the greater community. This program was readily accepted and used by the local IDU community. In January 1990 the NSEP hours were extended to 12 midnight, Monday to Friday. The longer opening hours and non-threatening initial point of contact provided by the NSEP further encouraged access to KRC's broader range of health care services, particularly by those IDU sex workers who worked on the streets at night.

By 1990 many brothel workers were required by their employers to provide a 'work certificate' verifying that they had undergone an STD screen on a weekly basis in order to work. A large number of workers chose to use screening services such as those provided by KRC, which was soon performing up to 40 worker STD screens each day. The waiting room was often crowded with brothel workers waiting, however long, for their 'passport' to employment. It was of serious concern that street workers who were not 'regulated' in this way would be less willing to wait in the queue for KRC services.

Ensuring KRC access for street workers was considered a

priority, as they were perceived to be at increased risk of HIV and other transmissible infections. Sex workers on the street did not have the support of a brothel policy of condom use among their clients (with some brothels reportedly employing 'bouncers' to ensure policy compliance). Street workers were more likely to engage in injecting drug use (Perkins 1991) with its inherent health risks. Drug-dependent workers reported that, while being drug-affected made the work more bearable, it sometimes compromised their ability to negotiate safe sex with clients. They also reported that on occasions when they needed to earn money urgently, to pay for drugs to reduce symptoms of drug withdrawal, they were more likely to accept the frequent offers of more money for sex without a condom. Such offers were often accompanied by threats of physical violence. Furthermore, it was the experience at KRC that street workers tended in the main to seek STD screening only with symptomatic STDs, rather than on a regular basis; leaving asymptomatic STDs, which are common (Tait 1980, p 37), likely to be untreated.

To address the concern that the escalation of regular STD screening of brothel workers over time could reduce KRC access for street workers, the centre requested additional funding to allow it to open in the mornings (from 9 a.m.) in order to provide a Well Workers Clinic. The clinic commenced in March 1990 and employed a female medical officer and two nurses working in an extended 'primary practitioner' role to meet the sexual screening and health needs of brothel workers, on both an appointment and a drop-in basis. According to KRC attendance statistics at the time, introducing the clinic had the desired effect of shifting brothel worker screening into the mornings, so that the afternoons became less busy and therefore more accessible to the more 'at risk' clients.

In December 1990, as a result of a survey of STDs among sex workers at KRC (see below), the centre ceased the arbitrary weekly STD screening of brothel sex workers. Instead, it recommended that sex workers, working from establishments that supported mandatory condom use, be screened every two weeks for the first six months and monthly thereafter. Meanwhile, an emphasis was placed on safer sex practices, extending in particular to the personal relationships of sex workers. This recommendation was welcomed by workers who had often felt resentful of the frequent-screening requirements dictated by their brothel managements. The initial concerns of brothel managements were allayed as other STD screening services made corresponding changes over the ensuing months. The reduction in the overall STD screening load at KRC also further increased access to the centre's services by the more 'at risk' clients.

In response to the same survey KRC also established a weekly Thai Sex Worker Clinic with a Thai interpreter, to improve communication regarding safer sex practices. Although the Sydney Sexual Health Centre already offered similar clinics which were well attended, a significant number of Thai workers continued to attend KRC for STD screening, despite referral. It soon became apparent that one of the reasons why these Thai workers seemed to prefer to remain with KRC, despite the referral efforts, was precisely because KRC *did not provide an interpreter service every day*. There was apparently a perception among these Thai workers that interpreters, who were often well-known members of their own small communities, might breach confidentiality — even though interpreters employed by the NSW Health Department all practise under a professional code of conduct which respects confidentiality of client information. Women working illegally in Australia on tourist visas also had concerns that they might be reported to the Immigration Department. Despite much reassurance, these Thai workers continued to attend KRC on every day that the interpreter was not there! After six months the Thai Clinic was discontinued and the centre returned to a telephone interpreter service on an ad hoc basis. KRC also made further efforts to encourage management's support of condom use in brothels employing workers of non-English-speaking background.

KRC OUTREACH SERVICE

In April 1990, following a recommendation of a report commissioned by the NSW Health Department AIDS Bureau (the Reid-Philpot Report), the management of the Mobile Outreach Program ('AIDS Bus') established at the Albion Street (AIDS) Centre in 1986 was transferred to KRC. It was appreciated that there was significant overlap in the client base of the 'AIDS Bus' and KRC, such that their amalgamation could potentially provide greater efficiency in both service to clients and professional support for outreach workers.

The 'AIDS Bus' was the first mobile outreach service of its kind in the world (Griggs and Gold 1989), with nurses and counsellors providing an HIV prevention, testing and psychosocial support service to clients on the streets of Kings Cross and Darlinghurst. In particular, the 'AIDS Bus' targeted male sex workers where they worked at 'The Wall' in Darlinghurst and also transgender sex workers in Premier Lane, Darlinghurst (colloquially referred to as 'Trannie Lane'). These people had previously used services at KRC in a limited way. Outreach workers worked from the bus and also on foot, making contact with clients at refuges, safe houses, strip clubs, bars and other venues frequented by the target population. They were also rotated to work shifts at KRC's fixed site. Providing familiar faces in both settings allowed more effective referral of the more difficult-to-reach outreach clients to KRC where appropriate, and vice versa.

KRC AT THE FIRE STATION

On 30 November 1992 KRC was relocated to the old Darlinghurst Fire Station on a 25-year lease negotiated with the NSW Fire Brigades Department. This move was to meet the physical space requirements of the much expanded KRC service, no longer met by the original site. Despite relocation from Kirketon Road itself, the name 'KRC' was retained.

The move to larger premises, away from the residential area, also enabled KRC to pilot the use of methadone as a harm reduction strategy to reduce risk behaviour among IDUs. The Methadone Project commenced in August 1993, targeting 'at risk' IDUs who had not sought treatment before or who had difficulty fitting into existing programs. Preliminary results from an evaluation of the project indicate that KRC has successfully recruited a significantly younger, 'methadone treatment-naive' IDU population compared to other programs overall, and that the extended dispensing hours (9 a.m.–8 p.m.) have been particularly appropriate for IDU street workers who work by night and sleep by day.

The addition of methadone treatment at KRC has in some respects completed the original objective of the 'one-stop-shopping'

Table 16.1

New Clients Registered at KRC

	ARY	ARY%	IDU	IDU%	SWS	SWS%	SWB	SWB%	Other	Other% A
					Target Groups					
Apr-Dec '87	124	12	345	33	58	5	124	12	522	50
Jan-Jun '88	138	14	374	37	72	7	165	16	460	45
Jul-Dec '88	97	7	670	48	48	3	133	9	530	38
Jan-Jun '89	47	4	443	36	34	3	251	21	544	44
Jul-Dec '89	71	8	379	43	62	7	183	21	323	57
Jan-Jun '90*	190	13	758	51	73	5	288	21	390	26
Jul-Dec '90†	508	19	1104	42	256	9	259	10	356	14
Jan-Jun '91	241	19	601	47	31	2	248	19	253	20
Jul-Dec '91	278	22	587	48	38	3	199	16	224	18
Jan-Jun '92	346	26	605	46	49	4	184	14	231	18

*   Introduction of Extended NSEP and Well Workers Clinic
†   Introduction of Mobile Outreach Program (AIDS Bus)

Table 16.2

Daily Attendances at KRC

	Total daily attendances	ARY	ARY%	IDU	IDU%	SWS	SWS%	SWB	SWB%	Other	Ot
						Target Groups					
Jan-Jun '88	40	5	13	4	9	12‡	31‡			17	
Jul-Dec '88	45	2	4	5	11	14‡	29‡			24	
Jan-Jun '89	57	2	33	4	7	27‡	47‡			22	
Jul-Dec '89	66	2	3	24	37	6	9	23	15	10	
Jan-Jun '90*	98	4	2	55	56	10	24	28	29	10	
Jul-Dec '90†	134	16	12	95	70	12	9	27	20	8	
Jan-Jun '91	134	20	15	93	71	11	8	24	18	7	
Jul-Dec '91	130	38	28	99	74	13	10	21	16	6	
Jan-Jun '92	147	36	24	114	76	13	9	21	14	7	

*   Introduction of Extended NSEP and Well Workers Clinic
†   Introduction of Mobile Outreach Program (AIDS Bus)
‡   Breakdown of SWS/SWB not available

Key
ARY   'At Risk' Youth
IDU   Injecting Drug User
SWS   Sex Worker, Street
SWB   Sex Worker, Brothel

Note: Percentage of total attendances exceeds 100% due to overlap among target groups.
        Attendance statistics prior to Jan '88 not available.
        Attendance rate post-June '92 stabilised.

model of primary health care provision developed at KRC. (Appendix 2 lists KRC services available at the end of 1993.) However, it seems unlikely that the story will end there!

EVALUATION OF SERVICES

Various data have been collected which allow us to look at aspects of KRC operations.

TARGET GROUP DISTRIBUTION AMONG NEW CLIENTS AND DAILY ATTENDANCES

Tables 16.1 and 16.2 demonstrate that initiatives such as NSEP, the Well Workers Clinic and the Outreach Program significantly increased access to KRC by 'at risk' youth, IDUs and street sex workers. The number of clients attending the centre who were not within the target populations ('Other') also decreased progressively, indicating better focusing of KRC services to the target populations over time.

SOME SOCIO-DEMOGRAPHIC CHARACTERISTICS OF SEX WORKERS SEEN AT KRC

Table 16.3 indicates that among sex workers who have attended KRC, injecting drug use is most prevalent among street workers (82%) compared to brothel workers (16%). While the prostitute clients of KRC are predominantly female (84%) and predominantly work in brothels (74%), in relation to the overall sex worker population males and street workers may be overrepresented (see Perkins 1991).

Table 16.3
Socio-demographic Characteristics

	Female (%)	Male (%)	Trans (%)	IDUs (%)(a)	Total (%)
Street	421 (53)	303 (38)	63 (5)	653 (82)	797 (23)(b)
Brothel	2402 (95)	110 (4)	15 (1)	400 (16)	2537 (74)(c)
Both	84 (72)	29 (25)	2 (2)	74 (63)	117 (3)(d)
Totals	2907 (84)	442 (13)	80 (2)	1127 (33)	3451

(a) 1873 clients had missing data for IDU status
(b) Row totals do not add up as there was missing sex data for 10 street sex workers
(c) Row totals do not add up as there was missing sex data for 10 brothel sex workers
(d) Row totals do not add up as there was missing sex data for 2 street and brothel sex workers

KRC SERVICE UTILISATION BY SEX WORKERS

A study funded by a Commonwealth AIDS Research Grant and conducted at the University of New South Wales in 1990 included a survey of 280 prostitutes in New South Wales and the Australian Capital Territory. Among venues where they had checkups, 31.8 percent cited KRC.

Table 16.4
Venues Used by Sex Workers for Checkups

Venue	n	%
Private doctor's surgery	140	50.0
STD clinic at Sydney Hospital	30	10.7
STD clinic at Parramatta Hospital	19	6.8
STD clinic at Liverpool Hospital	5	1.8
STD clinic at Prince of Wales	43	15.4
Kirketon Road Clinic	89	31.8
AIDS Centre, Albion Street	5	1.8
Taylor Square Clinic	12	4.2
Other (women's health centres, community health centres etc.)	13	4.6

The authors of the study note: 'The high preference for the Kirketon Road Centre in Kings Cross is as much due to its relaxed attitude towards prostitute women, the casual dress and manners of staff and informal method of its service, in which appointments are not necessary'. The authors also cite KRC along with private doctors as 'venues where prostitutes feel at ease, and feel their confidentiality is secure' (Lovejoy et al. 1991).

In 1992, in a survey of services to the sex industry, 295 female, 67 male and 21 transsexual sex workers recruited in New South Wales were asked which agencies they found useful. Overall KRC was nominated most often as being useful, among 17 health and welfare services, to the sex industry (Lovejoy et al. 1992).

Table 16.5
Agencies useful to sex workers

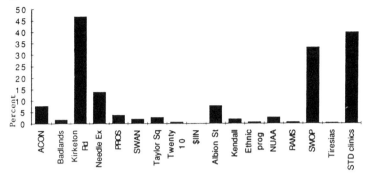

Female sex workers

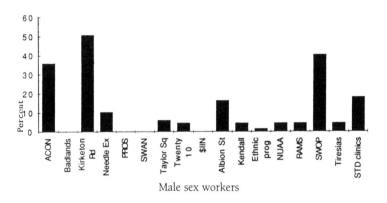

Male sex workers

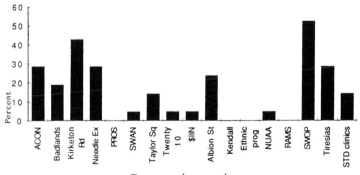

Transsexual sex workers

Source: R. Perkins, personal communication

EPIDEMIOLOGICAL CHARACTERISTICS OF SEX WORKERS SEEN AT KRC

In 1990 a survey was undertaken at KRC with respect to the occurrence of STDs among regularly screened brothel sex workers over a six-month period. Among 3012 STD screens 12 gonorrhoeal and 33 chlamydial infections were diagnosed. These occurred mainly among sex workers from non-English-Speaking Backgrounds (NESB), the majority from Thailand. While representing only 19 percent of the episodes of screening, NESB workers had 58 percent and 84 percent, respectively, of the two forms of infection diagnosed. Overall, more than 50 percent of these STDs were diagnosed at first visit to KRC, and the source of the infection was mostly from casual sex partners outside the work setting. The very low overall incidence of STDs, clustering among NESB sex workers at first visit, suggested that weekly STD screening of *all sex workers* was an inappropriate policy.

In June 1991 a survey was undertaken to determine the prevalence of human immunodeficiency virus (HIV) infection among 1212 IDUs who underwent their first KRC HIV-antibody test (Buckley et al. 1991). Overall, the HIV prevalence was 3.1 percent; 4.2 percent in males and 2.0 percent in females. The prevalence was higher in female IDUs who reported sex work (2.5%) — all of whom were street workers — than in those who didn't (1.6%). Male sex work was not associated with a higher HIV prevalence.

In 1992 a similar study investigated the prevalence of hepatitis C virus (HCV) infection among 201 IDUs who attended the centre for HCV-antibody testing (van Beek et al. 1994). For the 94 IDUs who reported sex work the prevalence of HCV infection was 56 percent, compared to 62 percent in the remainder (107) of the sample. This difference was not statistically significant, suggesting that engaging in sex work was not a risk factor for HCV infection.

WORKING WITH SEX WORKERS

For professional health care workers with limited experience in working with sex workers, establishing of an accessible, acceptable primary health care service for the sex industry presented a challenge. After seven years in the business, it would seem that being non-judgemental in approach and assuring client confidentiality are key elements for success. Ironically, our lack of personal contact with the industry has also been perceived to be an asset, particularly in terms of assuring clients that we are advocates of their health status and are not bound by competing interests.

Sex workers in general live double lives: one life as sex workers and another life as everyday people within the wider community. Most sex workers are determined to keep these lives separate for fear of the stigma commonly associated with sex work, despite its being a perfectly legal way in which to earn a living. This separation seems to be a continuing source of stress and anxiety for many sex workers. The personal and ongoing contact provided by regular sex worker screening at KRC allows a rapport to develop between health worker and sex worker. It is perhaps one of the few occasions where there is open acknowledgment of the two lives of sex workers, and it provides a safe and confidential opportunity for them to freely discuss any resulting stresses.

The sex industry has been exemplary in its adoption of STD/HIV prevention measures over time (Perkins 1991), but the risk of complacency developing is ever present. There is still work to be done. KRC looks forward to continuing to meet the challenge.

17

RESEARCH FIELDWORK AMONG SEX WORKERS

Amanda Wade and Gabrielle Mateljan

This chapter describes what is involved in field research on prostitution. We have been employed as research assistants in prostitution studies carried out over a period of four years at the School of Sociology, University of New South Wales, under the supervision of Frances Lovejoy and Roberta Perkins. In this time we have gained considerable knowledge of the functions of prostitution in various workplaces (Wade 1992).

We are responsible for contacting prostitute subjects in parlours (brothels), on streets or in private apartments where they work, and for obtaining data on their individual backgrounds, working experiences and opinions on sex work. Our usual method of collecting this information is by survey, often involving the distribution of self-administered questionnaires, but we also conduct in-depth interviews for qualitative research. Our current project, which commenced early in 1993 and is funded by the National Health and Medical Research Council, is a study of so-called private prostitutes (or 'call girls') and requires both quantitative and qualitative research methods.

PREPARING TO WORK IN THE FIELD

As in all our studies we began this project by planning a strategy for reaching all private sex workers across New South Wales and by producing a workable and comprehensive questionnaire. Our questionnaires are always designed with the aim of streamlining the survey process and not making the forms a burden to fill in. Firstly, we design them for completion within half an hour; any longer and the respondent no longer finds it fun, just tedious. This restriction of time means that we have to limit our questions to the bare essentials, however tempted we might be to acquire a plethora of social data from our informants. We have never had to pay subjects for information because our questionnaires are not a chore and are designed in an interesting way similar to questionnaires printed in women's magazines — which we have frequently observed sex workers filling in as a means of passing time in a brothel. Also, sex workers know us and are familiar with our work; they recognise that in helping us with our research they are also helping themselves, since our findings bring facts that will support their rights and interests.

Secondly, we have always found it essential to have the questions written in simple language so as to be understood by the least educated of our informants. Occasionally we encounter a worker who is illiterate and this has to be handled with discretion and tact. We plan visits to the state's geographical regions in advance and establish a timetable for covering these areas. Although our principal informants in the present study are private workers, we decided to survey brothel workers as well for a control group. Since the project's main concern is health the questionnaire seeks information on lifestyle, sexual health, sources of STD screening, past and present drug usage (including tobacco, alcohol, intravenous drugs, prescribed medication and other drugs) and general well-being. As social researchers we are also interested in the informant's personal history and cultural and social background to determine to what extent these might have a bearing on outcomes of health and well-being.

Once preparations for the survey are complete we begin our fieldwork by contacting our informants in their working venues. Our initial fieldwork involves calling upon some old contacts to serve as a pilot sample for testing the questionnaire. But once this is done, and the questionnaire altered as required, the real fieldwork begins in earnest. Most private workers are contacted by phone, because of the discreet nature of their business, and questionnaires with pre-paid self-addressed envelopes are posted to them. The brothel workers, however, are contacted by visits to their premises, usually at night when the shift carries most workers. The following is a typical night's work. We load up the car with questionnaires, self-addressed envelopes, and letters of introduction explaining who we represent and the purpose of our visit, and set off to do our door-knocking much like the Avon lady. The next stage is gaining access to the establishment. We receive many and varied reactions from receptionists opening the door. But, since most are now familiar with us from previous visits or know of Roberta Perkins and her work, we are most often received hospitably. In less familiar or new establishments we are often mistaken for outreach workers from a sexual health clinic or SWOP (Sex Workers Outreach Project) and asked for condoms and packets of lubricant. This may, at first, cause confusion all round. Sometimes we are met with suspicion or even a hostile reaction at the door, and have found that this is due to con-cern on the part of management or staff that we may be police, tax-ation officers, immigration officers or representatives of some other government department. If this occurs we quickly reassure them that we are none of these. We explain who we are and ask if we can leave questionnaires and envelopes to enable staff to participate at their leisure. We are aware that in these cases only some of the ques-tionnaires might be completed and returned to us through the post; no doubt some are unceremoniously deposited in the garbage bin.

INSIDE THE PARLOUR

Mostly, however, we are greeted warmly and are seated comfortably in the reception area with a cup of coffee, where we explain the purpose of our visit to the receptionist, manager or owner. After some time engaged on these formalities we are ushered into the staff room (usually simply known as the girls' room), where we introduce the project and the questionnaires to all the women pre-sent there. However, gaining access to this inner sanctum depends on how well we have built up a rapport with management in the first instance. This rapport is usually achieved by general chitchat and by discussing the current state of business in the parlour trade. The latter, of course, is of great interest to management and we are assumed to have a wide knowledge on the subject since we travel across the state visiting parlour after parlour. Often the conversation might drift around to issues concerning a neighbouring parlour or the local police, or dealing with disease, industrial relations or staffing problems.

We never forget that we are in someone else's territory and that the boss, like any person in charge of any other business, deserves the deference due to the manager of the establishment. However, in some places the initial formalities are not necessary as we are immediately greeted by management and taken straight to the staff room, or to the lounge room which is common ground for both staff and clients. In the latter case we respect the clients' presence so as not to intrude on the business. This is a work environment and both management and staff are indulging us with their time. The atmosphere in the girls' room is generally more congenial for conversing with the workers than is the lounge room where clients may eavesdrop. As with the management, the conversation usually begins with pleasantries or exchanging of information on the sex industry before turning to the business at hand. Sometimes a worker is called out to attend a client in the middle of our interview with her. In such circumstances we have no choice but to wait half an hour or an hour for her return, unless we can visit another parlour nearby during this period. More often, though, we will leave the questionnaire and envelope for her to post to us at her convenience.

For many of the workers, most especially the Asian workers who are often far from their homeland, the girls' room is a home away from home, complete with fridge, cooking facilities, bathroom accessories, lounge chairs and often lockers. Some places supply food, while others have just the bare minimum of tea and coffee. Workers provide their own comfortable clothing, grooming items, videos, books, food and beverages and, sometimes, condoms, lubricant and sex toys. In some establishments workers sleep on the premises for a few days, especially in country areas where they have travelled long distances to the brothel. In any case the hours are usually long and tedious and our presence is often a welcome interlude. We are often the only source of any kind of information about the wider business of the sex trade. Over time we have developed an intimate knowledge of industry jargon which helps the staff to relate easily to us.

We like workers to complete the questionnaire on the spot, but some prefer to take it home and others find answering the more intimate questions rather disturbing, as these require confidential information on private sexual behaviour, early sexual experiences, rape, incest and drug usage. We try to 'get in step' with the atmosphere of the place by listening to the general topics of conversation. Every place has its own 'feeling' and system of operation. Often the talk concerns decreasing income and clientele. However, most sex workers manage to maintain a positive outlook and a cheerful approach. Often they talk about what they do in the bedroom, their likes, their dislikes, problems with clients, unusual occurrences, tricks of the trade. They swap tips, mention their personal lives, children, holidays, goals and dreams, and discuss very freely what is going on. Generally, the girls' room is a supportive environment, and we like to think we contribute to that while we are there. As the workers complete our questionnaires there are often queries to be answered or explanations required, which is why we prefer to be on the spot. Our role is to be helpful and totally non-judgemental.

As we mentioned before, a few workers are illiterate — in these cases we play along with the pretence that they have forgotten their glasses or whatever and we go through the form question by question. If we are asked what happens to the questionnaires we find it helpful to show them our tables of statistics from previous studies or to show them a copy of Roberta Perkins' book *Working Girls* (1991), explaining to them how the data is used to support their cause and improve services to them. It is important for us to stress that we have respect for confidentiality and anonymity, as many workers have 'other lives' and their work may be completely secret from husbands or lovers, family, children, friends or neighbours. We have found that most workers have to 'psyche themselves up' for work and usually have a 'work persona' which may be very different from their usual personality. Adopting a 'work persona' allows these women to become another self for a period of time, enabling them to dissociate work life from their private life. This in turn allows them freedom to portray themselves as a sexual being, as a necessary part of their job — and for some people it is a major step in their personal growth. For others, this split persona can be detrimental to personal emotional stability. Most sex workers liken going to work to an actor playing a role in the theatre. This is not to suggest that sex workers force themselves to perform acts that are abhorrent to them. There is always a choice as to what is done or not done in the room, even if the worker is being pressured by management into doing something she is unable or unwilling to do. There is always the option to leave the job.

Depending on how or where the worker is working (ie street, parlour, escort or private) she may see a large number of clients in one night, or one client for a number of hours. In the latter situation, had she met her client under other circumstances, she would probably have little interest in his life. But when at work — and being a professional — she thinks of the money and does her best not to appear bored. Sometimes it is worse than this; as one woman confided to us: 'It's not the fucking that's hard; it's being nice to someone you wouldn't normally even spit on that's difficult'. On the other hand, workers sometimes form friendships with clients and even, occasionally, relationships. The point here is that workers behave differently at work from the way they behave in the rest of their life. Most workers are not sexually promiscuous, but at work they might see as many as fifteen men in one evening. This obviously requires a change of mindset from an average domestic life of shopping for groceries and picking up the kids from school. Most female workers seem to manage quite well, combining their roles successfully.

When we are in the girls' room it is imperative that we do nothing to threaten or disturb the fragile balance of the 'work persona'. This is not only because we want to get our questionnaires filled out in the best circumstances possible, but also because we do not want to interfere in any way with a worker's ability to do her job well. If a sex worker is flustered or distressed in any way this mood can continue to affect her for the rest of the shift, and this can produce resentment towards us. Some workers will use various tactics to 'shut us out' (eg pointedly ignoring us, redoing their makeup or furiously brushing their hair on the opposite side of the room) until they see how the other staff react and what the group response is going to be. In every parlour there is usually a 'ringleader' among the workers who might or might not be popular; but in any case once we discover this dominant personality one of us always makes a point of speaking to her directly. The other women in the room join in after a while and before long someone has started filling in a questionnaire. Once one person has started, everybody usually gets enthusiastic and more relaxed and our work is done quickly from that point on.

The number of staff on shift varies enormously and so do the surroundings, from basic to luxurious. Attitudes to management, clients, each other and self vary also. In some places there are rules and regulations about everything imaginable and in others there are only minimum rules. This can apply to dress codes also. Sex workers choose whichever type of place they feel most comfortable with, or as one woman said: 'Work where your face fits'. It takes some people years to figure out where their 'face fits' most appropriately, as they either don't know themselves or have yet to find the image that best suits them.

OTHER SITUATIONS

The pressures of brothel work (handing over half one's income, maintaining a high standard of grooming, spending large amounts on clothes and wigs, appearing friendly and attractive at all times) encourage many workers to move away from the parlour scene and into a 'private' situation, working by appointment from an apartment or sometimes their own home. For many this is empowering, as it is often the first time they have had control not only over their income but also over which clients they see and which they refuse. The negative aspects of this type of work are that it can be isolating, dangerous if the worker is alone, time-consuming — and emotionally draining having to continually answer the phone in a pleasant manner with abusive, foul-mouthed or disrespectful callers on the other end. Often clients do not keep the appointments they have made. The system of making appointments over the phone and getting the client to indicate his location protects the worker; it is assumed that if a client is a dangerous lunatic he is not going to go to the trouble of calling back and confirming his movements.

Most workers in private situations have not experienced any

violence from clients. However, we encountered one woman working in Canberra who had a terrifying tale to tell. She had gone to a
private home on an escort call, driven by her husband; once inside
the house the client seemed to go into a rage and attacked her, bit-
ing and almost severing her nose. This sort of incident is not common and most private workers, both male and female, enjoy the
freedom of being able to juggle their work and social schedules
more effectively.

The advent of mobile phones has been a boon to private and
escort workers, allowing the private worker to divert calls if necessary without any guilt about missing possible bookings, and providing the escort worker with greater mobility. Among private
workers, some do escort calls, but most stick to their own comfortable surroundings, with regular clients whom they have seen
many times before. Escorts sometimes work for themselves through
advertisements in the local newspapers, but more usually are
employed by an escort agency. In this case they are 'on call' during
specified evenings until the early hours of the morning. This means
that when a booking comes via the receptionist at the agency the
worker has half an hour or so to arrive, beautifully presented, at the
location, most usually a hotel room.

These different ways of working are not mutually exclusive, and
some workers regularly rush home from a shift at the parlour to get
themselves organised for an evening 'on call' for an agency.

The working life of the private prostitute makes survey research
difficult for fieldworkers. As we have pointed out, contacts are usually made over the phone followed by mailing of questionnaires,
which means that the rate of returns is usually lower than in the
case of brothel workers.

Our research also brings us among the most visible of sex workers, the street prostitutes. Although they represent a fairly small
percentage of all workers, it is street workers who most often spring
into the public mind when prostitution is mentioned. The main
advantage of working on the street is that it is open to anyone,
young or old, ugly or beautiful, of any race, colour, inclination or
sexual identity. A significant number of street workers are, of
course, intravenous drug users. As there is no shift work with parlour rules and regulations to endure, the street worker has much

greater freedom than the brothel worker has. Business is conducted on a one-to-one basis and is usually fairly fast, enabling the drug-dependent worker to run off and 'score' drugs whenever it is convenient or necessary.

Researching on the streets has its own problems, not least of which is trying to convince a drug-affected worker to fill in a questionnaire. Generally, street working is not conducive to filling in forms, so we usually attempt to see street workers when they have gathered in their houses or private hotels before they venture out on the street. Research fieldwork among male and transgender (transsexual) street prostitutes has similar problems to that among female workers.

Despite the many risks in their environment street workers demonstrate remarkable control. A young university graduate we met one night in Kings Cross had experienced a situation in which she was threatened by a client with a knife. She simply said to him: 'Oh, darling! How can we have a good time with that thing there? Do put it away.' The client acquiesced, she continued with the job calmly and saw the client out as usual. This is the kind of anecdote we are told as we walk around chatting to different workers on the street.

Our advice to future researchers in this field is to go in with an open mind, a ready smile and a sympathetic ear. Respect those whom you speak to, remember where you are — someone else's workplace — and be ready to adapt to any situation.

18

OUTREACH AS A SUPPORT STRATEGY
Geoffrey Fysh

Outreach is not a new phenomenon associated with the commencement of the HIV epidemic. But I would suggest that work in HIV education and support has expanded the parameters of outreach and professionalised it to some degree. Outreach is essentially the mobilisation of education, support or other services and the provision of these services on the 'home turf' or in the workplace of the target population by skilled peers. Outreach workers have a mandate to go where the target population congregates or moves to, rather than necessarily setting up services at a fixed site.

The skills involved in being an effective outreach worker are extensive, and include:

- driving and navigation
- communication and negotiation
- interpersonal skills
- assertiveness

- time management
- abilities to relate to a broad-ranging population
- small group work skills
- cross-cultural awareness
- abilities to work with issues of sexuality
- basic non-directive counselling skills
- appropriate referral skills
- ability to assess situations and act accordingly
- current knowledge about a range of relevant issues and subjects

One of the primary differences between education and support work done at a fixed site and outreach work is that outreach workers have little or no control over the environment in which they work, unlike other educators who can manipulate environments ensuring that they are safe and conducive to learning. Outreach workers often have to work in brief encounter situations where interruptions are frequent. In the sex industry, situations also occur where workers or others involved have their own agenda and use the time spent with an outreach worker meeting needs that may bear no relationship to the work being attempted.

Typically, contacts with sex workers on the street are brief and nothing is discussed in depth unless the workers indicate that they wish to do so. For 'survival', workers health and well-being are often low on their list of priorities. Hunger, homelessness, legal questions, police harassment and violence may be the priorities (Kjeldsen 1991). If possible the street worker and outreach worker will retire to a more favourable place such as a coffee shop or bar in order to speak confidentially and at length. Much more likely the contact will last about two minutes, if not less. Outreach staff have to respect that they are in the worker's environment, and that as her or his reason for being there is to make money the very presence of an outreach worker may well impede business.

Outreach in brothels is very different in that there is more than one stakeholder involved, a group dynamic exists, and you are to some degree removed from the public. An important part of the commercial safe sex equation is the presence and power of a third party (or gatekeeper). Gatekeepers can either block or facilitate safe behaviours; they are more often than not the manager or owner of the establishment that a sex worker works in (Alexander 1992). As with working generally with women in the context of HIV/AIDS, you must be realistic in the sense that you must target the individual and not the culture in which they exist. Owners, managers, receptionists or any other people deemed to be in charge in an establishment control the extent of contact between outreach workers and sex workers. The outreach workers must be skilful in dealing with these gatekeepers, breaking down any resistance they may have to outreach contact and to some degree meeting their needs as non-sex work employees or employers who happen to work in the sex industry. Rapport and trust are essential for ensuing development of a relationship with the sex workers in the establishment. A team of two outreach workers will be more effective as one can devote time to the manager, owner or receptionist while the other spends time with the workers. Once rapport and trust exist the two workers can move swiftly from entry to the establishment to engaging the workers, with little interference from gatekeepers. In some establishments, though, it's more a case of working around these people than of working with them. Unlike outreaching on the street, the outreach team often have more time to spend with brothel workers, and can discuss in more depth the issues of concern to those workers present. The environment is by no means controlled by the outreach workers, however, and the team must deal with factors such as competitive group dynamics, group resistance, constant interruptions from phones and doorbells, workers coming and going because they are on shift, and gatekeepers manipulating situations in a coercive manner. And yet often it may be appropriate for an outreach worker to spend time alone with an individual worker for privacy and confidentiality to be maintained.

All these considerations underline the tenet that outreach is a team effort and that the solo outreach worker is disadvantaged both professionally and in terms of personal safety.

GUIDING PRINCIPLES FOR OUTREACH

While outreach is individualised as much as possible in working with the sex industry, there are three fundamental guiding principles for effective work. These are harm reduction, self determination, and peer based delivery of services.

Harm Reduction

Harm reduction as it applies to the sex industry in the broadest sense must be adhered to. Workers who inject drugs must be given options that allow them to continue to use drugs in a fashion that does minimal harm to themselves and to others in their lives such as drug-using and sexual partners. Pragmatically, harm reduction must also apply to sex work itself. Outreach programs whose end goal is the retirement of sex workers from the industry will meet with negligible success. Workers must be allowed to explore their work options and if necessary encouraged and provided with support to change to safer working environments. For example, for a female worker who is fed up with penetrative sex and with working on the streets, working in a brothel doing hand relief may be a realistic option. It is also crucial that individual workers themselves determine the levels of harm that may occur in their working environment. Although we know through violent-incident rates that street work is the most dangerous form of sex work in Australia, that does not mean that it cannot be the preferred option of some workers. Choosing sex work has to be recognised as a valid vocational choice if the outreach team wish to develop a close relationship with sex workers that is based on trust.

Self-determination

Self-determination for people in the sex industry needs to be fostered. Sex workers are involved in an industry that is fraught with dangers to self-esteem and many people require empowerment to help them act at various levels. Outreach workers must provide options and not solutions to sex workers. It is the fundamental right of workers to determine the goals and outcomes they will strive for in life. The outreach team promote safety and dignity as rights if workers so choose them.

Peer-based Initiatives

Perhaps most importantly, outreach to the sex industry must be peer-based. To work effectively within the unique culture and the sites where commercial sex occurs, outreach workers need to be well informed about sex work and sex workers and to be free from prejudice or discomfort concerning the industry. The most appropriate people to perform the duties involved are people who are part of the sex industry. Background, empathy and sensitivity all enable peers to be free from judgement and condescension when making contact with people in the industry (Beckstein 1990). Initiatives and strategies that have their starting point in the lived experience of the local sex industry are essential. Active participation of influential peers is an essential prerequisite if sustainable development of health promotion initiatives is the aim, as treating sex workers as passive recipients of health promotion will not work (Wiseman 1989).

COMMUNICATION

Considerable skill in communication is needed when working with people in the sex industry, including subtlety and extreme sensitivity. The outreach worker is attempting to initiate and maintain contact with individuals or an establishment, build trust and rapport, ascertain what the needs of the individuals or groups are and, hopefully, meet those needs while introducing the issues on the outreach agenda (Beckstein 1990). The outreach worker is also continually assessing the direction and impact of the contact in the light of the knowledge and understanding of the person being contacted. Importantly, the outreach worker continually needs to validate knowledge that the person already has and to foster sharing of such knowledge with the person's immediate peers in the establishment or other work area. As already stated, no two outreach contacts are alike and the team must adapt to the needs in each circumstance. When meeting a hostile response the outreach team must use a variety of non-directive communication skills in working towards a positive outcome for that particular contact.

A crucial communication skill is that of 'joining', making that first contact with someone in a way that facilitates rapport. Skilful outreach workers will make eye contact, smile, adopt non-protective arm and body postures, and maintain a stance of relaxed confidence with those they meet (Beckstein 1990). Sex workers, especially, tend to make immediate judgements on the basis of non-verbal contact with somebody who has entered their space — usually uninvited. Once some rapport is established the outreach worker must listen carefully to be able to 'individualise' the information being given and to elucidate both the sex worker's existing knowledge and positive behaviour and the needs being expressed — often awkwardly. Open-ended questions may be used to facilitate the flow of information, as questions that require a yes/no response will get exactly that — a yes or no response that tells the outreach worker little or nothing of the person's knowledge, behaviour or needs.

To complete a productive and successful contact the outreach worker must use communication skills to build trust. Acceptance, affirmation and unconditional support are the keys. The process will develop once the sex worker understands that she or he is talking to a peer who knows at first hand about the sex industry; but the relationship needs to develop into one where support is openly given to the sex worker and where the outreach team are trusted to provide correct and useful information in a non-judgemental way.

PREPARATION

It is very important to be prepared for each outreach contact and, as already stated, contacts must be individualised. Often an establishment or a worker will request something specifically from the outreach team and, while a busy team making repeated multiple contacts might easily forget the request, the worker(s) won't — they expect and deserve to have reasonable requests met. It is also important to remember that the social dynamics in each establishment are different, and that being prepared to deal with issues of control, cross-culturalism, low self-esteem, misogyny, isolation in the workplace etc. is essential. Common courtesies will help the team build rapport — remembering people's names, remembering issues discussed on the last visit, showing familiarity that isn't sycophantic, and indicating an interest in returning. Length of the visit is dependent on each establishment and what is going on at the time of the visit, but anything beyond half an hour (unless you are specifically invited to stay on for a particular reason) can become invasive.

Although I have stressed the need for preparation in performing outreach work, it is equally important to be spontaneous during the contact and to react to the needs being expressed by the individual workers and establishments. For example, if you have been prepared to discuss hepatitis B with the workers in an inner city establishment but in fact they express a desire (overtly or covertly) to talk about taxation, then taxation becomes the issue to be covered first and hepatitis B can follow if there is time. An effective outreach team will be able to follow the mood of the people they are working with and attempt always to meet their immediate needs.

OUTREACH AS A BRIDGE

For many workers in the sex industry, contact with an outreach worker will be their first point of contact with a service provider other than the more traditional medical services they may receive at, say, a sexual health centre. With street workers, their first contact with an outreach worker on the street may lead to an expectation that all their needs can be met by that one person or team. Possibly this contact with an outreach worker is the first support they have received, and as a consequence their expectations may be unrealistic (Kjeldsen 1991). Linking sex workers in need, particularly young 'survival' workers, to relevant support and service delivery agencies is crucial. Outreach workers more than any other health educators are working at the frontline of health promotion, and they are the link between people engaging in high risk behaviours and the organisations that provide risk-reduction information and support (Deren et al. 1992).

While many workers in the sex industry actively limit their links to service provision agencies, it is the responsibility of the outreach workers to continue to make available to these isolated and marginalised members of the community appropriate and useful referral. Because of the nature of the industry sex workers are and will continue to be duly critical of organisations that they are referred to, highlighting the need for 'sex worker-friendly' organisations.

OUTREACH AS AN INAPPROPRIATE STRATEGY

Outreach as a theoretical strategy for taking information and support to people who don't traditionally access services is a positive starting point, but it is possible that outreach in practice might achieve the opposite — driving marginalised people further away from useful services. In some areas of Sydney, sex workers have reported to outreach teams that they are 'fed up with the do-gooders who chase them around the street'. In this instance it is likely that these predominantly street-working people are being contacted by several outreach teams on any one night. Usually these sex workers are highly visible and therefore highly accessible to the teams. There obviously needs to be some coordination of outreach so that frequency of contact doesn't become invasive and a privacy issue.

Outreach can also fall outside the guiding principles outlined in this chapter. An ineffective team might, for example, appear alien to sex workers, act inappropriately in their space and further isolate them from services available. Alienation of the sex industry from the rest of society is dangerous and undermines public health initiatives, as alienated owners, managers or workers may feel little or no responsibility to act for the general good of the public (Wiseman 1989).

As long as workers in the sex industry continue to be a highly stigmatised part of the labour force they will continue to under-use services. We have a responsibility to continue to make available appropriate and useful services for them in their workplaces, in a non-judgemental and open manner. Outreach is still the best strategy we have for providing certain services to sex workers. But we must continue to strive for highly skilled, peer-based outreach teams that are able to assist sex workers in their efforts to work and live with safety and dignity.

A CONCLUDING NOTE
Frances Lovejoy and Roberta Perkins

This book has covered an immense area in the study of prostitution. In this final chapter we will comment on some of the more prominent issues raised by the chapter authors.

HEALTH, SOCIAL AND POLICING ISSUES

The health of sex workers and their clients was a dominant concern for many of the authors. Sexually transmitted diseases dominate any consideration of health issues in sex work. In the last century, as Raelene Frances (Chapter 1) points out, Contagious Diseases Acts were used to harass female prostitutes. Christine Harcourt (Chapter 11) discusses STD distribution in prostitute and non-prostitute populations in Australia and overseas. In recent times, as Geoffrey Fysh (Chapter 18) indicates, the threat of AIDS has been a major consideration in most sex work outreach programs. Ingrid van Beek (Chapter 16) describes the work of the Kirketon Road Clinic which provides a full range of AIDS, STD, gynaecological and general women's and men's health services to a prostitute clientele. Roberta Perkins (Chapter 8) notes the generally responsible behaviour of female prostitutes in restricting the spread of STDs, including AIDS, through safe sex practices. Garrett Prestage (Chapter 9) confirms that male prostitutes also tend to be well informed on sexual health issues and to practise safe sex. But, as Carol Stevens (Chapter 13) points out, there are still a few sex workers who are not well-informed about HIV transmission and practise unsafe sex. Linda Brockett and Alison Murray (Chapter 10) describe the plight of Thai contract sex workers who may face the greatest risks of contracting AIDS.

Sex work is often linked in the public mind with substance abuse, including alcohol, tobacco and illegal and prescription drugs. Rachel Sharp (Chapter 12) discusses what is known about the doubly clandestine population of intravenous drug-using prostitutes and suggests that epidemiologically they have not so far proved to be a major vector of HIV transmission in Australia.

But STDs are only a part of sex worker concerns. As Louise Webb and Janice Elms (Chapter 15) point out, physical safety has long been a major problem for sex workers. It is not sufficient to expect prostitutes to solve this problem themselves through undergoing training in assertiveness, negotiation or martial arts or through carrying their own defensive weapons. It is up to the general public, through their representation on juries, to demonstrate that persons who attack, rape and kill prostitutes should be treated with the same severity as those who attack, rape and kill people who are not prostitutes. Sexual harassment has now been recognised as an intolerable workplace practice in other industries; workers' rights need to be extended to the sex industry.

Relatively little attention has been paid to the long-term effects of boredom, stress and inter-staff tension on prostitutes, although these have been recognised as potential sources of health problems for workers in other industries. Prostitutes often work in far from ideal conditions. And, as Caroline Barlow (Chapter 7) describes it, alcohol is more likely to be available in the workplace than are nutritious snacks; this coupled with the strong pressures to look slimly attractive may lead to eating disorders.

In recent years the range of prostitution services has greatly diversified; skill in both sex and interpersonal relations is now challenging the previously desired qualities of youth and physical attractiveness. The continued presence of older, higher earning sex workers and the development of a trade union consciousness may help to shift the emphasis from work crises like sexually transmitted diseases, drug overdoses and physical assault to the occupational health and safety conditions already achieved by other workers: adequate meal breaks, clothing appropriate to the weather, safe and pleasant working conditions and access to sick leave. If self-employed or casual workers continue to predominate, sex worker organisations should perhaps devote more time to advising on appropriate sick leave insurance schemes.

As a final comment on health issues we emphasise that, far

from sex workers being a health threat to the rest of society, the general public, especially condom-resistant clients, together with others in the community much less health conscious than sex workers are, continue to pose a major health threat to prostitutes. By shopping around for the most marginal, vulnerable workers who may be bullied into condomless sex, some clients are wilfully exposing the workers, themselves and other condom-resistant clients to the threat of AIDS and a variety of other STDs.

Male prostitution is a form of sex work too often overlooked in the public mind. And, as Garrett Prestage (Chapter 9) points out, the literature and research on sex work quite frequently fail to recognise the role of male sex workers. Unfortunately, this publication has not altogether avoided the failing. Many of the chapters addressing non-specific aspects of prostitution, such as those on oral history, feminism, social work and research fieldwork, do not integrate male and female sex work. But overall the book does provide greater discussion of male and transsexual sex workers than most works on prostitution. It is hoped that future writers and researchers on the subject will give more thought to *all* forms of sex work when discussing prostitution per se.

A number of the authors express concern about police behaviour. Jeddah Jakobsen and Roberta Perkins (Chapter 2) draw our attention to police assaults upon prostitutes in the past, Roxy Blain (Chapter 5) informs us about police control over the sex industry in South Australia and Western Australia and Roberta Perkins (Chapter 8) points to police corruption. On the other hand, Mike Lazarus (Chapter 4) tells us there is another side to police relations with sex workers: that of policemen concerned for the welfare of prostitutes and law-enforcers more interested in preventing crime than in catching criminals 'red handed'. Unfortunately, though, there continue to be too many police officers who assume that prostitution is somehow 'unnatural' or anti-social behaviour that must be stamped out.

As this book was being prepared a series of events occurred in the New South Wales industrial city of Newcastle that well illustrate this last point. One of the city's senior police officers at great expense vigorously used provisions in the *Disorderly Houses Act* in an effort to close down the town's five brothels; this in spite of the

Police Department's general inactivity on this law while awaiting a parliamentary decision to repeal it. No one in Newcastle could remember when police last took action against these houses, the oldest of which had been operating for more than 20 years. In an entirely separate incident this same senior police officer falsely arrested a mining engineer during a Christmas party (*Newcastle Herald* 19 February 1994). This event received a great deal of local publicity and the police officer in question was transferred to another town. His parting shot as he left Newcastle was that somehow the brothel owners had conspired to get him disgraced (*Newcastle Herald* 4 March 1994). Then in the early hours of 19 March 1994 over fifty Newcastle policemen with search warrants took an unprecedented action by raiding all five brothels simultaneously, removing ledgers and other paper work, confiscating all monies taken that evening and arresting eighteen women. In another unprecedented action a local newspaper carried the names of all these women in its next edition!

This kind of police behaviour is totally unwarranted. While, as we have seen in Mike Lazarus' chapter, much can be achieved with the cooperation of prostitutes, the actions of Newcastle police have set relations with the sex industry back many years. Raelene Frances' historical review (Chapter 1) indicates what can happen when police use a heavy hand: the sex industry falls into the grip of organised crime syndicates and drugs are introduced. If we are to achieve a more enlightened society in the future the police, among others, must rethink their relationship with the sex industry and seek to communicate with prostitutes in a cooperative relationship rather than a belligerent one.

LEGISLATIVE REFORM

Many of the opinions expressed throughout this book support the view that social attitudes to prostitution need to change. In his Foreword Paul Wilson suggests that the first step towards reaching this goal is through reforming and standardising the prostitution legislation across Australia. Roxy Blain (Chapter 5) tells us of the kind of legal confusion sex workers face when they move interstate to work. However, as Marcia Neave (Chapter 3) warns, law reform should not just aim to achieve uniform legislation across all

Australian jurisdictions but should make sure it does not favour the customer and public morality at the expense of the sex worker's safety. Reform should also remove the kind of gender and racial biases in law enforcement that Raelene Frances (Chapter 1) mentions. Mike Lazarus (Chapter 4) shows us how effective police can be in preventing crime through communicating with prostitutes and the community in a relaxed legal climate. On the other hand, Caroline Barlow (Chapter 7) alerts us to just how discriminatory law enforcement can be with police and local councils using discretionary powers even where prostitution is mostly decriminalised. Jeddah Jakobsen and Roberta Perkins (Chapter 2) point out how the media reinforces negative stereotypes when prostitution is criminalised. But, as we have indicated above, the Newcastle police raids and the publishing of the names of the prostitutes arrested was delivering a double penalty of criminal record and public shaming. Law reform is urgently needed to avoid such unnecessary actions in the future.

But legislative reform is likely to have many repercussions beyond mere law enforcement. As Christine Harcourt (Chapter 11) demonstrates, it could assist the sex industry in its health initiatives. And as Linda Brockett and Alison Murray (Chapter 10) indicate, reforming immigration laws could mean migrant workers gaining control over their working conditions. Rachel Sharp (Chapter 12) suggests similar possibilities for drug-using prostitutes following the repeal of certain drug laws.

Judicial attitudes must also change in response to law reform and consider the role of sex workers in a more positive light. Such a change could result, for instance, in a more rational response to rape cases involving prostitutes as victims than has hitherto been shown. And the same with even more serious crimes, as in the tragic case of slain victim Jasmin Lodge, a 17-year-old Kings Cross sex worker, which was concluded in the Supreme Court on 21 March 1994. Jasmin was strangled to death in February 1993 by a 29-year-old client, who claimed he had acted in self-defence because she drew a knife. But no knife was produced as evidence. Yet, on the basis of this man's dock statement, the jury returned a verdict of manslaughter rather than murder. Obviously, such factors as Jasmin's lifestyle as a prostitute and a drug user were considered more pertinent to the case than were the actions of the client. Legislative reform will make court decisions of this kind a thing of the past.

In their analyses of female, male and transsexual prostitution Roberta Perkins (Chapter 8) and Garrett Prestage (Chapter 9) make it clear that ordinary men and women engage in commercial sexual activities as sex workers or as clients. Their backgrounds, particularly the women's, are indistinguishable from other people's. Their sexuality, rather than reinforcing notions of deviant behaviour, actually demonstrates the great diversity in human sexual behaviour per se. Given these facts and the fact that little separates commercial from non-commercial sexual behaviour apart from a cash transaction, it seems irrational to continue legally punishing one or the other party on the basis of a mutually consensual act between two adults. Parties to such an act in other circumstances are not victimised. Since the law is designed to protect individual rights, and since the transaction of prostitution is itself not illegal, the logical conclusion is that modern law should adopt the principle of the ancient Roman law in protecting the prostitute's rights in respect of this transaction.

This book therefore is yet another reminder to legislators in Australia that the time has come to reform the prostitution laws across the country. Firstly, it is imperative that all jurisdictions agree to a basic legal framework that will eliminate the present ludicrous situation of confusing and contradictory legislation among the states. Secondly, given the evidence provided throughout this book, we suggest that serious consideration be given to decriminalising prostitution. This does not necessarily imply complete legal laissez-faire, for we are certain that the sex industry would support regulatory environmental legislation similar to that of other industries. But, it should cover all current forms of sex work, including private residential and street prostitution as well as brothel work. To arrive at a practical solution satisfactory to all concerned it is important that the sex industry itself be consulted and that, provided it does not detrimentally impinge upon the community at large, a legal formula devised by government in consultation with the sex industry should be adopted for all of Australia.

IS PROSTITUTION ON THE WAY OUT?

Given the comments by sex workers and researchers throughout the book indicating drastic declines in sex business, can we assume that prostitution is about to disappear in the near future? We think not. We feel that prostitution definitely has a future. So far this resilient industry has survived religious repression, police corruption, organised crime exploitation, sexually transmitted diseases, mandatory safe sex, criminalisation and decriminalisation, full employment and recession, greater availability of alternative sexual recreations, technologically improved pornography such as videos, greater availability of contraception to women in general and greater acceptance of extramarital sex.

At the same time, major changes in the wider society have been reflected in prostitution. Credit cards are more widely used in paying for sexual services, implicitly acknowledging that prostitution is a normal commercial activity. As living standards have increased, brothels have added the trappings of suburban consumerism — colour television and video for waiting clients, spa baths and 'luxurious' surroundings. The acceptance of advertisements for escort services, first in underground magazines and more recently in newspaper classifieds, has made possible not only the more independent off-street work but also the greater differentiation of services offered. After more than a century of active trade unionism it is only relatively recently that sex workers have had the opportunity to join a work collective; this has still to be translated into industrial action. Multiculturalism in the wider society is reflected in a wider ethnic mix of both sex industry investors and sex workers. As women and children leave the institution of the family for the workforce or the street, and as state welfare is more grudgingly distributed to the very poor, new groups are entering prostitution for reasons of economic survival.

Just as women have been seen less as victims of marriage in the wider society the female prostitute has been seen less as a titillating victim of men's indiscriminate lust. Old-fashioned feminists and moralists notwithstanding, the modern female sex worker does not spend her nights in drugsodden misery, meekly handing over her fabulous earnings to a sadistic pimp; she is increasingly likely to have chosen to remain in the industry because it offers flexible hours (which may fit with study or family commitments), reasonable but not wonderful pay, and a degree of independence in employment.

Given this resilience in the face of the social changes of the last few decades, is prostitution facing any serious challenges to its long-term survival?

As long as prostitution operates on the edge of the clandestine economy it will be vulnerable to wowser-inspired legislation; this could be created to protect child workers further, to enforce safe sex practices or to protect female workers from standover pimps. In recent years the industry has diversified to offer a greater range of services; it is possible that the outrage of politicians or pressure groups at any one service could render all sections of the industry vulnerable.

Furthermore, the trend in most areas of economic activity has been towards greater concentration of capital. Prostitution on the whole remains in the hands of self-employed individuals or owners of small brothels. Removal of anti-pimping legislation would possibly pave the way for greater standardisation of sexual service provision through public companies or franchises. This would be in keeping with the growing interest in international sex tourism, which may well favour a more standardised product — as some tourists favour hotel chains. Moves towards a higher concentration of sex industry ownership would probably have the effect of reducing flexibility of working hours, encouraging more full-time work, reducing wage rates in exchange for more secure and regular employment, and reducing employment opportunities for marginal workers such as juveniles, transsexuals, intravenous drug users, older women and workers of non-English-speaking backgrounds. Such moves might be welcomed by policy-makers because of worries about AIDS and other STD transmission or because of a belief that tax collection rates would increase with a shift to PAYE and company tax.

Although prostitution is stereotypically portrayed as the provision of sexual services for men by women, there is the possibility of substantial change in the future. More men are becoming sex workers and, through both professional gimmickry (eg dungeons and whips) and a shift from ejaculatory sex to less exhaustible forms, are overcoming their biological limitations for this work. And women in the general population are now less likely to be limited in their pursuit of sexual pleasure by marriage or the lack of monetary resources; these women, along with bisexual and homosexual men, provide a market for male prostitutes which may expand significantly in the future.

Prostitution remains one of the last great reservoirs of employment whenever State welfare and the regular labour market fail to provide. That, at least, is unlikely to change in the years ahead.

NOTES

Chapter 3

1   The *Criminal Law Amendment Act* 1885 (Eng) was enacted to suppress brothels and 'to make further provision for the protection of women and girls'.

2   See for example An Act for the Prevention of Vagrancy and for the Punishment of Idle and Disorderly Persons 1835 (NSW) s 2; Police Offences Statute 1865 (Vic) s 35.

3   *Contagious Diseases Act* 1879 (Tas); *Act for the Suppression of Contagious Diseases* 1868 (Qld) (31 Vict No 40).

4   In Western Australia and Tasmania this offence applies only to 'common prostitutes'. In theory this requires the status of common prostitutes to be established, but in practice this is unlikely to be contested.

5   A similar situation applies in Victoria, for brothels without planning permits. See Part B, Table 2.

6   Criminal Code (Qld) s 229E(1).

7   Criminal Code (Qld) s 229D(2)(b).

8   Criminal Code (Qld) s 229K(2).

9   Criminal Code (Qld) s 229J(5).

10   Criminal Code (Qld) s 229M.

11   Criminal Code (Qld) s 229N.

12   Criminal Code (Qld) s 229N(2).

13   Criminal Code (Qld) s 229I(3).

14   *Crimes Act* 1900 (NSW) s 91A.

15   *Prostitution Act* 1979 (NSW) s 5.

16   *Prostitution Act* 1979 (NSW) s 7.

17   *Prostitution Act* 1979 (NSW) s 8.

18   *Offences in Public Places Act* 1979 (NSW) s 5.

19   Melbourne Metropolitan Planning Ordinance, Part 1, Cl 2. Inserted by Amendment No 61, Part 2, amended by Amendment No 104, Part 2A.

20   *Prostitution Regulation Act* 1986 (Vic) ss 3, 15, 22(1)(d).

21   *Prostitution Regulation Act* 1986 (Vic) s 12.

22   *Prostitution Regulation Act* 1986 (Vic) s 63.

23   In particular Part 3 (the licensing provisions) and s 77(b) repealing some *Vagrancy Act* offences were not proclaimed.

24   *Prostitution Regulation Act* 1992 (NT) s 3.

25   *Prostitution Regulation Act* 1992 (NT) s 22.

26   *Prostitution Regulation Act* 1992 (NT) s 6.

27   *Prostitution Regulation Act* 1992 (NT) s 24.

28   *Prostitution Regulation Act* 1992 (NT) ss 41, 42.

29   *Prostitution Regulation Act* 1992 (NT) s 9.

30   *Prostitution Regulation Act* 1992 (NT) s 20(2) (A similar requirement applies to prostitutes: s 28(3).)

31   *Prostitution Act* 1992 (ACT) s 7.

32   *Prostitution Act* 1992 (ACT) s 6.

33   *Prostitution Regulations, Subordinate Law No 19 of 1993,* s 4.

34   *Prostitution Act* 1992, (ACT) s 4.

35   *Prostitution Act* 1992, (ACT) s 20.

36   See for example Victoria, *Final Report of Inquiry into Prostitution* (1985) Ch 2; Parliament of New South Wales, *Report of Select Committee of the Legislative Assembly Upon Prostitution* (1986) Ch 1.

Chapter 8

1   This refers to prostitution in which sex workers identify as prostitutes and consider this occupation to be essential to their income. It usually refers specifically to street, brothel and private ('call girl') prostitution among female sex workers.

Chapter 9

1   The author was previously known as Garry Bennett and some of his writing can be found under that name.

2   There is a growing tendency to replace the term 'transsexual' with 'transgender' as the former is a medical term to which some 'trannies' object. The other concern with the term 'transsexual' is that trannies change their gender, not their biological sex.

Chapter 10

1   This chapter concentrates on female Thai sex workers since no organised male prostitution exists in Thailand and no equivalent contract system for the immigration of men operates. Also there is no ethnic specific prostitution designed for male sex workers.

2   *Hinch* (Channel 10, August 1991).

3   Estimated through outreach visits to sex establishments.

4   Many commercial sex establishments demand 'fit for work' certificates.

5   For example, two Thai women with heart-related illnesses sought treatment at the Sydney Sexual Health Centre in September 1991.

6   This figure indicates number of visits rather than number of workers : many workers attend several times over a six-month period.

7   'Half-French' is a sex industry term for oral sex without ejaculation, 'sex' is vaginal intercourse.

8   In a twelve-month period we had visited this parlour on several occasions to follow up visits to clinics by Asian women suffering from repeated STDs contracted while working there.

9   Observation by health workers and shown through medical records.

BIBLIOGRAPHY

Adler P. 1953 *A House is Not a Home* Rinehart: New York.

Agacfidan A., Badur S. & Gerikalmaz O. 1993 'Syphilis prevalence among unregistered prostitutes in Istanbul, Turkey' (letter) *Sexually Transmitted Diseases* vol. 20 pp 236–7.

Agoston T. 1945 'Some psychological aspects of prostitution: pseudo-personality' *International Journal of Psychoanalysis* no. 26.

Ahmed H. J., Omar K., Adan S. Y. et al. 1991 'Syphilis and human immunodeficiency virus seroconversion during a 6-month follow-up of female prostitutes in Mogadishu, Somalia' *International Journal of STDs and AIDS* vol. 2 pp 119–23.

Aitkin J. 1978 'The prostitute as worker' *Women and Labour Conference Papers* pp 240–8.

Alexander P. 1992 'Key issues in sex work related HIV/AIDS/STD prevention interventions' *AIDS Health Promotion Exchange* vol. 1 pp 4–7.

Alford K. 1984 *Production or Reproduction? An Economic History of Women in Australia, 1788–1850* Oxford University Press: Melbourne.

Allen J. 1984 'The making of a prostitute proletariat in early twentieth century New South Wales' in *So Much Hard Work* (ed. K. Daniels) Fontana/Collins: Sydney.

_____ 1987 'Policing since 1880: some questions of sex' *Policing in Australia: Historical Perspectives* (ed. M. Finnane) UNSW Press: Sydney.

_____ 1988 'Rose Scott's vision: feminism and masculinity, 1880–1925' in *Crossing Boundaries: Feminisms and the Critique of Knowledges* (eds B. Caine, E. A. Grosz & M. de Lepervanche) Allen & Unwin: Sydney.

_____ 1990 *Sex and Secrets. Crimes Involving Australian Women Since 1880* Oxford University Press: Melbourne.

Altman D. 1971 *Homosexual: Oppression and Liberation* Penguin: Middlesex.

Arnot M. 1985 *The Law and Prostitution in Victoria, 1834–1980* Historical background paper for the Victorian Government's *Inquiry into Prostitution*.

_____ 1987 'Prostitution and the state in Victoria, 1890–1914', MA thesis, University of Melbourne.

_____ 1988 'The oldest profession in New Britannia' in *Constructing a Culture* (eds V. Burgmann & J. Lee) McPhee Gribble/Penguin: Fitzroy.

Australian Bureau Of Statistics (ABS) 1986 *Census Of Population and Housing in Australia*.

_____ 1992 *Social Indicators* Cat. 4101.0.

Australian Capital Territory 1991 *Select Committee on HIV, Illegal Drugs and Prostitution* Interim Report, ACT Legislative Assembly.

Aveling M. 1992 'Bending the bars: convict women and the state' in *Gender Relations in Australia: Domination and Negotiation* (eds K. Saunders & R. Evans) Harcourt, Brace & Jovanovich: Sydney.

Backhouse C. 1985 'Nineteenth century Canadian prostitution law: reflection of a discriminatory society' *Histoire Sociale/Social History* XVIII (36) November.

Bacon J. 1976–77 'The real estate industry in women' *Vashti: A Women's Liberation Magazine* vol. 17 pp 5–6.

Barclay E. 1974 'Queensland's Contagious Diseases Act 1868' *Queensland Heritage* vol. 12 no. 10 pp 27–34; vol. 3 no. 1 pp 21–9.

Beckstein D.L. 1990 *AIDS Prevention in Public Sex Environments — Outreach and Training Manual* Santa Cruz AIDS Project.

Bell D. 1983 *Daughters of the Dreaming* McPhee Gribble/Allen & Unwin: Sydney and Melbourne.

Bell L. (ed.) 1987 *Good Girls/Bad Girls: Feminists and Sex Trade Workers Face to Face* Seal: Toronto.

Bellis D. J. 1993 'Reduction of AIDS risk among 41 heroin addicted female street prostitutes' *Journal of Addicted Diseases* vol. 12 no. 1 pp 7–23.

Bennett G. 1983 *Young and Gay: A Study of Gay Youth in Sydney* Twenty-Ten: Sydney.

Bennett G., Chapman S. & Bray F. 1989 'Sexual practices and "beats": AIDS related sexual practices in a sample of homosexual and bisexual men in the western area of Sydney' *Medical Journal of Australia* 18 Sept. vol. 151 pp 309–14.

Berger P. & Luckmann T. 1966 *The Social Construction of Reality* Penguin: Middlesex.

Biles A. 1980 'Propositions on prostitution' *Scarlet Woman* vol. 10 pp 18–22.

Blackmore C. A., Limpakarnjanarat K., Rigau-Perez J.G. et al. 1985 'An outbreak of chancroid in Orange County, California: descriptive epidemiology and disease-control measures' *The Journal of Infectious Diseases* vol. 151 pp 840–4.

Blaikie G. 1980 *Wild Women of Sydney* Rigby: Adelaide.

Borthwick P. 1992 'Research report on "Round the Parlours": the Streetwize comic on HIV/AIDS prevention for Asian sex workers', unpublished report.

Brandt A.M. 1987 (2nd edition) *No Magic Bullet* Oxford University Press: New York.

Brockett L. 1992 'Annual Report', unpublished report of Multicultural Health Promotions Project, Sydney Hospital.

Brockett L. & Murray A. 1992 'Sydney's Asian sex workers. AIDS and the geography of a new underclass' *Asian Geographer* Oct.–Nov.

Buckley R., van Beek I., Roach A., Imrie A. & Kaldor J. M. 1991 'Patterns of HIV prevalence among injecting drug users seeking primary health care', (abstract), Paper presented at IIIrd Annual Conference on Medical and Scientific Aspects of HIV/AIDS, Wollongong, Nov. 1991.

Bullough V. L. & B. 1967 *Women and Prostitution: A Social History* Prometheus: Buffalo, NY.

Bullough V. L., Elcano B., Deacon, M. & Bullough B. (eds) 1977 *A Bibliography of Prostitution* Garland: New York.

Buning E. C. 1990 'The role of harm reduction programmes in curbing the spread of HIV by drug injectors' in *AIDS and Drug Misuse* Routledge: London.

Buning E. C., Coutinho R. A., van Brussell G. H. A., et al. 1986 'Preventing AIDS in drug addicts in Amsterdam' (letter) *Lancet* vol. 1 p 1435.

Burgmann V. & Lee J. (eds) 1988 *Constructing a Culture* McPhee Gribble/Penguin: Fitzroy.

Burley N. & Symanski R. 1981 'Women without: an evolutionary and cross-cultural perspective on prostitution' in *The Immoral Landscape* (ed. R. Symanski) Butterworths: Toronto.

Burns T. 1973 'Leisure in industrial society' in *Leisure and Society in Britain* (eds M. Smith, S. Parker & C. Smith) Allen Lane: London.

Calderon, E. J., Gomez-Lucia E., Aguado I. et al. 1991 'Absence of HTLV-I and HTLV-II infection in prostitutes in the area of Seville, Spain' *European Journal of Clinical Microbiologically Infectious Diseases* vol. 10 no. 9 pp 773–5.

Cameron D. W., Ngugi E. N., Ronald A. R. et al. 1991 'Condom use prevents genital ulcers in women working as prostitutes' *Sexually Transmitted Diseases* vol. 18 pp 188–91.

Caprio F. & Brenner D. 1961 *Sexual Behavior: Psycho-Legal Aspects* Citadel: New York.

Carmichael G. 1992 'So many children: colonial and post-colonial demographic patterns' in *Gender Relations in Australia: Domination and Negotiation* (eds K. Saunders & R. Evans) Harcourt, Brace & Jovanovich: Sydney.

Caron S. L., Davis C. M., Wynn R. L. & Roberts L. W. 1987 'America responds to AIDS, but did college students? Differences between March 1987 and September 1988' *AIDS Education and Prevention* vol. 4 no. 1 pp 18–28.

Cheney B. 1988 'Prostitution — a feminist jurisprudential perspective' *Victoria University of Wellington Law Journal* vol. 18 p 239.

Clark C. M. H. 1956 'The origins of the convicts transported to eastern Australia, 1787–1852' *Historical Studies* vol. 7 no. 26 pp 121–35, May; vol. 7 no. 27 pp 314–27 November.

Cleo March 1991.

Cohen J. 1994 'Smith and Strong: a tale of two women' *The West Magazine* 29 January, pp 14–17.

Commonwealth Government 1993 *National HIV/AIDS Strategy, 1993–94 to 1995–96*.

Conte D., Ferroni P. & Lorini G. P. 1987 'HIV and HBV infection in intravenous drug addicts from northeastern Italy' *Journal of Medical Virology* vol. 22 pp 299–306.

Cooper D. A., Dodds A. J. 1986 'AIDS and prostitutes' (letter) *The Medical Journal of Australia* vol. 145 p 55.

Criminal Justice Commission (CJC) 1991 'Regulating morality? An inquiry into prostitution in Queensland', Research and Co-ordination Division.

Daniels K. 1984 'Prostitution in Tasmania during the transition from penal settlement to civilised society' and 'St Kilda voices' in *So Much Hard Work* (ed. K. Daniels) Fontana/Collins: Sydney.

_____ 1993 'The flash mob: rebellion, rough culture and sexuality in the female factories of Van Diemen's Land' *Australian Feminist Studies* no. 18, Summer.

Daniels K. & Murnane M. 1979 'Prostitutes as "purveyors of disease": venereal disease legislation in Tasmania, 1868–1945' *Hecate* vol. 5 no. 1 pp 5–21.

Davidson R. 1980 *Prostitution in Perth and Fremantle and on the Eastern Goldfields,*

1895–1939 MA dissertation, University of Western Australia: Perth.

_____ 1983 '"As good a bloody woman as any other bloody woman": prostitutes in Western Australia, 1895–1939' in *Exploring Women's Past* (ed. P. Crawford) Sisters Publishing Company: Melbourne.

_____ 1984 'Dealing with the "social evil": prostitution and the police in Perth and on the eastern goldfields, 1895–1924' in *So Much Hard Work* (ed. K. Daniels) Fontana /Collins: Sydney.

Davies S. 1989 'Working their way to respectability: women, vagrancy and reform in late nineteenth century Melbourne' *Lilith* no. 6, Spring.

Davis N. 1971 'The prostitute: developing a deviant identity' in *Studies in the Sociology of Sex* (ed. J. M. Henslin) Appleton-Century-Crofts: New York.

Davison G., Dunstan D. & McConville C. 1985 *The Outcasts of Melbourne: Essays in Social History* Allen & Unwin: Sydney.

D'Costa L. J., Plummer F. A., Bowmer I. et al. 1985 'Prostitutes are a major reservoir of sexually transmitted diseases in Nairobi, Kenya' *Sexually Transmitted Diseases* vol. 12 pp 64–7.

De Beauvoir S. 1979 *The Second Sex* Penguin: Harmondsworth.

Decker J. F. 1979 *Prostitution: Regulation and Control* Rothman: Littleton.

Delacoste F. & Alexander P. (eds) 1987 *Sex Work: Writings by Women in the Sex Industry* Cleis: San Francisco.

Department of Health and Community Services, Victoria 1993 'Surveillance of sexually transmissible diseases in Victoria, 1992' Public Health Branch, Melbourne.

Deren S. et al. 1992 'AIDS outreach workers: an exploratory study of job satisfactions/dissatisfactions' *AIDS Education and Prevention* vol. 4 no. 4 pp 328–37.

Dixon O. F. 1982 *The Report of O.F. Dixon* (WA Ombudsman).

Dixson M. 1975 *The Real Matilda: Women and Identity in Australia, 1788 to 1975* Penguin: Ringwood.

Donovan B. 1984 'Gonorrhoea in a Sydney house of prostitution' *The Medical Journal of Australia* vol. 140 pp 268–71.

_____ 1990 'Female sex workers and HIV infection in Australia: so far so good' *National AIDS Bulletin* vol. 4 no. 17–19.

Donovan B., Bek M., Pethebridge A. M. & Nelson M. J. 1991a. 'Heterosexual gonorrhoea in central Sydney: implications for HIV control' *The Medical Journal of Australia* vol. 154 pp 175–9.

Donovan B., Harcourt C., Bassett I. & Philpot, C. R. 1991b 'Gonorrhoea and Asian prostitution: the Sydney Sexual Health Centre experience' *The Medical Journal of Australia* vol. 154 pp 520–1.

Echevarria S., San Miguel G., Pelayo T. et al. 1993 'Risk for hepatitis C virus (HCV) and human immunodeficiency virus (HIV) infections among prostitutes' (letter) *Genitourinary Medicine* vol. 67 pp 321–5.

Egger S. & Harcourt C. 1993 'Prostitution in New South Wales: the impact of deregulation' in *Women and the Law* (eds P. Westeal & S. McKillop) AIC conference proceedings, number 16, Australian Institute of Criminology: Canberra.

Erickson P. 1987 *The Steel Drug: Cocaine in Perspective* Lexington Books: London.

European Working Group on HIV Infection in Female Prostitutes 1993 'HIV infection in European female sex workers: epidemiological link with use of petroleum–based lubricants' *AIDS* vol. 7 pp 401–8.

Evans R. 1975 'Harlots and helots' *Exclusion, Exploitation and Extermination: Race Relations in Colonial Queensland* (eds R. Evans et al.) Australia and New Zealand Book Company: Sydney.

———— 1984 '"Soiled doves": prostitution in colonial Queensland' *So Much Hard Work* (ed. K. Daniels) Fontana/Collins: Sydney.

———— 1987 '"Don't you remember Black Alice, Sam Holt": Aboriginal women in Queensland history' *Hecate* vol. 8 no. 2 pp 7–21.

Farley T. A., Hadler J. L. & Gunn R. A. 1990 'The syphilis epidemic in Connecticut: relationship to drug use and prostitution' *Sexually Transmitted Diseases* vol. 17 pp 163–8.

Filla R. 1975 'Life as a prostitute' in *The Other Half, Women in Australian Society* (ed. J. Mercer) Penguin: Ringwood.

———— 1975 'Towards an understanding of prostitution' *Social Deviance in Australia* (eds A. R. Edwards & P. Wilson) Cheshire: Melbourne.

Foucault M. 1980 *The History of Sexuality: Introduction* Vintage: New York.

Frances R. 1993 'Gender and labour in Australia: the case of prostitution', Paper presented to the Australian–Canadian Labour History Conference, Sydney.

Freeman J. 1989 'The feminist debate over prostitution reform' *Berkeley Women's Law Journal* no. 75.

French D. & Lee L. 1989 *Working: My Life as a Prostitute* Gollancz: London.

Gagnon J. & Simon W. 1973a *Sexual Conduct* Hutchinson & Co: London.

———— 1973b 'Psychosexual development' in *Human Sexuality: Contemporary Perspectives* (eds M. Borosage & P. Morrison) Mayfield Publishing Co: California.

Game A. & Pringle R. 1983 *Gender at Work* Allen & Unwin: Sydney.

Gerull S. & Halstead B. (eds) 1992 *Sex Industry and Public Policy: Proceedings of a Conference Held 6–8 May 1991*, Australian Institute of Criminology: Canberra.

Gibbens T. C. N. 1971 'Female offender' *British Journal of Hospital Medicine* September.

Glover E. 1953 'The abnormality of prostitution' in *Women* (ed. A. Krich) Dell: New York.

Golder H. & Allen J. 1979–80 'Prostitution in New South Wales, 1870–1930: restructuring an industry' *Refractory Girl* vols 18/19 pp 17–25 Dec./Jan.

Goldman E. 1969 (1917) 'The traffic in women' in *Anarchism and Other Essays* (by Emma Goldman) Dover: New York.

Goode M. 1991 *The Law and Prostitution Information and Issues. Paper Prepared for SA Government.*

Greenwald H. 1970 *The Elegant Prostitute* Walker: New York.

Griggs L. & Gold J. 1989 'The development of a street based outreach program to reach young male, female and transsexual street based prostitutes in Sydney', Australia Paper presented at the *Fifth International Conference on AIDS, Montreal, Canada.*

Grosz E. (forthcoming) 'Ontology and equivocation: Derrida's politics of sexual difference' in *Derrida and Feminism* (ed. N. Holland) University of Texas Press: Houston.

Hantrakul S. 1983 'Prostitution in Thailand', Paper presented to *Women in Asia Workshop*, Monash University, Melbourne, July 22–24.

Harcourt C. 1989. 'Prostitutes show responsible response to human immunodeficiency virus threat' *Today's Life Science* September pp 58–62.

Harcourt C., Edwards J. & Philpot R. 1988 'On the "Grim Reaper" campaign' (letter) *The Medical Journal of Australia* no. 149.

Harcourt C. & Philpot R. 1990 'Female prostitutes, AIDS, drugs and alcohol in New South Wales' in *AIDS, Drugs and Prostitution* (ed. M. Plant) Routledge: London.

Harcourt C., Philpot R. & Edwards J. 1989 'The effects of condom use by clients on the incidence of STDs in female prostitutes' *Venereology* vol. 2 pp 4–7.

Harding W. & Zinberg N. 1977 'The effectiveness of subculture in developing rituals and sanction for controlling drug use' in *Altered States of Consciousness* (ed. B. du Toit) A. A. Balkena: Rotterdam.

Hart G. 1992 'STD epidemiology in Australasia: syphilis and gonorrhoea' *Venereology* vol. 5 pp 115–20.

Hartnoll R., Lewis R., Mitcheson M., et al. 1985 'Estimating the prevalence of opiod dependence' *The Lancet* p 8422.

Hebdige D. 1979 *Subculture: The Meaning of Style* Methuen & Co: London.

Heng B. H., Lee H. P., Kok L. P., Ong Y. W. & Ho M. L. 1992 'A survey of sexual behaviour of Singaporeans' *Annals of the Academy of Medicine Singapore* vol. 21 no. 6 pp 723–9.

Henriques F. 1962 *Prostitution and Society, Vol 1: Primitive, Classical and Oriental* Grove: New York.

Hirsch P. 1990 *Development Dilemmas in Rural Thailand* Oxford University Press: Singapore.

Holden C. 1989 'Street-wise crack research' *Science* vol. 246 no. 4936 pp 1376–81.

Hollander X., Moore R. & Dunleavy Y. 1972 *The Happy Hooker* Dell: New York.

Holmes K.K., Mardh P-A, Sparling P. F. et al. (eds) 1990 *Sexually Transmitted Diseases* 2nd edition, McGraw-Hill: New York.

Hood D., Prestage G., Crawford J., Sorrell T. & O'Reilly C. 1994 *A Report on the Bisexually Active Non Gay Attached Research Project* Western Sydney Area Health Service: Sydney.

Hooykaas C, van der Velde F. W., van der Linden M. M. D. et al. 1991 'The importance of ethnicity as a risk factor for STDs and sexual behaviour among heterosexuals' *Genitourinary Medicine* vol. 67 no. 378–83.

Horan S. 1984 'More sinned against than sinning? Prostitution in South Australia, 1836–1914' in *So Much Hard Work* (ed. K. Daniels) Fontana/Collins: Sydney.

Horn P. L. & Pringle M.B. 1984 *The Image of the Prostitute in Modern Literature* Frederick Ungar: New York.

Huggins J. & Blake T. 1992 'Protection or persecution? Gender relations in the era of racial segregation' in *Gender Relations in Australia: Domination and Negotiation* (eds K. Saunders & R. Evans) Harcourt, Brace & Jovanovich: Sydney.

Hughes R. 1987 *The Fatal Shore: A History of the Transportation of Convicts to Australia, 1788–1868* Collins: London.

Hunt S. 1986 *Spinifex and Hessian: Women's Lives in North-Western Australia, 1860–1900* University of Western Australia Press: Perth.

Ismail S. O, Ahmed H. J, Grillner L. et al. 1991 'Sexually transmitted diseases in men in Mogadishu, Somalia' *International Journal of STDs and AIDS* vol. 1 pp 102–6.

Jackson S. & Otto D. 1980 'From delicacy to dilemma: a feminist perspective' in *So Much Hard Work* (ed. K. Daniels) Fontana/Collins: Sydney.

Jaget C. (ed.) 1980 *Prostitutes, Our Life* Falling Wall: Bristol.

Jama H., Hederstedt B., Osman S. et al. 1987 'Syphilis in women of reproductive age in Mogadishu, Somalia: serological survey' *Genitourinary Medicine* vol. 63 pp 326–8.

James J. & Meyerding J. 1977 'Early sexual experience and prostitution' *Archives Of Sexual Behavior* vol. 7 no. 1.

Jana S., Chakraborty A. K., Chatterjee B. D. et al. 1993 'Knowledge, attitude of CSWs toward STD/HIV and prevalence of STD/HIV among CSWs', Ninth International AIDS Conference, Berlin, abstract number WS–C08–4.

Jebb M. & Haebich A. 1992 'Across the great divide: Gender relations on Australian frontiers' in *Gender Relations in Australia: Domination and Negotiation* (eds K. Saunders & R. Evans) Harcourt, Brace & Jovanovich: Sydney.

Jeffreys S. 1985 'Prostitution' in *Women Against Violence Against Women* (eds D. Rhodes & S. McNeill) Only Women Press: London.

John T.J., Babu P. G., Saraswathi N.K. et al. 1993 'The epidemiology of AIDS in the Vellore region, Southern India' *AIDS* vol. 7 pp 421–4.

Johnston C. 1985 'Prostitution law reform in New South Wales: two shuffles forward, one stumble back' in *Being A Prostitute* (eds R. Perkins & G. Bennett) Allen & Unwin: Sydney.

Jones R. 1984 'STD in prostitutes' (letter) *Medical Journal of Australia* vol. 140 pp 303–4.

Jordan J. 1992 *Working Girls: Women in the New Zealand Sex Industry* Penguin: Auckland.

Kaptue L., Zekeng L., Djoumessi S. et al. 1991 'HIV and chlamydia infections among prostitutes in Yaounde, Cameroon' *Genitourinary Medicine* vol. 67 pp 143–5.

Kawana T. 1992 'Sexually transmitted diseases in Japan' *The Asia–Pacific Venereologist* (IUVDT Asia–Pacific Newsletter) vol. 1 pp 3–5.

King N. 1988 *Daughters of Midas: Pioneer Women of the Eastern Goldfields* Hesperian Press: Perth.

Kinsey A.C., Pomeroy W.B., Martin C.E. & Gebhard P.H. 1953 *Sexual Behavior in the Human Female* Saunders: Philadelphia.

Kippax S., Cooper D., Prestage G., Crawford J. & Tindall B. 1994 *A Report on the Findings from the Initial Round of Interviews for the Sydney Men and Sexual Health Project* National Centre in HIV Social Research and National Centre in HIV Epidemiology and Clinical Research, Sydney (forthcoming).

Kjeldsen M. 1991 'Outreach work with young men on the rent scene in central London' in *Outreach Work with Men Who Have Sex With Men* (eds P. Aggleton, S. Jordan, P. Stoakes & T. Wilton) Southmead Health Authority and the Health Education Authority.

Koenig E. R. 1989 'International prostitutes and transmission of HIV' (letter) *The Lancet* vol. i pp 782–3

Kreiss J. K., Koech D., Plummer F. A. et al. 1986 'AIDS virus infection in Nairobi prostitutes' *New England Journal of Medicine* vol. 314 pp 414–8.

Kreiss J. K., Kiviat N B., Plummer F. A. et al. 1992 'Human immunodeficiency virus, human papillomavirus, and cervical intraepithelial neoplasia in Nairobi prostitutes' *Sexually Transmitted Diseases* vol. 19 pp 54–9.

Krogsgaard K., Gluud C., Pedersen C. et al. 1986 'Widespread use of condoms and low prevalence of sexually transmitted diseases in Danish non-drug addict prostitutes' *British Medical Journal* vol. 293 pp 1473–4.

Lake M. 1988 'Convict women as objects of male vision: an historiographical review' *Bulletin of the Centre for Tasmanian Historical Studies* vol. 2 no. 1 pp 40–8.

Limpakarnjanarat K., Mastro T. D., Yindeeyoungyeon W. et al. 1993 'STDs in female prostitutes in Northern Thailand' Ninth International AIDS Conference, Berlin abstract number PO–C10–2820.

Lin V. & Pearce W. 1990 'A workforce at risk' in *The Health of Immigrant Australia: A Social Perspective* (eds R. Reid & P. Trompf) Harcourt, Brace & Jovanovich: Sydney.

Lombroso C. & Ferrero G. 1895 *The Female Offender* Fisher Unwin: London.

Longstreet S. (ed.) 1970 *Nell Kimball: Her Life as an American Madam* Macmillan: New York.

Lovejoy F., Perkins R., Corduff Y., Dean M. J. & Wade A. 1991 *AIDS Preventative Practices Among Female Prostitutes and Their Clients and Private Risk,* Parts 1 & 2 (Report to Department of Health, Housing and Community Services) University of New South Wales: Sydney.

Lovejoy F., Sharp R., Prestage G. & Perkins R. 1992 *Impact Evaluation Project: HIV/AIDS Education for Sex Workers and Brothel Managers in the Sex Industry* (Report to NSW AIDS Bureau) University of New South Wales and Macquarie University: Sydney.

Loxley W. & Davidson R. 1991 'Why do injecting drug users take risks? Barriers to safer injecting and sexual behaviour in Perth' *National Aids Bulletin* Oct. pp 32–8.

Lule G. S. & Gruer L. D. 1992 'Knowledge of HIV and condom use among heterosexual patients at a Glasgow genito-urinary medicine clinic' *Health Bulletin* vol. 50 no. 1 pp 39–46.

Luthy R., Ledergerber M. B., Tuber M. & Siegenthaler W. 1987 'Prevalence of HIV antibodies among prostitutes in Zurich, Switzerland' *Klinische Wochenschrift* vol. 87 pp 287–8.

Mabey D. C. W., Tedder R.S., Hughes A. S. B. et al. 1988 'Human retroviral infections in The Gambia: prevalence and clinical features' *British Medical Journal* vol. 296 pp 83–6.

Macdonald C. 1986 'The "social evil": Prostitution and the passage of the Contagious Diseases Act (1869)' in *Women in History: Essays on European Women in New Zealand* (eds B. Brookes, C. Macdonald & M. Tennant) Allen & Unwin: Wellington.

Madeleine 1919 *Madeleine: An Autobiography* Harper: New York.

Mak R., Plum J. & van Renterghem L. 1990 'Human immunodeficiency virus (HIV) infection, sexually transmitted diseases and HIV-antibody testing practices in Belgian prostitutes' *Genitourinary Medicine* vol. 66 pp 337–41.

Mann J., Tarantola D. J. M. & Netter T. W. (eds) 1992 *AIDS in the World: A Global*

Report Harvard University Press: Cambridge, Mass.

Markos A. R., Wade A. A. H. & Walzman M. 1992 'The adolescent female prostitute and sexually transmitted diseases' (editorial review) *International Journal of STDs and AIDS* vol. 3 pp 92–5.

Martin G. 1978 *The Founding of Australia: The Argument about Australia's Origins* Hale & Iremonger: Sydney.

Martin J. 1984 'Non-English-speaking women: production and social reproduction' in *Ethnicity, Class and Gender in Australia* (eds G. Bottomley & M. de Lepervanche) Allen & Unwin: Sydney.

Marx K. 1975 'Economic and philosophic manuscripts of 1844' in *Early Writings* (K. Marx) Penguin: Middlesex.

_____ 1976 *Capital, A Critique of Political Economy*, Volume 1, Penguin: Middlesex.

McConaghy N. 1993 *Homosexuality/Heterosexuality: Sissiness and Tomboyism in Sexual Behavior: Problems and Management* Plenum Press: New York.

McConville C. 1980 'The location of Melbourne's prostitutes, 1870–1920' *Historical Studies* vol. 19 no. 74 pp 86–98.

_____ 1985 'From "criminal class" to "underworld"' in *The Outcasts of Melbourne* (eds G. Davison, D. Dunstan & C. McConville) Allen & Unwin: Sydney.

McCoy A. 1980 *Drug Traffic: Narcotics and Organised Crime in Australia* Harper and Row: Sydney.

McGrath A. 1984a '"Spinifex fairies": Aboriginal women workers in the Northern Territory, 1911–39' in *Women, Class and History: Feminist Perspectives* (ed. E. Windschuttle) Fontana: Melbourne.

_____ 1984b '"Black velvet": Aboriginal women and their relations with white men in the Northern Territory, 1910–40' in *So Much Hard Work* (ed. K. Daniels) Fontana/Collins: Sydney.

_____ 1987 *'Born in the Cattle': Aborigines in Cattle Country* Allen & Unwin: Sydney.

McKeganey N. & Barnard M. 1992 'Selling sex: female street prostitution and HIV risk behaviour in Glasgow' *AIDS Care* vol. 4 no. 4 pp 395–407.

McKeganey N., Barnard M., Leyland A. et al. 1992 'Female streetworking prostitution and HIV infection in Glasgow' *British Medical Journal* vol. 305 pp 801–4.

McKnight C. 1976 *The Voyage to Marege: Macassan Trepangers in Northern Australia* Melbourne University Press: Melbourne.

McLeod E. 1982 *Women Working: Prostitution Now* Croom Helm: London.

Mickler S. E. 1993 'Perceptions of vulnerability: Impact on AIDS-preventive behavior among college adolescents' *AIDS Education and Prevention* vol. 5 no. 1 pp 43–53.

Millett K. 1971 *The Prostitution Papers: A Quartet for Female Voices* Basic Books: New York.

Mills H. 1984 'Prostitution and the law. The question of decriminalisation' in *So Much Hard Work* (ed. K. Daniels) Fontana/Collins: Sydney.

MMWR (Morbidity and Mortality Weekly Report) 1987 'Antibody to human immunodeficiency virus in female prostitutes' *MMWR* vol. 36 pp 157–61.

Moore C. 1992 'A precious few: Melanesian and Asian women in Northern Australia' in *Gender Relations in Australia: Domination and Negotiation* (eds K. Saunders & R. Evans) Harcourt, Brace & Jovanovich: Sydney.

Moore D. 1992 *Recreational Drug Use, with Particular Reference to Amphetamines,*

Extasy and LSD, Amongst a Social Network of Young People in Perth National Centre for Research into the Prevention of Drug Abuse.

Morlet A., Darke S., Guinan J. et al. 1990 'Intravenous drug users who present at the Albion Street Centre for diagnosis and management of HIV infection' *Medical Journal of Australia* vol. 152 pp 78–80.

Mugford S. 1988 'The significance of recreational drug users: the example of the cocaine study' *Proceedings of the First National Drug Indicators Conference* 10–12 May, pp 303–22.

Murray A. 1991 *No Money No Honey: A Study of Street Traders and Prostitutes in Jakarta* Oxford University Press: Singapore.

Nance C. 1979 'Women, public morality and prostitution in early South Australia' *The Push From the Bush* vol. 3 pp 33–42.

National Centre in HIV Epidemiology and Clinical Research 1991 *Australian HIV Surveillance Report* vol. 7 (supplement 2) pp 1–2.

_____ 1993 *Australian HIV Surveillance Report* vol. 9 no. 4.

Nayyar K. C., Cummings M., Weber J. et al 1986 'Prevalence of genital pathogens among female prostitutes in New York City and in Rotterdam' *Sexually Transmitted Diseases* vol. 13 pp 109–17.

Neave M. 1988 'The failure of prostitution law reform' (Text of John Barry Memorial Lecture) *Australian and New Zealand Journal of Criminology* no. 192.

Ngugi E. N., Plummer F.A., Simonsen J.N. et al. 1988 'Prevention of transmission of human immunodeficiency virus in Africa: effectiveness of condom promotion and health education among prostitutes' *The Lancet* vol. II pp 887–90.

Nkya W. M. M. M., Gillespie S.H., Howlett W. et al. 1991 'Sexually transmitted diseases in prostitutes in Moshi and Arusha, Northern Tanzania' *International Journal of STDs and AIDS* vol. 2 pp 432–5.

Oldfield E. C., Rodier G. R. & Gray G. C. 1993 'Endemic infectious diseases of Somalia' *Clinical Infectious Diseases* no. 16 (supplement 3) p S143.

O'Leary J. n.d. 'Prostitution as sex work — A step forward or backwards' Unpublished paper, University of New England.

Overall C. 1992 'What's wrong with prostitution' *Signs: Journal of Women in Culture and Society* vol. 17 no. 4 pp 705–24.

Overs C. 1989 'Prostitution: we call it sex work now' *Lilith: A Feminist History Journal* vol. 6 pp 64–8.

Oxley D. 1988 'Convict Women' in *Convict Workers* (ed. S. Nicholas) Cambridge University Press: Sydney.

Palacio V., de Sanjose V. S. et al. 1993 'Cervical neoplasia and sexually transmitted diseases among prostitutes in Oviedo Spain' (letter) *International Journal of STD and AIDS* vol. 4 pp 121–3.

Parent-Duchatelet A. J. B. 1857 'De la prostitution dans la Ville de Paris' *Bailiere de Fils* Paris.

Parliament of New South Wales 1986 *Report* of the *Select Committee of the Legislative Assembly Upon Prostitution.* (Chairman, P. Rogan MP).

Pateman C. 1988 *The Sexual Contract* Polity: Cambridge.

Pearson G. 1987 'Heroin and unemployment' in *A Land Fit for Heroin: Drugs in Britain in the 1980s* (eds N. Dorn & S. South) Macmillan: Basingstoke.

Pepin J. et al. 1991 'HIV-2 infection among prostitutes working in The Gambia: association with serological evidence of genital ulcer diseases and with generalized lymphadenopathy' *AIDS* vol. 5 pp 69–75.

Perkins R. 1989a 'Wicked women or working girls: the prostitute on the silver screen' *Media Information Australia* Feb no 51.

____ 1989b 'Working girls in "wowserville": prostitute women in Sydney since 1945' in *Australian Welfare: Historical Sociology* (ed. R. Kennedy) Macmillan: Melbourne.

____ 1991 *Working Girls: Prostitutes, Their Life and Social Control* Australian Institute Of Criminology: Canberra.

____ 1992 'Being and becoming "working girls": an oral history of prostitutes in Sydney, 1935–1985' in *All Our Labours: Oral Histories Of Working Life In Twentieth Century Sydney* (ed. J. Shields), NSW University Press: Sydney.

____ 1994 *Health Aspects of Female Private Prostitutes in New South Wales* Report to the National Health and Medical Research Council, Canberra.

Perkins R. & Bennett G. 1985 *Being a Prostitute: Prostitute Women and Prostitute Men* Allen & Unwin: Sydney.

Perkins R., Corduff Y. & Lovejoy F. 1990 'Prostitutes, their lovers and the AIDS debate on prostitution and women' *National AIDS Bulletin* vol. 4 no. 5 pp 14–7.

Perkins R., Griffin A. & Jakobsen J. 1994 *Transgender Lifestyles and HIV/AIDS Risk* (Report to Federal Department of Health and AFAO) University of New South Wales: Sydney.

Perkins R., Lovejoy F., Dean M. J. & Wade A. 1991a 'AIDS preventative practices among female prostitutes' *National AIDS Bulletin* vol. 5 no. 8 pp 28–32.

____ 1991b 'Female prostitutes and other women in non-commercial sex situations' *National AIDS Bulletin* vol. 5 no. 9 pp 39–41.

Perkins T. 1979 'Rethinking stereotypes' in *Ideology and Cultural Production* (eds M. Barrett, P. Corrigan, A. Kuhn & J. Wolff) Croom Helm: London.

Pheterson G. (ed.) 1989 *A Vindication of the Rights of Whores* Seal: Seattle.

Philpot C. R., Harcourt C. L., Edwards J. M. 1991 'A survey of female prostitutes at risk of HIV infection and other sexually transmissible diseases' *Genitourinary Medicine* vol. 67 pp 384–8.

Philpot C. R., Harcourt C. L., Edwards J. M. & Grealis A. 1988 'Human immunodeficiency virus and female prostitutes, Sydney, 1985' *Genitourinary Medicine* vol. 64 pp 193–7.

Phongpaichit P. 1982 *From Peasant Girls to Bangkok Masseuses* ILO: Geneva.

Pineda J. A., Aguado I., Rivero A. et al. 'HIV-I infection among non–intravenous drug user female prostitutes in Spain. No evidence of evolution to pattern II' *AIDS* vol. 6 pp 1365–9.

Plant M. (ed.) 1990 *AIDS, Drugs and Prostitution* Tavistock/Routledge: London.

____ 1991 'AIDS, drugs and commercial sex' *The International Journal on Drug Policy* vol. 2 no. 2 pp 25–7.

Plourde P. J., Plummer F. A., Pepin J. et al. 1992 'Human immunodeficiency virus type 1 infection in women attending a sexually transmitted diseases clinic in Kenya' *The Journal of Infectious Diseases* vol. 166 pp 86–92.

Plummer F. A., Ngugi E. N. 1990 'Prostitutes and their clients in the epidemiology and control of the sexually transmitted diseases' in *Sexually Transmitted Diseases* (eds K. K. Holmes et al.) McGraw-Hill: New York.

Potterat J. 1992 'Socio-geographic space and sexually transmissible diseases in the

1990s' *Today's Life Science* December pp 16–31.

———— 1993 'Prostitution: a global public health issue' (conference report) *Venereology* vol. 6 p 85.

Potterat J., Rothenberg R. & Bross D. C. 1979 'Gonorrhoea in street prostitutes: epidemiologic and legal implications' *Sexually Transmitted Diseases* vol. 6 pp 58–63.

Prestage G. 1992 *Report on the Western Beats Study, Stage 2*, National Centre of HIV Social Research, Macquarie University: Sydney.

Prestage G. & Hood D. 1993 'Targeting non-gay attached homosexually-active working class men', Paper presented at the Social Aspects of AIDS Conference, London.

Ramachandran S. & Ngeow Y. F. 1990 'The prevalence of sexually transmitted diseases among prostitutes in Malaysia' *Genitourinary Medicine* vol. 66 pp 334–6.

Randall T. 1969 *Hooker* Award: New York.

Reynolds H. 1982 *The Other Side of the Frontier: Aboriginal Resistance to the European Invasion of Australia* Penguin: Harmondsworth.

———— 1990 *With the White People: The Crucial Role of Aborigines in the Exploration and Development of Australia* Penguin: Harmondsworth.

Robinson P. 1979 'The first forty years' in *In Pursuit of Justice: Australian Women and the Law, 1788–1979* (eds J. Mackinolty & H. Radi) Hale & Iremonger: Sydney.

———— 1985 *The Hatch and Brood of Time* Oxford University Press: Melbourne.

———— 1988 *The Women of Botany Bay* Macquarie: Sydney.

Robson L. 1963 'The origin of the women convicts sent to Australia, 1787–1852' *Historical Studies* vol. 11 no. 41 pp 43–53.

———— 1965 *The Convict Settlers of Australia: An Enquiry into the Origin and Character of the Convicts Transported to New South Wales and Van Diemen's Land, 1787–1852* Melbourne University Press: Melbourne.

Rose D. B. 1992 *Hidden Histories: Black Stories from Victoria River Downs, Humbert River and Wave Hill Stations* Aboriginal Studies Press: Canberra.

Rosen R. 1982 *The Lost Sisterhood: Prostitution in America, 1900–1918* John Hopkins University Press: Baltimore.

Rosenbaum M. 1985 *Women on Heroin* Rutgers University Press: Brunswick NJ.

Rubin G. 1984 'Thinking sex: notes for a radical theory of the politics of sexuality' in *Pleasure and Danger: Exploring Female Sexuality* (ed. C. Vance) Routledge and Kegan Paul: Boston.

Ruijs G. J., Schut I. K., Schirm J. & Schroder F. P. 1988 'Prevalence, incidence, and risk of acquiring urogenital gonococcal or chlamydial infection in prostitutes working in brothels' *Genitourinary Medicine* vol. 64 pp 49–50.

Rutter O. 1937 *The First Fleet* Cockerel Press: London.

Ryan M. P. 1991 'AIDS in Thailand' (letter) *The Medical Journal of Australia* vol. 154 pp 282–4.

Samarakoon S. 1993 'STD among female prostitutes attending the Central Venereal Diseases Clinic (CVDC), Colombo, Sri Lanka', Ninth International AIDS Conference, Berlin, abstract number PO-C14-2891.

Samra Z., Dan M., Segev S. et al. 1991 'Prevalence of sexually transmitted pathogens among women attending a methadone clinic in Israel'

Genitourinary Medicine vol. 67 pp 133–6.

Sanger W. 1937 (1858) *The History of Prostitution* Eugenics: New York.

Saunders K. & Taylor H. 1987 'The impact of total war upon policing: the Queensland experience' in *Policing in Australia: Historical Perspectives* (ed. M. Finnane) New South Wales University Press: Sydney.

Scates B. 1993 '"Knocking out a living": survival strategies and popular protest in the 1890s depression' in *Debutante Nation: Feminism Contests the 1890s* (eds S. Magarey et al.) Allen & Unwin: Sydney.

Schedvin M. S. 'Prostitution in South Australia: a proposal for reform, 1842' *The Push from the Bush* vol. 4 pp 33–8.

Schwarcz S. K., Bolan G. A., Fullilove M. et al. 1992 'Crack cocaine and the exchange of sex for money or drugs: risk factors for gonorrhoea among black adolescents in San Francisco' *Sexually Transmitted Diseases* vol. 19 pp 7–13.

Scutt J. 1979 'The economics of sex: women in service' *Australian Quarterly* vol. 51 no. 1 pp 32–46.

Sharp R. 1992 'Structural factors and dysfunctional injecting drug use: The implications for treatment agencies' *Proceedings of the Winter School in the Sun,* Queensland Alcohol and Drug Foundation, July.

Sharp R., Davis M., Dowsett G. W., Kippax S., Hewitt K., Morgan S. & Robertson W. 1991 *Ways of Using: Functional Injecting Drug Users Project* NSW Department of Health and Macquarie University Centre for Applied Research: Sydney.

Shaw A. G. L. 1966 *Convicts and the Colonies* Faber & Faber: London.

Sheldin M. G. 1990 'An ethnographic approach to understanding HIV/high risk behaviours: prostitution and drug use' *NIDA Research Monographs* vol. 93 pp 134–49.

Shrage L. 1989. 'Should feminists oppose prostitution?' *Ethics* vol. 99 pp 347–61.

Silbert M. H. & Pines A. M. 1982 'Entrance into prostitution' *Youth and Society* vol. 13 no. 4.

Simoes E. A., Babu P. G., Jeyakumari H. M. & John T. J. 1993 'The initial detection of human immunodeficiency virus I and its subsequent spread in prostitutes in Tamil Nadu, India' *Journal of Acquired Immune Deficiency Syndrome* vol. 6 pp 1030–4.

Simons G. L. 1975 *A Place of Pleasure: The History of the Brothel* Harwood-Smarth: Lewes.

Sissons D. C. S. 1976–7 'Karayuki-San: Japanese prostitutes in Australia, 1887–1916' *Historical Studies* vol. 17 pp 323–41, 474–88.

Smith B. 1988 *A Cargo of Women: Susannah Watson and the Convicts of the Princess Royal* New South Wales University Press: Sydney.

Smith G. L. & K. F. 1986 'Lack of HIV infection and condom use in licensed prostitutes' (letter) *The Lancet* vol. ii p 1392.

Stary A., Kopp W. & Soltz-Szots J. 1991 'Medical health care for Viennese prostitutes' *Sexually Transmitted Diseases* vol. 18 pp 159–65.

Stott N. C. H. 1983 *Primary Health Care: Bridging the Gap Between Theory and Practice* Springer-Verlag: Berlin.

Sturma M. 1978 'Eye of the beholder: the stereotype of women convicts, 1788–1852' *Labour History* May, vol. 34

Sullivan B. 1992 'Feminist approaches to the sex industry' in *Sex Industry and*

Public Policy (eds S. Gerull & B. Halstead) Australian Institute of Criminology: Canberra.

Summers A. 1975 *Damned Whores and God's Police: The Colonization of Women in Australia* Penguin: Ringwood.

Sydney Sexual Health Centre & Parramatta Sexual health Clinic 1991 'The Asian sex industry in Sydney'. (a Multicultural Health Promotion Project) unpublished report to the NSW AIDS Bureau.

Tabet P. 1991 '"I'm the meat, I'm the knife": sexual service, migration and repression in some African societies' *Feminist Issues* Spring, pp 3–21.

Tait I. A. et al. 1980 'Chlamydial infection of the cervix in partners of men with NGU' *British Journal of Venereal Diseases* vol. 56 p 37.

Thomas R. M., Plant M. A. & M. C. & Sales D. I. 1989 'Risks of AIDS among workers in the sex industry: some initial results from a Scottish study' *British Medical Journal* 15 July, vol. 299 no. 6692 pp 148–9.

Thomas W. I. 1923 *The Unadjusted Girl* Harper Bros: New York.

Traisupa A., Wongba C. & Taylor D. N. 1987 'AIDS and prevalence of antibody to human immunodeficiency virus (HIV) in high risk groups in Thailand' *Genitourinary Medicine* vol. 63 pp 106–8.

Traore–Ettiegne V., Ghys G. P. D., Diallo M. O. et al. 1993 'High prevalence of HIV infections and other STD in female prostitutes in Abidjan' Ninth International AIDS Conference, Berlin. abstract number WS-C08-3.

US Department of Health and Human Services 1991 *Sexually Transmitted Disease Surveillance, 1990*, CDC: Atlanta, Georgia.

van Beek I , Buckley R., Stewart M., MacDonald M. & Kaldor J. M. 1994 'Risk factors for hepatitis C virus infection among injecting drug users in Sydney' *Genitourinary Medicine* (in press).

van de Perre P., Clumeck N. & Carael M. 1985.'Female prostitutes: a risk group for infection with human T-cell lymphotrophic virus type III' *The Lancet* vol. ii pp 524–7.

van der Hoek J. A. et al. 1988 'Prevalence and risk factors of HIV infections among drug users and drug using prostitutes in Amsterdam' *AIDS* vol. 1 pp 55–70.

van Haastrecht H. J. A., Fennema J. S. A., Coutinho R. A. et al. 1993 'HIV prevalence and risk behaviour among prostitutes and clients in Amsterdam: migrants at increased risk for HIV infection' *Genitourinary Medicine* vol. 69 pp 251–6.

van Onselen C. 1980 'Prostitutes and proletarians, 1886–1914', Paper delivered to conference on 'Class Formation, Culture and Consciousness: the Making of Modern South Africa', University of London, January.

Vega J., Levine W., Estensorro M. et al. 1993 'High STD prevalence among commercial sex workers in La Paz, Bolivia' Ninth International AIDS Conference, Berlin, abstract number PO-C10-2818.

Victorian Government 1985 *Report on Inquiry into Prostitution* (Inquirer: M. Neave).

Wade A. 1992 'From the inside' in *Sex Industry And Public Policy* (eds S. Gerull & B. Halstead), Australian Institute Of Criminology: Canberra.

Waldorf D. 1980 'A brief history of illicit drug ethnographies' in *Ethnography: A Research Tool for Policy Makers in the Drug and Alcohol Fields* (eds C. Alkins & G. Beschner) NIDA: Rockville.

Walkowitz J. 1980 *Prostitution and Victorian Society: Women, Class and the State* Cambridge University Press: Cambridge.

_____ 1992 *City of Dreadful Delight: Narratives of Sexual Danger in Late Victorian London* University of Chicago Press: Chicago.

Walters J. M. 1985 'Taking care of business' *Life with Heroin: Voices from the Inner City* Lexington Books: Lexington.

Ward H., Day S., Dunlop L. et al. 1992 'Commercial sex and HIV risk: a six year study of female sex workers' Eighth International AIDS Conference, Amsterdam, abstract number PoC 4186.

Warren J. 1993 *Ah Ku and Karayuki-San: Prostitution in Singapore, 1870–1940* Oxford University Press: Oxford.

Wasserheit J. N. 1992 'Epidemiological synergy: interrelationships between human immunodeficiency virus infection and other sexually transmitted diseases' *Sexually Transmitted Diseases* vol. 19 pp 61–77.

Western Australian Community Panel on Prostitution, 1990 *Report*.

Williams N. & Jolly L. 1992 'From time immemorial? Gender relations in Aboriginal societies before "white contact"' in *Gender Relations in Australia: Domination and Negotiation* (eds K. Saunders & R. Evans) Harcourt, Brace and Jovanovich: Sydney.

Willis P. 1979 'Shop floor culture, masculinity and the wage form' in *Working Class Culture* (eds J. Clarke, C. Critcher & R. Johnson) Hutchinson: London.

Winick C. & Kinsie P. 1971 *The Lively Commerce: Prostitution in the United States* Quadrangle: Chicago.

Winter M. 1976 *Prostitution in Australia* Purtaboi: Sydney.

Wiseman T. 1989 'Marginalised groups and health education about HIV infection and AIDS' *AIDS: Representation, Social Practices* (eds P. Aggleton, G. Hart & P. Davies) Falmer Press: New York.

Wodak A. 1991 'Australia: preventing HIV spread among injecting drug users' *The Lancet* 23 Feb. p 337.

Wong M. L., Tan T. C., Ho M. L. et al. 1992 'Factors associated with sexually transmitted diseases among prostitutes in Singapore' *International Journal of STDs and AIDS* vol. 3 pp 332–7.

Woolley P. D., Bowman C. A. & Kinghorn G. R. 1988 'Prostitution in Sheffield: differences between prostitutes' *Genitourinary Medicine* vol. 64 pp 391–3.

World Health Organisation (WHO) 1988 *A Brief Summary of Its Work* Department of Community Services and Health: Canberra.

Zekeng L., Feldblum P. J., Oliver R. M. & Kaptue L. 1993 'Barrier contraceptive use and HIV infection among high-risk women in Cameroon' *AIDS* vol. 7 pp 725–31.

CONTRIBUTORS

Caroline Barlow owns and operates two parlours in the inner city and suburbs of Sydney. She is involved in ongoing discussions within the sex industry in an endeavour to bring normal business regulations to the parlour trade and to help change the legal status of parlours as well as parlour owners.

Roxy Blain has worked for nine years in the sex industry, having been employed in brothels and self-employed in private prostitution in three states of Australia. She offers her clients a diversity of services, including straight sex, massage, escort and home visit services, fantasy work and bondage & discipline, as well as non-sexual services such as companionship, kindness and advice.

Linda Brockett is completing her MA in geography at the University of Sydney. She has worked extensively with Thai sex workers both in Sydney and in Thailand, and was the Multicultural Health Promotions Project Officer at the Sydney Sexual Health Clinic, Sydney Hospital, from 1991 to 1993. She also works with the Sex Workers Outreach Project (SWOP) in Sydney.

Janice Elms is completing her Master's in counselling at Macquarie University and is now researching commercial sex workers. Janice is a Canadian who achieved her Bachelor's degree at Brock University in St Catherine, Ontario. She has worked in the areas of social housing, education and youth accommodation both in Canada and in Australia.

Raelene Frances lectures in history at the University of New South Wales. She is associate editor of *Labour History*, author of *The Politics of Work: Gender and Labour in Victoria 1880-1940* and co-author of *Women at Work in Australia from the Goldrushes to World War II*. In 1980 she completed an MA thesis on the history of prostitution in Western Australia to 1940 and is now researching a larger study of prostitution in Australia from 1788.

Geoffrey Fysh has had over 15 years experience working in and for the sex industry. He worked for five years in Sydney as a street sex worker, before going on to be one of the initial Project Officers employed by the Australian Prostitutes Collective. He has also worked on a mobile outreach bus providing medical, educational and support services to sex workers, injecting drug users and at risk youth, and for four and a half years has been employed as the Project Manager of the Sex Workers Outreach Project (SWOP) in New South Wales. Geoffrey is also trained by a Mistress in developing Master skills, which he intends using in part-time sex work to help finance his university course in a Master's degree.

Steven Goodley is 28 years old and has been active in the gay scene for some years now. In the past he has worked in hotels and as a plumber, as well as for a newsagent. He has been a sex worker for four years, working only in parlours.

Christine Harcourt is enrolled in a PhD program in the School of Community Medicine, University of New South Wales, and holds a Commonwealth AIDS Research Grants Committee (CARG) postgraduate scholarship. She is employed in the Academic Unit in Sexual Health Medicine in the Sydney Sexual Health Centre, Sydney Hospital, where she has been involved in a number of studies on prostitution and public health. Chris has published a dozen articles in various medical journals.

Jeddah Jakobsen is completing her MA at Queensland University. She has taught in various capacities in South Australia, has been employed to write a history of the Queen Victoria Hospital in that state and is an artist in various media, especially film and video, with exhibitions in Sydney and Adelaide. Jeddah worked as a research assistant on a transgender (transsexual) project at the University of New South Wales in 1993.

Mike Lazarus is a police sergeant and has been a member of the New South Wales Police Service for 16 years. He holds a BA from the University of Sydney and a Master of Commerce from the University of New South Wales. He is currently undertaking a Command Development Programme, which will result in a postgraduate degree from Wollongong University. In 1990 he created the largest Beat Unit in the state at Kings Cross and in 1993 created the Beat Unit at the Rocks Police Patrol in Sydney. He has been involved in a number of committees, including planning of the Cops Programme and a sub-committee creating the South Region Strategic Plan. In the private sector he created a five year marketing plan which was adopted by the Jewel Food Store Pty Ltd.

Frances Lovejoy is a senior lecturer in sociology at the University of New South Wales whose research interests include women's issues, discrimination, and sexuality. Since 1990 she has been chief investigator in research projects on prostitution and AIDS funded by CARG, NH&MRC and the NSW AIDS Bureau.

Gabrielle Mateljan worked in a number of occupations, including dental technician, air hostess, dance instructor, dental sales representative, owner of a dance studio and catering manager, before being employed in 1992 as a research assistant at the University of New South Wales , where she has been involved in fieldwork among female, male and transsexual prostitutes on the streets, in brothels and in private apartments.

Alison Murray has a PhD in human geography and is the author of the book *No Money No Honey: A Study of Street Traders and Prostitutes in Jakarta*. She has worked with the Sex Workers Outreach Project since 1992 and is a Research Fellow in the Research School of Pacific and Asian Studies, Australian National University.

Marcia Neave has held a personal chair in the Law Faculty at Monash University since 1991 and was formerly the John Bray Professor of Law at Adelaide University. She was dean of the Adelaide Law School, 1987-89, and was part-time commissioner with the Law Reform Commission of Victoria until its abolition. She is a member of the Australian National Council on AIDS and of the National Health and Medical Research Council. In 1985 she chaired an Inquiry into Prostitution for the Victorian Government and has an ongoing interest in prostitution law reform. She has written extensively in the areas of property law, family law and trusts.

Roberta Perkins has been researching female prostitution for 15 years and has produced three books, contributed four chapters to other books and published 16 articles in academic journals, newspapers and popular periodicals on the subject. She has also been a long-time activist for prostitute rights. She is employed as a senior research officer in the School of Sociology, University of New South Wales, where she has been doing research projects on prostitution and AIDS over the past four years.

Garrett Prestage (formerly Garry Bennett) is completing a PhD in sociology. He has worked as a youth worker and a staff training officer for the NSW Department of Youth and Community Services, has been a tutor in sociology at the University of Sydney, and co-authored *Being a Prostitute*. In 1992 he was a senior research assistant at Macquarie University on gay research projects and at the University of New South Wales on prostitution research projects. Since then he has been the coordinator of the SMASH study, looking at clinical and socio-behavioural aspects of HIV/AIDS among Sydney gay and bisexual men, at the National Centre in HIV Epidemiology and Clinical Research.

Rachel Sharp is a professor of education at the University of New England, researching in the areas of education and health. She has authored, co-authored or edited a number of books and articles, including an evaluation of social inequality in contemporary Australia. She has recently been working on HIV/AIDS issues and is currently participating in studies of young gay men who inject drugs and of the educational needs of rural men who have sex with men. She has helped to evaluate the educational campaigns targeting the sex industry in New South Wales.

Carol Stevens has a BA (psych) from the University of New South Wales and a background in research on sexual behaviour.

Barbara Sullivan is presently a post-doctoral research fellow in political science at the Research School of Social Sciences, Australian National University. She has recently completed a PhD dissertation at the University of Queensland on the political regulation of the sex industry in Australia since 1945.

Ingrid van Beek graduated in medicine at the University of New South Wales in 1982 and received an MBA on an exchange program at New York University in 1988. She has been a resident medical officer at St Vincent's Hospital in Darlinghurst, has worked in anaesthetics at the Marie Stopes Women's Health Clinic in London, and has been a medical officer at Kirketon Road Centre in Kings Cross since its commencement in April 1987. Two years later she was appointed Director of Kirketon Road Centre, a position she holds to this day.

Amanda Wade has lived in Kings Cross for many years and includes sex workers and drug users among her many friends. She has worked as a printer and a proofreader. Her vast experience and knowledge of the people of the Cross have proved invaluable in her position as a research assistant on prostitution studies at the University of New South Wales over the past four years. She also wrote a chapter for the Australian Institute of Criminology's publication, *Sex Industry and Public Policy*.

Louise Webb is a lecturer in social work and an honorary fellow in the School of Social Work, University of New South Wales. She worked with London street sex workers between 1976 and 1982 and was national coordinator of PROS (Program for Reform of the Laws on Soliciting) in the United Kingdom. Since coming to Australia Louise has worked as a social policy consultant as well as an academic.

Paul Wilson is a criminologist and dean of humanities and social sciences at Bond University. He is the author of over 25 books, including *The Sexual Dilemma*, *The Other Side of Rape* and *The Man They Called A Monster*. He recently gave the Sir John Morris Memorial Lecture on 'Sexual Crimes and Sexual Behaviour in Australia', and was convenor of the Australian Institute of Criminology's landmark conference on the sex industry in 1991.

APPENDICES

Appendix 1

Committee findings; Chapter 7 of the Rogan Report: Health Aspects of Prostitution; prostitutes and health services:

7.7.23 Prostitutes suffer from a variety of illnesses and conditions related to their work and lifestyle, in addition to the publicly recognised sexually transmitted diseases (STDs). Further it appears that current health services are not well adapted to the needs of prostitutes, and that many of the workers avoid traditional health and welfare centres.

7.7.24 On the basis of the evidence before it the Committee agreed that there is a need for 'more flexible outreach and "drop in" services... In addition to clinical services, health services should include preventive services, health education programs, support and counselling services'...etc.

7.7.25 Many of the most serious health problems encountered by prostitutes as a group have a greater impact on streetworkers, and those who work out of poorly run brothels and cheap rooms in the inner-city areas   These   are also the people least likely to visit the established STD clinics and health care centres.

7.7.26 Some of these problems could be overcome by establishing a health care centre in Kings Cross which would not be solely identified with an STD clinic, but would also offer general health care, counselling, and contraceptive advice. Regular screening for STDs should be offered to prostitutes, together with more frequent Pap smears (to detect cervical cancer) — say six-monthly instead of the annual or two-yearly smear usually recommended; and hepatitis B vaccine. The Health Department submission suggests that these needs could be met either through the establishment of a special-purpose centre or by augmenting of existing health services in the area.

7.7.27 A centre dealing with a variety of personal and public health needs under one roof might also play an educative and advisory role in any attempt to improve the amenity and public health aspects of life in the Kings Cross-Darlinghurst area.

APPENDIX 2

KRC Services at end 1993

* assessment and management of general health issues.
* HIV antibody testing, pre and post-test counselling.
* primary medical and psychosocial management of HIV infection, and AIDS related conditions.
* sexual health screening and treatment of sexually transmissible infections.
* hepatitis A & B virus screening and vaccination.
* hepatitis C virus screening and liver function monitoring.
* women's health screening, Pap smears and breast examination.
* family planning advice, contraception, pregnancy testing, antenatal care and referral.
* medical and psychosocial assessment and management of transgender issues and referral.
* drug and alcohol counselling and referral.
* methadone treatment and referral.
* crisis and ongoing counselling.
* social welfare assistance and referral (housing, income support, employment, training and legal).
* mobile (bus) and on-foot street outreach.
* sterile injecting equipment, water, swabs, condoms and lubricant.

INDEX